Hegemony and Power

Hegemony and Power

Consensus and Coercion in Contemporary Politics

Edited by Mark Haugaard and
Howard H. Lentner

LEXINGTON BOOKS

A division of
ROWMAN & LITTLEFIELD PUBLISHERS, INC.
Lanham • Boulder • New York • Toronto • Oxford

LEXINGTON BOOKS

A division of Rowman & Littlefield Publishers, Inc.
A wholly owned subsidiary of The Rowman & Littlefield Publishing Group, Inc.
4501 Forbes Boulevard, Suite 200
Lanham, MD 20706

PO Box 317
Oxford
OX2 9RU, UK

British Library Cataloguing in Publication Information Available

Library of Congress Cataloging-in-Publication Data

Library of Congress Control Number:

ISBN-13: 978-0-7391-1502-2 (cloth : alk. paper)
ISBN-10: 0-7391-1502-2 (cloth : alk. paper)
ISBN-13: 978-0-7391-1503-9 (pbk. : alk. paper)
ISBN-10: 0-7391-1503-0 (pbk. : alk paper)

Printed in the United States of America

♾™ The paper used in this publication meets the minimum requirements of American
National Standard for Information Sciences—Permanence of Paper for Printed Library
Materials, ANSI/NISO Z39.48–1992.

Contents

Postmodern and Feminist Approaches to Hegemony and Power

Conclusion

Acknowledgments

With one exception the main chapters of this book were presented as papers at a meeting of the International Political Science Association's Research Committee on Political Power held in June 2004 at the Graduate School and University Center of the City University of New York. The editors wish to thank all of those who contributed to the success of the conference through sponsorship, financial assistance, and administrative support.

The meeting was jointly sponsored and partly financed by the Ph.D. Program in Political Science, whose executive officer is Professor Ruth O'Brien, and by the Ralph Bunche Institute on International Studies, directed by Professor Thomas Weiss. Provost William Kelly and Dean of Sponsored Research Brian Schwartz also provided financial assistance. Robert Biondi and Nancy Okada and her staff gave excellent administrative support before and during the meeting. We also thank Tim Thomai for his help in making hotel arrangements for visitors from abroad. We are grateful to Anoush Koshkish for his participation in the meeting and for his hospitality following it.

We also express our thanks to Rob Carley, the acquisitions editor at Lexington Books, for his confidence in our work, and we appreciate the support of his successor Joseph Parry and Production Editor Catherine Forrest for helping to bring the work to publication.

Introduction

Chapter 1

Conceptual Confrontation

Mark Haugaard

From being a relatively obscure technical term, hegemony has emerged as a significant concept in contemporary discourse. A Google search on hegemony scores over
six million hits. By way of comparison, Marxism scores five million, neoliberalism
just under a million, and neoconservatism a mere two hundred thousand. Gramsci,
the social theorist upon whose work most contemporary interpretations of hegemony rest, scores 2.5 million against 5 million for Marx, 1.7 million for Durkheim,
and a mere 300 thousand for Engels.

While hegemony has been used by academics for over half a century, in both
international relations and social theory, since 1989 there has been a sudden surge
in the popularity of concept. In the late 1980s Kennedy's *The Rise and Fall of the
Great Powers* became immensely popular. The central argument in that work was
that, in terms of international power, the problem confronting the US was how to
manage decline. Eighteen years later, this argument appears entirely implausible.
The main concern today is the emergence of the unrivaled dominance of the US in
world politics. The US stands more and more like Rome to the Classical world or
Britain to the 19th century. Yet, there is something unsatisfactory about the comparison. Rome and Britain were empires. Is the US an imperial power or something
qualitatively different? There are those who argue that the US is indeed an empire.
Another interpretation is that the US is a hegemonic power or, less clear cut, that
the US is hegemonic and/or imperial at different times depending upon the policy
and administration.

The events of 1989 also confirmed a process that had been taking place since
the late Seventies within the European Left. Radical politics became post-Marxist,
which entailed a move into postmodern social theory. Central to this was the realization that the locus of power is substantially more complex than was previously
thought. Power belongs neither to the state nor to the bourgeoisie. The only classical Marxist to have understood this was Gramsci. In essence, his theory of hegemony is a theory of the dispersal of power, which post-Marxists could build upon.

What is riding on the concept of hegemony? In his recently popular book
Hegemony or Survival (2004) Chomsky used the term hegemony interchangeably

with empire and dominance, suggesting that hegemony is some kind of rationalization for imperial self-interest. However, any sophisticated theoretical examination shows hegemony as a substantially subtler concept than mere rationalization.

Hegemony in Ancient Classical Discourse

As will be explained in greater depth in Chapter 2, the term hegemony is of Greek origin and was used in the classical world to designate leadership (*hegemonia*) of a military alliance that was voluntarily entered into. Aristotle classified political systems according to a binary logic whereby one form is legitimate and the other a corruption of the latter. The distinguishing criteria in this binary opposition are whose interests are being served. Accordingly, Monarchy is government by *one* in the interests of *all*, while Tyranny is government by *one* in the interest of *one* and so on, for Aristocracy versus Oligarchy, and Polity versus Democracy. Within this scheme, hegemony is the legitimate political form that serves common interests, while empire is purely in the interest of the dominating party.

In Pericles and Isocrates we find a further refinement of hegemony as a fusion of power and knowledge, whereby hegemony is conceptualized in opposition to unregulated power, as manifest through coercion and violence. Once the coercive power of the hegemon is fused with knowledge, an alliance of states is created in which the power of the hegemon is governed by a perception of common interest and respect for the less powerful in the alliance. In such an alliance, the objective is to increase the autonomy of all parties, not to compromise the autonomy of the less powerful in order to increase the autonomy of the more powerful. The latter is the principle of empire. Respect for the autonomy of others entails that the collective power of the alliance is always derived through consent among the various parties (Lentner 2005). In contrast, since empire does not presuppose consent the dominant party governs through coercion.

Hegemony in Gramsci's Social Thought

After the Classical period the term largely disappears from the discourse of social and political theory until its use in Marxism, especially in the work of Gramsci. In his thought, the Classical dualism is continued whereby hegemony entails some level of consent and remains in conceptual opposition to coercive domination. However, the picture is made somewhat more complex by the observation that the bourgeoisie maintain their power through hegemony, which is obviously not as legitimate government in the interests of the proletariat. According to Marxist orthodoxy, only the latter and not the former can represent collective interests.

In this characterization of both communism and bourgeois capitalism as hegemonic, there are two things going on. The Greek characterization of hegemony was largely one in which hegemony constituted a desirable relationship of mutual autonomy between hegemon and those who are led. In Gramsci this normative evaluation remains *only* with regard proletarian hegemony. There is also a secondary empirical—what I would call *sociological*—observation concerning the actual relationship between the bourgeoisie and the subaltern, or subordinate, classes. The theoretically unsophisticated view of the relationship between the bourgeoisie and subaltern classes would solely be in terms of coercion. In this model those who dominate coerce the dominated either through the threat of violence or material depravation—either military or economic domination. However, Gramsci perceived that, as an empirical fact, on a sociological level, it had to be conceded that bourgeois domination is largely based upon the *consent*, rather than the coercion, of subaltern groups. The bourgeoisie do not dominate by virtue of their control of the military or the economy but rather through a series of consensual alliances with other classes and groups. This sociological claim of course drives a conceptual wedge into the core of the concept of hegemony. Both the bourgeoisie of a liberal society and the proletariat of a communist society, exercise hegemonic control sociologically speaking (based upon empirically observable consent), but only the latter is also normatively desirable. Only proletarian hegemony is both sociologically and normatively hegemonic.

The idea that bourgeois hegemony is based upon consent of the governed classes and yet is normatively undesirable raises the conceptually interesting idea that social actors can actively consent to their own domination in instances where such domination is contrary to their interests. This is, of course, different from the Greek hegemonic alliance, where it is assumed that the reason for consent is that it is in everyone's interest. The theoretically pertinent question is, of course, why do subaltern groups consent to their own domination if it is contrary to their particular interests?

In Gramsci's view, historically the bourgeoisie are the first class to move from coercive power to hegemonic power, which makes them substantially more powerful than any previously dominant class. The contrast between their domination and that of other classes is clearly seen in the contrast between the success of the 1917 Russian revolution and the impossibility of such a revolution in Western societies. Pre-1917 Russia was pre-bourgeois, and all that was necessary in order to gain the reins of power was to meet the coercion of the old regime with greater coercion, thus to gain control of the state. In contrast, such a simplistic strategy would not work in Western bourgeois society because the power of the state is rooted in a much more complex web of consent, which Gramsci attributes to "civil society." Gramsci contrasted the two as follows:

> In the East the State was everything, civil society was primordial and gelatinous; in the West, there was a proper relation between State and civil society, and when the State trembled a sturdy structure of civil society was at once revealed. The state was only an outer ditch, behind which there stood a powerful system of fortresses and earthworks. (Gramsci 1971: 238).

As is argued by Fontana in Chapter 2, the description of civil society as primordial and gelatinous is intended to imply that it is so highly underdeveloped as to be almost absent. In contrast, the powerful system of fortresses and earthworks is intended to suggest that this is where real power lies. Central to this contrast is the move from a coercive state to a modern state that educates society (Gramsci 1971: 260). The key to the creation of bourgeois domination and consent is the use of state power to get other classes to make sense of the world in a bourgeois way. Subaltern groups become socialized into the bourgeois order of things through an educational process whereby this way of perceiving reality becomes naturalized—as inherent in the "natural order" of things. This socialization should not be perceived in narrow terms as indoctrination or confined to formal schooling. Rather, people's overall interpretative horizon is shaped through everyday interaction.

In an argument which is reminiscent of both Gellner (1983) and Bourdieu (1991), Gramsci analysed the process whereby the Florentine dialect became Italian. His view of this process is instructive in understanding the workings of hegemony.

As Ives (2004: 102-125) notes, prior to unification there was no singular Italian language but a multiplicity of minor Latin-based languages spoken in the Italian peninsula. A political decision was taken to make Florentine the official language of Italy because it was associated with high culture and literature. Thus this dialect was known to the educated classes, although it was spoken as an everyday language by as little as two percent of the population. This meant that the linguistic dialects and mannerisms that were relatively easily attainable by the elite became the "correct way" to speak. The association between Florentine, now Italian, and some great classics, including Dante and Boccaccio, meant that this was not some arbitrary linguistic form which was contingently elevated but represented a "superior civilization." The language of school became consistent with the taken-for-granted knowledge of the bourgeoisie but inconsistent with that of the rural peasantry. However, the latter did not see this as the imposition of an alien cultural form (which is what it was) but as socialization into a higher civilized and educated form of speech. Consequently, they consented to the imposition of bourgeois speech upon their children.

Speech is, of course, not an empty set of arbitrary labels that are applied to the world, but also a way of interpreting the world. Thus subaltern groups, in effect, consent to the imposition of a bourgeois characterization of reality. Not only that, they also implicitly consented to the idea that a person's worth, as manifest in their ability to speak "correctly," be evaluated according to cultural linguistic norms which were essentially alien to them. A person who expressed him or herself clearly and with ease in Italian (as opposed to some rural dialect) became "obviously" educated, thus knowledgeable, hence likely to interpret the truth correctly. Those who expressed themselves haltingly or in an unnatural way in this linguistic form betrayed their origins. This created an incentive to internalize "proper" Italian. Thus linguistic competition was created which was, essentially, a form of embourgeoization, which was not based upon coercion but consent.

What we have said concerning language applies to the wider socialization of society as a whole. For Gramsci everyone is a "philosopher" in the sense that our perceptions of reality are interpretations of the world. He writes as follows:

> It must first be shown that all men are "philosophers,"…This philosophy is contained in: 1) language itself, which is a totality of determined notions and concepts and not just of words grammatically devoid of content; 2) "common sense" and "good sense"; 3) popular religion and, therefore, also in the entire system of beliefs, superstitions, opinions, ways of seeing things and of acting,… (Gramsci 1971:323)

This philosophy of everyday life is a product civil society which shapes the context of social action. The binary "common sense" and "good sense" is worthy of note: the "common sense" of bourgeois society is "good sense," while the "common sense" of parochial peasant society or working class neighborhoods has the same lower status as a local dialect. In the minds of the subaltern classes, the overall result is the coexistence of two conceptions of the world. One part is a hegemonic bourgeois order that is affirmed and aspired to discursively. The other, which is less visible, is representative of the subaltern classes' actual perception of the world as it would be without hegemony. The latter manifests itself fleetingly in social practices that do not receive discursive validation with the result of a disjuncture between theory and social practice (Gramsci 1971: 326).

The hegemonic way of perceiving the world is disseminated both through schools and by educated classes generally—technicians, doctors, lawyers and anyone who has received further education. Gramsci refers to this group as "organic intellectuals" who, unintentionally, by their socialization, effectively disseminate bourgeois hegemony.

If bourgeois social order is to be replaced by an alternative socialist vision of society, the counterhegemonic strategy task is to replace the bourgeois perception of the world, perpetuated by organic intellectuals, with a vision of society more suited to the interests and practices of the subaltern classes. The way that this can successfully be accomplished is to use the cognitive dissonance created by the gap between theory and practice. The key to counterhegemony is to formulate a vision which is consonant with the everyday social practices of the subaltern classes. In this sense, counterhegemony is a form of consciousness raising whereby discursive form is given to existing social practices.

In *Gramsci's Political Thought*, Femia usefully distinguishes proletarian and bourgeois hegemony by calling the former "integral" hegemony and the latter "decadent" or "minimal" hegemony (Femia 1987: 46). "Integral hegemony" represents a true "collective will," while decadent hegemony constitutes a distortion of the collective will due to the fact that the consent of the subaltern classes is not a true consent based upon a clear understanding of their own interests and social practices. In the case of "integral" hegemony the disjuncture between the normative and empirical sociological claim is overcome. It is both an empirical fact that the subaltern classes express consent to the hegemonic relationship and it is normatively correct or just that they should do so.

Hegemony and the World Order

As developed so far, we have a fourfold typology, based on the empirical dichotomy Hegemonic/Imperial and the normative dichotomy Positive/Negative as well as a Classical/Gramscian interpretive dichotomy, against which to interpret the claim that a specific actor is hegemonic. With regard to international politics, the assertion that the US is hegemonic, implies one of the following.

1. Classical Imperial/Negative. The US appears hegemonic but is really imperial. Based upon the Classical view of hegemony, this claim is a normatively negative evaluation to the effect that the US is the dominant party in a web of alliances in which it uses its privileged position to pursue its own ends. In this scenario, the US is interpreted as not respecting the autonomy or interests of its partners. In terms of observable behavior, the pursuit of unilateral foreign policy would be dominant, and multilateralism would be pursued only when it suited US, as opposed to collective, interests.

2. Classical Hegemonic/Positive. The US is genuinely hegemonic. The claim could be a normatively positive one. In this scenario the US is the leader of an alliance of states pursuing collective interests and respecting the autonomy of other states. In this interpretation, the US would be seen to pursue genuinely multilateral strategies relative to collective goals. In instances of conflict between the US and collective interests, the US would be expected to back, or give due weight to, the latter. The US would also be expected to respect the autonomy of members of the alliance, which (to use Kantian language) would entail never using others as a means to an end but always respecting them as an end in themselves.

3. Gramscian Hegemonic/Negative. The US is hegemonic in the same sense as the bourgeoisie are. This model is a sociological empirical claim to the effect that other states and actors consent to the US position of dominance. However, this consent does not represent their true interests and/or it constitutes an affirmation of a discourse which is essentially alien to their social practices.

In order to apply this model to the US, it is necessary to use Gramsci's account as a metaphor. Gramsci was writing about classes within nation states, while the US is a state and the arena is the world as a whole. However, if the concept of globalization has any meaning, it is a claim to the effect that the globe itself constitutes a social system which is largely replacing the nation state as a container of power (Malesevic and Haugaard 2002: 1-11). The conceptual equivalent of civil society of the nation state would be global culture and economy.

In this interpretation, people across the world are being socialized into making sense of reality in a manner that is functional to US dominance. As in the Gramsican model, this need not entail direct "brainwashing." Rather it takes place through the absorption of specific cultural norms of global society, which render certain forms of agency legitimate and logical, while demoting others as "local" and "irrelevant"—the functional equivalents of local dialects in the Italian language example.

In this model, counterhegemony would be the attempt to undermine US hegemony through opposing ideologies that give expression to everyday social practices. These would be local in the sense of being consonant with everyday practices yet global in their capacity to displace the advance of US-backed global culture and economy. With their fusion of local issues and global action, new social movements (with mottos like "global is local") would suggest themselves as the conceptual equivalent of socialist intellectuals and activists in the Gramscian model.

4. *Gramscian Hegemony/Positive*. US domination is the metaphorical equivalent of the proletariat becoming hegemonic. This claim is one of "integral" hegemony in which sociological fact and normative rightness are consonant with each other. In this interpretation, the spread of ideas functional to the globalization of the world through Americanization is a liberating force that contributes to the creation of a worldwide "collective will" that constitutes a force for justice. The consent that underpins this is not contrary to anyone's interests but represents a discursive formulation of a bid for normatively positive values, such as liberty, freedom, and democracy. This view is consonant with modernization theory and appears to be implicit in much recent neoconservative ideology.

These four models are "ideal types" in the Weberian sense. These models will not be found in their pure form and do not follow a strict "either/or" logic. It is not the case that if, for instance, US hegemony is found to approximate model three that there are not aspects of one, two, and four present. The "ideal" refers to the way in which an idea, or hypothesis, enables us to make sense of reality, not "ideal" in the sense of being perfect or desirable. Empirical facts are ordered by ideas and gain relationship to other facts through that order. With all ideal types, one model will tend to make more sense than rival ones but some elements will fit different ideal types. In all probability, one of the ideal types has the capacity to make better sense of data than the rest: it will be more economical in explanation, have greater consistency and predictive power. In the case of an evolving relationship between actors, such as the US and the rest of the world, one may see a fluid dynamic relationship between models in which one is more appropriate than others at specific junctures.

Power and Hegemony

The Classical and Gramscian views of hegemony suggest that power should not be perceived as purely coercive. Recent developments in the power debate would tend to confirm this view. In understanding hegemony, the power literature of the last thirty years provides a rich resource that can expand our conceptual vocabulary in a way that was open neither to the Classical theorists nor to Gramsci.

In the literature there is no universal agreement upon what constitutes the essence of power. This led Lukes (1974) to claim that power was an "essentially contested" concept. I would prefer to argue (Haugaard 2002: 1-4) that it is what the philosopher Wittgenstein terms a "family resemblance" concept. There is no single essence that defines the concept but there are a number of overlapping characteristics, as in a large family, which define membership. Each theory has local usage which makes sense for that theory but is not entirely applicable in a different context.

Power is also what is called a scalar concept. That is to say, various oppositions which characterize the power debate are not necessarily mutually exclusive. There is a broad scalar opposition between those who argue that power is consensual, as "power to," while others, at the opposite end of the scale, view power as conflictual —"power over." The consensual theorists include Parsons (1963), Arendt (1970), and Barnes (1988). Those at the conflictual end of the spectrum are Weber (1978), Dahl (1957), Bachrach and Baratz (1962), Wrong (1979), Poggi (2001), Mann (1986), and Lukes (1974, 2005). Between these positions, moving from the consensual to the conflictual side, are Haugaard (1997, 2003), Giddens (1981, 1984), Morriss (1987, 2003), Foucault (1979, 1980, 1981), and Clegg (1989).

The second opposition is between those who have an agent-centered view of power, whereby A exercises power over B by making B do something which he would not otherwise do. At the other end of this scale there is the systemic and structural view of power, whereby power is the property of social systems. The agent-centered view includes Dahl (1957), Bachrach and Baratz (1962), and Lukes (1974, 2005) while the systemic would include Parsons (1963) and Foucault (1979, 1980, 1981). However, in keeping with the attempt over the last twenty years or so by most social theorists to combine agency and structure, many contemporary thinkers fall between these positions. They include Giddens (1984), Clegg (1989), Barnes (1988), and Haugaard (1997).

If we examine the concept of hegemony we can see the same basic scalar oppositions. Hegemony as empire is an entirely conflictual relationship of domination. On the other hand, hegemony as an alliance and as integral hegemony, is a consensual view of hegemony. The view of hegemony as modelled on the Gramscian perception of the bourgeoisie, would be representative of the in-between position where conflict and consensus are combined. The agent-centered view of power is appropriate to the Classical vision of specific autonomous actors forming alliances. The systemic view of power can be related to structuralist Marxism but is not consonant with Gramscian hegemony. This is best covered by the in-between position, where there is conceptual space both for the fact individual actors have certain levels of autonomy and their relations have a structural systemic form which is greater than any individually chosen acts.

The combination of the in-between positions, with regard both to conflict and consensus and to agency and system, has the greatest potential to deepen our understanding of the type of phenomena that Gramsci had in mind. This applies both to US hegemony and to making sense of hegemony by specific groups or classes. Obviously, I cannot, at this point, summarize the relevant theories and perspectives in this regard but, based upon the work of Giddens, Clegg and Haugaard, I mention a few salient points to be borne in mind.

When we think of social actors, be they individuals, groups, or collectivities (such as sovereign states), they act within a context. The latter includes two kinds of resources, material resources, such as armaments, and social resources, which derive their meaning from social systems. If we consider hegemony as only conflictual and coercive, we are claiming that the key resources are solely material. However, if we take a Gramsican view, we are arguing for social resources as a basis for power and, in combination, these two types of resources set up a dynamic which is inverse and affects autonomy.

Let us take a simple example: the idea of an International Criminal Court. This is a resource which actors can use to prevail over one another. Country A wishes to prosecute someone from country B and, in order to further that aim, collectively with others, helps to set up the court as a set of structures. If A uses these structures successfully in a specific act of agency (prosecution), a number of things take place simultaneously. First of all, we have both conflict and consensus. B may not wish to comply (conflict) but does so, which entails consent. The structures of the International Criminal Court have been reproduced, and so the actors have gained a new systemic aspect to their social reality. The power and autonomy of A has been increased, in the sense that A now has a greater capacity for action than before these institutions were set up. This power is not A's alone but is the property of a social system.

In the momentary episodic exercise of power, actor B, has been reduced to subaltern actor for the purposes of that interaction. However, there are long-term implications of this, which work the other way. Actor A may have gained momentary autonomy and power, but these structures have the future potential to compromise A's autonomy. State B now has the potential to prosecute some member of state A. When B prevails over A, it is B's autonomy which has been increased and A's which has been compromised. Consequently, gaining power through social resources both increases and decreases autonomy at one and the same time and is both enabling and constraining. If A and B (and a whole number of other actors) enter into routine prosecutions through the International Criminal Court, then new social resources have been created, which increase power by a combination of conflict (the prosecution) and consent (the structures reproduced). Simultaneously, they also recreate a new system with implicit constraints.

So far we have methodologically bracketed coercive resources. Imagine that, after a period of time, country B decides to prosecute some highly regarded figure from country A and the latter decides not to be structurally constrained into compliance. A has the largest military forces in the world and, thus, can afford not to comply. What happens then? The structures of the International Criminal Court are not reproduced. Consent in structures has essentially been overridden by conflict and the structures of the criminal court have lost force. However, in the future, A has actually lost a power resource. If A now wishes to prosecute someone from B, B will no longer comply because of a belief in the legitimacy of the structures. Of course, A may ensure compliance by threat of force but this is a substitution of one kind of power for another. Coercion and structural systemic power exist in opposition to each other. On the one hand we have social resources, which are structural and systemic in form while, on the other, we have coercive physically-based resources, which are corrosive to the former.

For a would-be hegemon this creates a dilemma. On the one hand it is possible to gain a kind of stand-alone autonomy which is entirely based upon coercive resources (hegemony as empire). Alternatively, the aspiring hegemon may participate in the creation of structural resources which increase the total amount of power in the system. However, this binds actor A into a set of obligations with regard to subaltern actors B.

What we have is essentially a dynamic model whereby momentary, episodic, exercises of power reproduce structures. Every reproduction reaffirms the existence of this resource by legitimating the system of ideas in which they are carried. We have both conflict and consent and autonomy and structure being reproduced at the same time. On the other hand there is the option of physical resources, which deliver autonomy without interdependence and constraint but are corrosive to consensual hegemonic relations.

Structure and Content of the Book

The book is divided into three parts: "Theoretical Bases of Hegemony and Power," "Hegemony and Power in International Relations and Political Life," and "Postmodern and Feminist Approaches to Hegemony and Power." The logic of this three-part division is to move from theory, to the applications of this theory in International Relations, and then to the transformation of this debate by feminist and postmodern contributions.

Chapter 2, by Benedetto Fontana, gives the reader a thorough understanding of the concept of hegemony in the work of Gramsci. By way of introduction, Fontana analyzes the genesis of hegemony in Greek thought, arguing that it entails consensual leadership and that it is in conceptual opposition to violence and domination. Central to his account of Gramsci's theorization of hegemony is the Machiavellian image of the Centaur, who is half-animal and half-human. This image captures a dualism between domination and leadership, force and consent, authority and hegemony, and violence and civilization. In liberal political theory the nightwatchman state is conceptualized as a coercive institution which exists to protect civil society. In this model the state embodies violence but is a necessary evil because humans are less than perfect. The consensus and liberty of civil society is protected, although not created, by the state. In contrast, in Gramsci civil society is also a product of state power. The state as educator draws society together through hegemony by forging a common alliance among potentially conflicting groups through the creation of a common, hegemonic worldview. Thus the view of the state is partly a Hegelian one in which the state exists to realize liberty and reason and partly a Hobbesian one in which the state is coercive. Within this vision, both hegemony and any potentially successful counterhegemony are not simply about gaining control of coercive resources. Rather, it represents a conflict between different ways of defining reality.

In Chapter 3, Mark Haugaard relates Gramsci's theory of hegemony to the contemporary power literature. He begins by outlining Gramsci's and Laclau and Mouffe's interpretation of hegemony. The latter derives from Foucault's account of discourse formations, as systems of thought which define the parameters of social interaction. To the Foucauldian vision, Laclau and Mouffe add the idea that these discourses presuppose significant exclusions, the maintenance of which is central to hegemonic practice.

In the main body of the chapter, Haugaard combines these insights with the work of Barnes, Giddens, and his previous research to create his own theory of the working of hegemony. Central to this is the idea that social structures are meaning-given and continually subject to contestation in social interaction. Such structures are not external to social agents but constitute part of their ontology. Essentially structural conflict is about different ways of being in the world and this battle of ontologies is what lies at the core of hegemonic and counterhegemonic strategy. By way of conclusion, Haugaard argues that hegemonic power is the theoretical opposite of violence and coercion.

In Chapter 4, Philip G. Cerny introduces the reader to the concept of hegemony in international relations through an analysis of US hegemony. His opening premise is that hegemony is an essentially contested concept, which cannot be covered by a single definition. In the IR literature a fundamental division exists between those who view hegemony largely as a preponderance of power, irrespective of consent and those who conceptualize it, following the Classical and Gramscian view, as a form of leadership rooted in consent. These views are not simply arbitrary choices but are based upon the nature of social order itself, whereby particular interpretations of hegemony are derived from focussing upon specific aspects of social order. In the systemic whole of actual social life these elements are, of course, interrelated and frequently inversely so. So, for instance, as we have already argued, hegemony as preponderance of power is actually inversely related to hegemony as consent.

The theory of social order that underpins this analysis is derived from Cerny's extension of Lukes' account of the three dimensions of power. Lukes' first dimension of power is simple episodic power, whereby A exercises power over B, when A makes B do something which B would not otherwise do. The second dimension of power is structural power, whereby certain social structures define relative relations of empowerment and disempowerment through the "rules of the game." The third dimension of power is the system of ideas in which these structures are embedded. Cerny calls this "infrastructural hegemony" and argues that it is hegemony from below, in the sense that it is rooted in the ideas and practices of social actors. This is the Gramscian view, while focus upon the first and second dimensions results in the simple preponderance of power view of hegemony.

Pursuance of dominance at these three levels is frequently at variance with one another. For instance, preponderance of power at the first level may be gained by supporting totalitarian regimes that are "good for business" or useful in a military alliance. However, at level three infrastructural hegemony presupposes the spread of American values across the globe and central to this is liberty and democracy. So, the former undermines the latter. In deciding which of these should have priority, Cerny argues that true power comes from infrastructural hegemony. Consequently, the long-term interests of the US as a hegemonic actor should lie in prioritizing decisions which reinforce this kind of hegemony.

In Chapter 5, Howard H. Lentner provides us with an overview and comparison of the uses of the concept of power and hegemony in the political science and the international relations literature. Central to his analysis is the insight that the two literatures are divided from each other by having different normative and empirically substantive premises.

The chief normative concerns of political scientists analyzing power are framed by democratic theory. For instance, Dahl develops his first formulations of power (1957) as a defense of democracy, while Lukes (1974) and Foucault (1979) develop theirs as part of a critique of the workings of democracy—which is what led Lukes to argue that power was essentially contested. In contrast, for international relations theorists the usual normative motivation is the desire to understand balance of power and the avoidance of war or genocide.

On the empirical level, political scientists think in terms of actors as individuals who wish to exercise power over each other within the context of a social order made up of social structures. The latter are rules (Giddens 1984) or systems of meaning (Clegg 1989, Foucault 1981, and Haugaard 1997). In contrast, in international politics the main actors are collectivities (mainly states but also organizations) that are working in a context of relative anarchy. This entails that social agents are confronted with the problem of continuity and survival in a way in which social actors are not, consequently defensive power becomes central. Given the absence of a strong social order in the international arena, structures tend to be thought of relationally, for instance, unipolar versus bipolar and multipolar relations.

While both groups of scholars are interested in the distribution of power, working from a normative agenda of democratic theory entails a restricted vantage point in which diffusion of power is considered normatively desirable, because it facilitates democracy, while concentration and dominance interferes with it. In contrast, for an international relations theorist, it is not clear in advance which distributions of power favor peace and stability. Consequently, the role of unintended effects of various distributions of power are analyzed in much greater depth in international relations.

Through the body of the article, Lentner uses these juxtapositions to great effect to provide a rich tapestry of contrasts. He concludes with an overall evaluation of the potential for cross-fertilization and exchange. While he clearly believes that the coming together of these debates would be hugely fruitful, he is only cautiously optimistic that it will take place because of the fundamentally different premises.

In Chapter 6 Henri Goverde examines the hegemonic relationship between the US and Europe. He begins from the image of Europe as Venus and the US as Mars and argues that this mirrors two views of hegemony. The European view is premised upon the Gramscian perception of hegemony as rooted in "civic culture." Empirically this presupposes shared norms of interaction which constrain both hegemon (US) and the subaltern actors. On a normative level this presupposes collective goals relative to which no actor can be a means to an end. The other vision of hegemony is simply as preponderance of power, which constitutes relations of domination. This view is dominant in the Administration of Bush Junior and with neoconservatives. However, they do not exhaust the totality of US opinion. Neoliberals see the rule of law as essential to a world economic order. Consequently, theirs is a neo-Gramscian position whereby the spread of common norms and civic culture constitute a significant aspect of globalization. The European view of hegemony and the neoliberal perception would lend themselves to multilateral foreign policy, while the view of hegemony as domination lends itself to unilateralism. Because the latter is dominant in the Bush Junior administration, we see the predominance of unilateralism. However, neoliberalism is also a significant player, consequently there are multilateral forces at play.

As we have argued, the view of power as domination leads to a long-term cost in terms of hegemonic power. It may increase immediate autonomy but also entails that systemic structures are not reproduced and the latter have the long-term potential to augment the power of the hegemon. George Bush Senior was of course conscious of this and, for instance, in the Gulf War made a substantially greater effort to create a collective will through the UN, than his son attempted with the invasion of Iraq. Given that hegemony as unilateralism has this cost in terms of effective power, it begs the question: why is this not immediately obvious to the Bush Junior administration? The answer which Goverde proposes is in terms of intellectual isolation created by "groupthink" psychology.

In Chapter 7 Tomohisa Hattori introduces his analysis of international aid and hegemony with some general arguments on the philosophy of social science. In this context, Hattori puts himself forward as a "critical realist."

The social sciences exist along a scalar continuum between positivism and constructivist relativism. The positivist views social life as real in the same sense as natural phenomena. In contrast, the social constructivist views social life as a manifestation of essentially arbitrary systems of meaning imposed upon social life by interpretation. The former position is flawed by its failure to distinguish the qualitative difference between natural objects and structures which do not simply exist out there but are the result of social practice. In contrast, social constructivists take the latter all too seriously, with the result that they wind up in a form of relativism whereby social life is no more than different language games. Critical realism attempts to bring these two positions together by arguing, on the one hand, that social life is indeed real and open to falsification in the way that the natural sciences are while, at the same time, perceiving that social phenomena are qualitatively different from natural phenomena. Social phenomena do not exist "out there" in the natural world in the same way as physical objects but are constituted through complex sets of relations. However, for a critical realist, this fact does not make them any less real. This critical realism informs Hattori's account of aid and hegemony. Hattori observes that there is a remarkable correlation between those who give charity worldwide and those who benefit most from global capitalism. Bilateral donor-recipient relations coincide with bilateral creditor-debtor relations in most cases. As we have seen, central to the Gramscian concept of hegemony is the coupling of conflict and consent. Hattori argues that the giving of charity is central to the process whereby consent is created to global capitalism. The dynamic which Hattori pinpoints is in terms of exchange theory and Bourdieu's analysis of habitus and capital. Essentially, donor-recipient relations appear like unreciprocated exchange, in which an active powerful agent helps a passive needy subject. This type of exchange is particular to capitalism and is also found in phenomena such as the welfare state. In other words, it is a systemic structural relationship. These relations do not have a stable existence in time and space but constantly have to be reproduced. In his account of symbolic power and various forms of noneconomic capital, Bourdieu argues that central to the perpetuation of a set of relations of domination is both a naturalization and obscuring of the exploitative aspect of those specific social forms. Giving charity and the acceptance thereof are practices constituting a complex ritual whereby the beneficiaries of globalization obscure their exploitative relationship with regard to the subaltern elements within the system. Thus they make it appear part of the natural order of things that they should be dominant. A set of constraints is created for the subaltern actors which renders them subaltern and through the ritual of accepting donation those constraints are legitimized. They are essentially drawn into a process whereby they misrecognize the systemic sources of their disempowerment.

The third part of the book brings together three constructivist interpretations of hegemony. Unlike Hattori, the three authors are comfortable with postmodern theorizations of reality construction.

In Chapter 8 Elina Penttinen opens her paper in a highly Foucauldian manner, which is intended to jolt the reader out of their taken-for-granted reality. Foucault either presents readers with the unfamiliar and tells them that it was once part of familiar taken for-granted-reality or, alternatively, presents them with the familiar and informs them that it is mistaken. Both techniques disorient and in the resulting reorientation the reader is forced to question her taken-for-granted reality. Penttinen begins with an account of the mundane: she is driving on a sunny day looking for the right gear, while listening to the radio. Then she hears the news that a bill to criminalize the buying of sexual services has been postponed. She thumps the wheel and exclaims "Yes!" in delight. The reader is bemused: this is a feminist author opposing the criminalization of prostitution in Finland, where most of the prostitutes are women trafficked from Eastern Europe—victims par excellence exploited by Western men of dubious sexual preferences. Penttinen should be horrified, not delighted: our taken-for-granted reality is insufficient to make sense of the situation.

Central to Foucault's perception of power is a distinction between deep conflicts and shallow conflicts. The former, are conflicts over systems of meaning where dominant structures are resisted. In contrast, shallow conflicts reproduce the existing structures of meaning. In a sense, shallow conflicts reproduce the structural consensus that underlies conflict. It can be argued that this is the consent that underpins hegemony. Once structures are consented to deep conflict is avoided by excluding certain systems of meaning. Thus existing relations of domination are reproduced.

It is Penttinen's hypothesis that the idea of protecting East European prostitutes by criminalizing prostitution represents a shallow conflict which, in the longer term, reinforces the existing hegemonic project. In masculinist discourse concerning protection, security, and nationhood, there is a longstanding tradition of the male protecting and providing security for the female, passive, nation. Male subjective agency is realized through binary opposition to the weak female in need of security. In the debate concerning the criminalization of prostitution, Eastern women are presented as passive objects in need of security. They are spoken for and protected. Anyone criticizing the protection of these women is, ipso facto, in favor of their insecurity and exploitation as prostitutes. The police point out that the criminalization of prostitution actually renders prostitutes more vulnerable than before, but such assertions are outside the discourse of the "true."

The model of "protecting these other women" taps into a familiar well-established masculinist discourse. The fact that Finnish feminists are using this hegemonic discourse means that they will be heard. However, the unintended consequence is that the dominant hegemonic discourse of an active subject who protects a passive object becomes reproduced. The reader who is disoriented by the introduction to Penttinen's article is confronted with the hegemonic nature of her taken-for-granted reality. Once this is realized, a reversal of meaning takes place, whereby what appeared as intuitively radical and progressive becomes visible as a moment of closure or an act of structuration to hegemonic domination.

In Chapter 9 Saul Newman interrogates the place of power in contemporary postmodern social theory. He structures his article around the theme of the displacement of the locus of power. The central debate between anarchists and Marxists concerned whether the state was the locus of bourgeois power (Marxists) or power and domination in general (anarchists). For Marxists the secret to emancipation was to displace bourgeois with proletarian control of the state. However, anarchists argued that the source of domination was state power itself, which should be dissolved. Gramsci's contribution was to perceive that bourgeois power was not coterminus with the state as narrowly defined but included civil society. Although, the three positions represent a gradual displacement of power, there still exists a "place" of power.

What is central to Foucault's work is the displacement of the locus of power. Power has no source and is everywhere in the micro practices of everyday life. Neither is power simply something negative which once overcome leads to emancipation. The subject who desires emancipation constitutes a subject who is the product of power in its positive form—as constitutive of reality.

While Newman welcomes the Foucauldian move, he notes that it throws up two problems for radical critique: a) there is no longer an obvious target of revolution and b) there is no privileged position for the subject from which to mount his critique. These are the essential conservative implications of Foucauldianism which have been noted by many including Taylor (1984) and Fraser (1985).

Newman's solution is to draw upon the work of Lacanian-inspired discourse theory, in particular Laclau, Žižek, and Lefort. Discourse theory is, of course, radically anti-essentialist. However, Lacan argues that there are "anchoring points" which constitute master signifiers in chains of metaphoric and metonymic movements between signifiers. These "nodal" points give the illusion of fixity, without which systems of meaning would disintegrate into an indefinite play of differences. Removal of these points would be akin to removing the woof from a tapestry. However, these signifiers are in themselves considered to be empty and defined by an essential lack. This means that meaning is only partly fixed and contestation is always an imminent possibility. Within this hegemony is constituted by the manner in which these essentially empty places structure the conditions of possibility.

Newman distinguishes between ethics and morality, arguing that the quest for universal moral norms constitutes the attempt to fill these empty spaces and thus contribute to the reproduction of hegemony. However, an ethic of antagonism and resistance takes place in that empty space by refusing the structuring logic of the moral. It is a counterhegemonic strategy to refuse to fill the empty space. Critical thought is a moment of madness that refuses the immanent logic of the void. For instance, nodal points such as equality and liberty are usually structured as having an oppositional logic. A critically ethical stance would be radical refusal to accept this logic. Equaliberty constitutes an ethical postmodern, counterhegemonic inter-pretative horizon.

Chapter 10 is a further theorization of postmodern perspectives on hegemony. Based upon the same authors as Newman, Kevin Ryan argues that in postmodern theory the void, the excluded, and the contingent, which are constantly present in the moment of the reproduction of meaning, constitute the conditions of possibility for a subversive act that is counterhegemonic. However, in postmodern thought the radical decentering of the subject entails that this moment can be conceptualized as analogous to a meeting between the edges of the tectonic plates on the earth's crust (my image). They throw up volcanoes, which are subversive acts, but in the longer term contribute to the creation of new hegemonic tectonics which, in themselves, are only a manifestation of hegemonic tectonic shifts. From a social theory perspec-tive, this is not only unsatisfactory in its radical denial of agency but, from the perspective of social critique, is unsatisfactory in that it offers no criteria for the social subject to pull up the flag of justice as a form of critique. However, the modernist corollary is equally unsatisfactory in presupposing what is, essentially, an undersocialized concept of agency (who resists from one's "true self") or an essentialist discourse (justice outside meaning).

Based upon the work of Haugaard, Ryan outlines a theoretical methodology which has the potential to provide a way through, without foundering either on the Scyla of postmodernism or the Charybdis of modernism. In Haugaard's work we find a social subject who is not a singular unified subject as in modern theory. The self is made up of interpretative horizons which are frequently incommensurable. The self who practices science or administers bureaucratic files is the same self who may be a religious being or a perfect lover. These interpretative horizons are not stitched seamlessly together in the individual. They remain separate through the ability of the competent social agent to switch interpretative horizons depending upon context: one may be a scientist in the morning, a bureaucrat in the afternoon, a religious practitioner at sunset, and a romantic poetic lover after dusk. While this may seem like a source of schizophrenia (and in some instances literally is), this also offers the potential for autonomy. This is not the radical, undersocialized autonomy of modernism, but autonomy gained from mirroring interpretative hori-zons against one another.

The resisting subject mirroring interpretative horizons against each other is structurally constrained. This constraint is not a subjectless force operating on its own but is derived from others as subjects. Power comes from the ability to act in concert with other subjects. Without this the would-be counterhegemonic subject is speaking a "private language," which is entirely impotent as a social intervention. The social subject is thus subject to the internal constraints of her own constitutive multiple interpretative horizons and the multiple horizons of others. However, the fact that others are similarly not unified selves opens the possibility for a contingency which is neither subjectless, as in postmodernism, nor based upon undersocialized subjects or essentialisms, as in modernism.

Relative to the four possible interpretations of hegemony outlined earlier, it is clearly the case that the authors in this work agree that the Gramscian image of bourgeois, or decadent, hegemony is the most challenging and pertinent aspect of hegemony for making sense of the contemporary world. Understanding how this combination of conflict and consent operates is one of the greatest challenges of contemporary social thought and I think it fair to say that each of these chapters substantially deepens our insight into the workings of this process.

Theoretical Bases of Hegemony and Power

Chapter 2

State and Society:

The Concept of Hegemony in Gramsci

Benedetto Fontana

Power and hegemony are important concepts in the study of politics. Power especially is crucial. Most thinkers regard power as the underlying and unifying concept of politics. In both normative and empirical theory it has played a central role in the formulation of theoretical frameworks and analytical models to describe and prescribe political behavior. From Aristotle and Thucydides, to Hobbes and Machiavelli, to Dahl, Arendt, and Foucault its meaning, definition, and utility have been debated and contested (Haugaard 2002; Goverde et al. 2000). Thus there is an enormous literature on power and its analysis, a literature that extends centuries to the origins of political thinking in the West.

Hegemony, however, has gained wide currency only in recent decades and today has become quite popular in academic as well as in public discourse. Though it may be traced all the way back to the ancient Greeks, it first emerged as a conceptual and theoretical tool in the post-War World II era as a consequence of the dissemination of the work of the Italian revolutionary and Marxist Antonio Gramsci (Williams 1960; Nardone 1971; Buci-Glucksman 1975; Anderson 1977; Adamson 1980; Germino 1990). Originally used by Gramsci within a specifically Marxist, European, and Western context, the term has been deployed throughout the humanities and the social sciences. It is found in various and widely different disciplines and fields of study, from political science (and its constituent subfields, especially international studies) to sociolinguistics, sociology, literary and cultural studies, to the field of education and pedagogy. Indeed, ideas originally formulated by Gramsci pervade contemporary political and cultural discourses.

This chapter will discuss Gramsci's concept of hegemony and its relation to his political thought. It will attempt to clarify and explicate its multilayered senses, and will try to unpack the complex of ideas that together form the concept. In so doing it addresses such questions as: why hegemony, that is, how and why did Gramsci come to talk about hegemony? Why was hegemony added to the discussion and analysis of bourgeois capitalist society regarding relations of domination and subordination, class conflict, revolution, and reform? And finally, in what ways, if at all, does it differ from such other terms as power, domination, subjection, dictatorship? Does it add new or novel intellectual and theoretical substance to the discourse of power?

Hegemony in History

Gramsci's thought is the product of three fundamental developments that came together in the first decades of the twentieth century: first, the debate within Marxism about the necessary and sufficient conditions for revolution; second, the victory of fascism, and the defeat of the left, in Italy and parts of Western Europe; and third, the Bolshevik revolution in Russia (Cammett 1967; Davidson 1977; Clark 1977). All three compelled Gramsci to rethink the theoretical and conceptual bases of Marxist political thought, especially its understanding of power and the state.

Before we take up hegemony in Gramsci, however, a discussion of the way hegemony was understood and used prior to Gramsci will be useful. It will both place contemporary notions of hegemony in context, and at the same time help to identify Gramsci's use of it. Moreover, it will be seen that Gramsci's notion was especially prefigured in that of ancient Greek thinkers (Fontana 2005, 2000, 1993). Hegemony derives from the Greek ἡγεμών (guide, ruler, leader) and ἡγεμωνία (rule, leadership) and generally means the preeminence or supremacy that a state, social group, or even an individual may exercise over others.

In ancient Greece one meaning attributed to the term hegemon is leader of a military alliance of the various city states freely and voluntarily entered into. A second related meaning of hegemon is a *polis* as the leader of an alliance constituted by a number of *poleis* which join together freely as a response to military threat. Thus hegemony may be seen as an interstate system where a given state exercises power and leadership over an alliance of reciprocally consenting states. Herodotus in his *Histories* relates the war of the Greeks against the Persians and sees the Greeks coming together under the hegemonic leadership of Athens and Sparta. Thucydides, too, in his *History of the Peloponnesian War*, often uses hegemony as a means to describe both a military and a political alliance of autonomous states. Thus the Delian League, originally established as a consensual alliance of free states under the hegemony of Athens as a means to repel the Persian threat against the common interests of the members, gradually turned into an Athenian Empire, in which allies were transformed into dependent subjects. From an alliance in which Athens' leadership served the common interest, the League was transformed into a form of rule in which power was exercised purely in the self-interest of Athens.[1]

Thus, with the ancient Greeks hegemony is used to describe an alliance in which a state attains preeminent military and political leadership. Such a hegemonic alliance is characterized by four fundamental elements (Ehrenburg 1960: 113-114; 1973). First, it has dual structure: the leading state or hegemon and its allies are structurally independent and distinct from one another. The second element is the absence of an alliance-wide or common citizenship. Each *polis* retains its own citizenship criteria. The third element pertains to the fluid nature of membership in the alliance: *poleis* joined or left the alliance periodically over time, and their membership depended upon both their perceived self-interest and the shifting power relations of the international environment. And the fourth element is the historical (but not conceptual or analytical) tendency of the hegemonic alliance to become transformed into an empire.

In addition, both Aristotle and Isocrates refer to hegemony and use it to make a dichotomy between despotic or imperial and hegemonic rule. In the *Politics* Aristotle establishes two fundamental forms of rule, despotic and political (or constitutional). The first refers to power exercised over unequals in the self-interest of those who exercise power, whereas the second refers to power exercised by and among equals in the common interest of all. The term hegemony is used when Aristotle wants to discuss the leadership of equals in the interest of all, and despotism is used when he discusses the domination of others in the ruler's self-interest (Aristotle 1998: 1277b, 1278b-1279b, 1333a39-1334a5). The distinction here is crucial: the first refers to rule or government of free and equal citizens, while the second describes the power exercised by a master over slaves. Aristotle directly opposes hegemony (understood as leadership) to despotism or domination. It is also important to point out that hegemony in Aristotle is intimately linked to his typology of regimes or constitutions, in which legitimate or just forms are contrasted with illegitimate and unjust types, where supremacy of the law and pursuit of the common good are the distinguishing criteria.

Hegemony is also important to the rhetorician Isocrates. In his *Panegyricus*, for example, Isocrates criticizes the Athenians' utilitarian transformation of the Delian League into the Athenian Empire, and simultaneously explains Athens' defeat by Sparta to its despotic rule over Greeks. Like Aristotle, he distinguishes hegemonic from despotic rule: the first is leadership exercised over consenting and autonomous allies, and the second is domination coercively exercised over conquered subjects. At the same time, Isocrates understands the exercise of hegemony as closely interwoven with the generation and formulation of moral/intellectual, cultural, and educational ideas. He sees Athens as the generator and organizer of such ideas, and thus as the logical and natural hegemonic leader. Athens is the school of Hellas, the teacher and guide (that is, the hegemon) not only of Greeks but of all peoples (Isocrates 2000: 20, 50).

The idea that Athens is the cultural, moral, and intellectual leader of Greece (an idea depicted by Thucydides in Pericles' Funeral Oration) suggests another meaning for hegemony, one different from those described above, yet related to them in important ways. This other sense is that of hegemony as a guiding or governing principle or idea. Again, we can find this in Isocrates. Elaborating on both Plato and Gorgias, Isocrates posits the preeminence of reason and discourse in all human and social affairs. Within the context of Athenian political and social institutions such a belief meant that rhetoric, public speech, and dialectical reasoning were seen to be crucial to both state and society. At the same time, the intellectual and moral controversies (such as those between Plato and the Sophists) spawned various schools of thought, each formulating opposing discourses and narratives which competed for recognition and preeminence (Guthrie 1971). In addition, Greek political thought emerged out of, and tried to grapple with, the perennial problem of the relative value of power and knowledge, and of the nature of their relation. The problem was how to wed knowledge (philosophy) and power (political leadership) such that a just and stable political order could be established. Power denuded of knowledge becomes mere violence and coercion, purposeless and mindless. At the same time, knowledge stripped of power lacks a social and political foundation and is thus ineffective. Thinkers such as Plato, Aristotle, and Isocrates delved into the ways that power and knowledge could mutually reinforce each other. In effect, hegemony understood as a governing or guiding principle underlines the purpose and direction of Greek political thought: to achieve a synthesis of power and knowledge, such that each would inform the other.

Since ancient political thought, and before Gramsci's social and political theory, only two usages of hegemony may be identified. The first, under the general name of "hegemonism," equated hegemony purely and simply with any form of domination or exercise of power (Scruton 1982: 200). Generally hegemony was viewed as the application of the term to international politics, in which hegemony referred to states possessing or exercising a preponderance of power, such that one state dominates and subjugates other states.

A second understanding of hegemony, one more closely related to that of the ancients and to that of Gramsci, appeared during the late nineteenth and early twentieth centuries in the course of the debates and polemics among the leaders of the Russian Social Democratic Party (Anderson 1976-77: 15-17). As socialists such as Plekhanov, Axelrod, Lenin, and Trotsky introduced into a socioeconomically and politically backward Russia a Marxist socialism originally designed for the advanced capitalist societies of the West, it became necessary to define the role of a minority working in an overwhelmingly peasant society, as well as to establish the relation between this class, the peasantry, and the national minorities of the Russian Empire (Haimson 1966). In the process they used hegemony to describe the leading role of the proletariat in a revolutionary system of alliances among the anti-tsarist forces. Thus Axelrod writes, "By virtue of the historical position of our proletariat, Russian Social Democracy can acquire hegemony (*gegemoniya*) in the struggle against absolutism" (Anderson 1976-77: 16). Lenin also called for the establishment of a "real hegemony" of the working class in Russia (Anderson 1976-77: 16). And he notes, "As the only consistently revolutionary class of contemporary society, it [the proletariat] must be the leader in the struggle of the whole people for a fully democratic revolution, in the struggle of *all* the working and exploited people against the oppressors and exploiters. The proletariat is revolutionary only in so far as it is conscious of and gives effect to this idea of the hegemony of the proletariat" (Anderson 1976-77: 17). It is clear that hegemony was understood by Lenin and Trotsky as a tactical alliance between the working class and other exploited groups (especially the peasantry), one to be directed at both the political absolutism of the tsars and the socioeconomic supremacy of the ruling groups. At the same time, it is also clear that the hegemonic leading role assigned to the working class was the product, not so much of a convergence of values and interests among the revolutionary groups, but rather of the value, weight, and position the proletariat was given in a Marxist and later Leninist theory of revolution. That is to say, the working class is hegemonic precisely because it is the carrier and bearer of the most advanced political and social knowledge. Thus, the hegemony of the working class presupposed and required the subordination of the allied groups and the loss of their political autonomy to the hegemon. In any case, the Bolshevik seizure of power in October 1917 and the subsequent armed dispersal of the Constituent Assembly in 1918 froze all political activity. The imposition of party dictatorship and revolutionary terror underlined the bankruptcy of alliance formation as a means to state power, and revealed hegemony as a mere political formula (to use Mosca's phrase) that masked the reality of domination and subjection.

Gramsci, using both the ancient Greek understanding of hegemony and the experiences of the Bolsheviks in Russia, develops the concept as a means to understand and to explain the strength and the resilience of modern bourgeois society. With hegemony Gramsci tries to capture the power dynamics and power differences within society, and to show the ways and means by which power persists and endures over time.

Hegemony in Gramsci

Gramsci's political and theoretical enterprise was to discover within a fragmented Italian and European reality the material and cultural forces that would lead to the formation of a new, more universal sociopolitical order (Buttigieg 1990; 1993; 1994). All this, of course, in order to develop the political, theoretical, and strategic means to organize and mobilize what he called the subaltern (subordinate) groups so that they might usher in a new form of state and a new order. It is ironic that today hegemony, developed by Gramsci in order to further the goals of socialist revolution, lives on as a theoretical and conceptual term while the mass and popular movement for which it was originally developed no longer exists.

In Gramsci hegemony means the supremacy of one group or class over other classes or groups; it is established by means other than reliance on violence or coercion. In the prison writings he used hegemony as a way of explaining political failure; and in his earlier writings hegemony is also used to describe the leadership position of the working class within an alliance of other classes. We should note that the second was a formulation used by Gramsci in the struggle for power, and the first was elaborated after the power struggle was lost, and thus was a means to explain the failure.

Gramsci emphasizes that politics and political activity are fundamentally centered on the attaining and maintaining of power. And power, according to Gramsci, is constituted by a dual or dyadic opposition: force and consent, violence and persuasion. Here Gramsci is consciously using Machiavelli's metaphor of the Centaur *The Prince* (Machiavelli 1985: ch. 18):

> Thus, you must know that there are two ways of fighting: one with laws, the other with force. The first is proper to man, the second to beasts; but because the first is often not enough, one must have recourse to the second. Therefore it is necessary for a prince to know well how to use the beast and the man. This was covertly taught to princes by ancient writers, who wrote that Achilles, and many other ancient princes, were given to Chiron the centaur to be raised. . . . To have as teacher a half-beast, half-man means nothing other than that a prince must know how to use both natures, and one without the other is not durable. (Translation somewhat altered).

Gramsci notes that the "dual perspective" pertains to the two levels or two elements of political action, which correspond to the "dual nature of Machiavelli's Centaur —half-animal and half-human. They are the levels of force and consent, authority and hegemony, violence and civilization, of the moment of the individual and that of the universal ('Church' and 'State'). . . ." (Gramsci 1975: 1576; 1971: 169-170; Fontana 1993).

These oppositions parallel Gramsci's characterization of the supremacy of a social group in terms of the exercise of moral and intellectual leadership over allied and associated groups, and of the exercise of domination—"even with armed force" —in order to subdue antagonistic groups. Here is the full reference:

> The methodological criterion on which our own study must be based is the following: that the supremacy of a social group manifests itself in two ways, as "domination" [dominio] and as "moral and intellectual leadership" [direzione]. A social group dominates antagonistic groups, which it tends to "liquidate," or to subjugate perhaps even by armed force; it leads kindred and allied groups. A social group can, and indeed must, already exercise "leadership" before winning governmental power (this indeed is one of the principal conditions for the winning of such power); it subsequently becomes dominant when it exercises power, but even if it holds it firmly in its grasp, it must continue to "lead" as well (Gramsci 1975: 2010-11; 1973: 57-58).

It should be noted that this formulation bears a striking resemblance to the distinction established by Aristotle and Isocrates regarding the exercise of political power: leadership or *hegemonia* is exercised over equals and allies in the interest of those over whom power is exercised, and domination or *despoteia* is exercised over enemies over unequals, such as slaves or "barbarians," in the interest of those who exercise power. The *dominio/direzione* dyad, moreover, parallels quite closely the ancient Greeks' (such as Isocrates' and Thucydides') understanding of an interstate alliance based on the voluntary consensus of free and autonomous members (Fontana 2000). Gramsci's reference to "kindred" and to "allied" must be linked to the important qualifier to his term "leadership," namely "moral and intellectual." It is the latter that determines the nature of the relation between leader and led, ruling and led; just as it is the latter that defines the meaning and content of what is kindred and allied.

Leadership (moral and intellectual) is again closely linked with hegemony in one of Gramsci's letters from prison, in which he says that "Croce emphasizes solely that moment in historico-political activity which in politics is called 'hegemony', the moment of consent, of cultural leadership, to distinguish it from the moment of force, of constraint, of state-legislative or police intervention" (Gramsci 1965: 616).

Gramsci's emphasis on the moment of consent, of persuasion, and of leadership leads him to construct a theory of intellectuals and their role. Intellectuals are the "organizers" of consent and persuasion. The stability, legitimacy and persistence of the over all sociopolitical system is achieved by means of moral, intellectual and cultural systems formulated by intellectuals. As such, intellectuals act as links or mediators between the subordinate groups and the elites (Gramsci 1971: 12). Intellectuals, for Gramsci, "exercise hegemony, which presupposes a certain collaboration, i.e, an active and voluntary (free) consent" on the part of the people (Gramsci 1971: 271).

In his discussion of intellectuals, Gramsci identifies civil society as the locus or space within which the organization of consent is generated (Bobbio 1975; Garin 1975; Nardone 1971; Buci-Glucksman 1975; Germino 1990; Buttigieg 1995; Adamson 1987; Texier 1989; Cohen and Arato 1992; Fontana 2006). He delineates "two major superstructural 'levels': the one that can be called 'civil society', that is the ensemble of organisms commonly called private, and that of 'political society' or 'the State'" (Gramsci 1971: 12). Hegemony is exercised within the first level, and "direct domination or command" is exercised within the second. These two levels are connected by intellectuals. They provide both vertical and horizontal mediation. That is, within both political society (such as administrative and public agencies) and civil society (such as sects, interest groups, political parties) intellectuals act as agents of reciprocal communication, and they simultaneously connect civil society with political society.

The dual nature of power is revealed more sharply in another letter of Gramsci, in which he again contrasts "political Society (or dictatorship, or coercive apparatus to ensure that the popular masses conform to the type of production and economy of a given moment)" to "civil society (or hegemony of a social group over the whole national society exercised through so-called private organizations, such as the Church, trade unions, schools, etc.) . . ." (Gramsci 1965: 481).

Thus we have a series of opposing, yet interrelated, dyads. One set, derived from Machiavelli's force/persuasion polarity, identifies as a general proposition the defining characteristic of politics:

Benedetto Fontana

Force	Consent
Authority[2]	Hegemony
Violence	Civilization (*Civiltà*)

A second set locates the foregoing within a particular historical and political context (namely, the Risorgimento and the formation of the Italian state): domination is opposed to leadership (moral and intellectual). The process of Italian unification relied too heavily on domination, and not sufficiently on leadership. Cavour and his party unified the peninsula by means of conquest and annexation. Because the popular masses—the overwhelming majority of which were peasants—were not mobilized and were excluded, the ruling groups established a state with an exceedingly narrow social and political foundation. Moreover, because the formation of a liberal state meant destroying the political and territorial power of the Papacy, the new state could not mobilize and deploy religion (the Catholic Church and its various ancillary organizations within society) to generate social and cultural support. Thus the Italian state was the result of an imposition from above (domination), rather than a product of a mass movement from below (moral and intellectual leadership).

Gramsci's reference to Machiavelli underlines several important points. First, politics occurs in the context of conflict, struggle, and contestation. As Machiavelli says, "there are two methods of *fighting* [my italics]. . . ." (Machiavelli 1985: ch. 18). Second, without consent or persuasion it would be impossible to wield effective force or violence, in the same way that force is necessary to guarantee or secure the use of persuasion. As Machiavelli puts it in *The Prince*, "when they [prophets, or innovators] . . . are able to use force, then it is that they are rarely in peril. From this it arises that all the armed prophets conquered and the unarmed ones were ruined . . . [for] the nature of peoples is variable, and it is easy to persuade them of something, but difficult to keep them in that persuasion. And thus things must be ordered in such a mode that when they no longer believe, one can make them believe by force" (Machiavelli 1985: ch. 6). Machiavelli's "armed prophet" corresponds to Gramsci's polarity domination/leadership. In addition, by equating political action with conflict and competition Gramsci points to the necessary and intimate connection with their opposites, namely community and consensus. Indeed, one presupposes the other.

Sheldon Wolin, in his famous *Politics and Vision*, describes politics, or the political, as constituted by two apparently contradictory, yet closely interwoven, elements, each mutually acting on the other (Wolin 2004). The first is the search for a common ground or *topos* within which the common or the public good may be engendered and attained. The second sees politics as a competition or struggle for advantage and for power, both in terms of material interest or economic goods, and in terms of competing or opposing values and beliefs. In the first, politics is seen as the activity by which community, consensus and shared values are developed. In the second, politics is the mechanism by which antagonistic groups attain and maintain power and supremacy. What connects the two is power. It underlies, and gives meaning to, both views of politics. The history of political thought in the West may be seen as a dialogue, and as a reciprocal interaction, between these two perceptions of politics. Since Plato's polemic against the Sophists, political thinkers have focused now on one, now on the other version of politics. Polemarchus' definition of justice (*Republic* 331E-336A), helping one's friends and harming one's enemies, anticipates Machiavelli's "two ways of fighting" and Gramsci's domination/leadership dichotomy.

Politics and political action comprise a dynamic interaction of social groups and structures continually forming and reforming in a continuous process of construction and deconstruction. In a kaleidoscope of multiple perspectives and multiple centers of power where centripetal and centrifugal forces are simultaneously in play power shifts and differences appear as instances of the variations in the relative proportion between conflict and consensus, force and persuasion. Transformations in the social group or social structure are contingent upon the nature and degree of integration or disintegration, mobilization or fragmentation, which in turn are determined by the perspective of the engaged actors as well as that of the observer. Moreover, the processes of the fragmentation and dissolution of a given social structure are simultaneously processes for the integration and dynamic growth of another and different structure. In the same way, what appears as group conflict and factional strife is, from a slightly different perspective, also the generation of community and social cohesion. In effect, the conflict generated by antagonistic factions is the mechanism by which those very factions not only come into existence but also, by developing into determinate and conscious political forces, might eventually form the basis of a new sociopolitical order. At the same time, the generation of community, consent, and moral and intellectual leadership within a given group is what enables it to engage in the struggle for power and advantage. The nature and degree of such consent, that is to say, the degree to which the ruling groups disseminate and proliferate "moral and intellectual" systems of belief throughout the subordinate groups, reflects and indicates their relative power in relation to antagonistic groups.

We should recall that Gramsci opposes political society to civil society, where the latter denotes the realm of consensus, persuasion, hegemony, and moral and intellectual leadership, and where the former denotes the realm of force, dictatorship, and coercion. These distinctions parallel the conventional and classical liberal and neoliberal (that is, Lockean and Hobbesian) dichotomy between state and society. Society represents the sphere of free contract, private property, and liberty, and where individuals and groups engage in economic, political and various other kinds (such as religious, cultural, etc.) of competition. And the liberal state, what Gramsci calls the "night-watchman state" (Gramsci 1975: 763-74) represents force and coercion: it provides the necessary force to guarantee and to secure the liberty and property which are the bases and the motive force for the competition. Thus we have:

State as force	State as consent
Political society	Civil society
Dictatorship	Hegemony

The distinctions correspond to Machiavelli's general formulation regarding the nature of power and of politics as the synthesis of force and consent, incarnated in the figure of the centaur.

Moreover, the Marxist and Leninist critique of liberalism and bourgeois society reproduces the distinction between state and society, and assigns to the state a purely negative, repressive and coercive character. In Marx and Lenin the state has no positive functions, its organization and purpose are merely to protect and to secure property and the market (Marx 1974; 1973; Engels 1968; Avineri 1971; Lichtheim 1970; Tucker 1969: 54-91). In this sense both liberals and their critics share the view of the state as a coercive apparatus. Here the state has no redeeming value: to the former it is an organization of coercive power, which, precisely because it is necessary to regulate and secure the "private" activities occurring within society, is dangerous to liberty and prone to abuse of its power; to the latter it is a repressive apparatus which, precisely because it is necessary to guarantee the stability and order of the socioeconomic order, is an instrument of the ruling groups.

The Integral State

Gramsci has a more nuanced, subtle, and articulated understanding of the state and of its relation to society. He returns to the Hegelian distinction between the two and in so doing gives the state a positive (that is, cultural, educational, and transformative) character. In a discussion of free trade and market competition Gramsci notes that the ideas of the "Free Trade Movement are based on a theoretical error . . . on a distinction between political society and civil society, which is made into and presented as an organic one, whereas in fact it is merely methodological. Thus it is asserted that economic activity belongs to civil society, and that the State must not intervene to regulate it. But since in actual reality civil society and State are one and the same, it must be made clear that *laisser-faire* too is a form of State 'regulation', introduced and maintained by legislative and coercive means" (Gramsci 1971: 159-60). The distinction between state and civil society, like that between domination and moral and intellectual leadership, is methodological and analytical and is not meant to reflect the social and political reality. Similarly, Gramsci expresses a similar notion when he points to Guicciardini's assertion that two elements are "absolutely necessary for the life of the State: arms and religion" (Gramsci 1975: 762-63; 1971: 170). Gramsci translates and modernizes Guicciardini's formulation into the now familiar polar terminology: "force and consent; coercion and persuasion; State and Church; political society and civil society; politics and morality (Croce's ethico-political history); law and freedom; order and self-discipline. . . ." (Gramsci 1975: 762-63; 1971: 170). This set of polarities is quite different from the very first set noted above, and it reveals a significant reevaluation of the nature of the state and civil society. In the first polarity, political society/dictatorship/domination was equated with the state, and hegemony/consent/persuasion was equated with civil society. This issues from the conventional liberal dichotomy. In this last series, however, the polarity political society/civil society, force/consent, no longer denotes the opposition between state and civil society, but is rather subsumed within the idea of the state itself. In effect, what Gramsci has accomplished is a broadening of the notion of the state. The state is now seen as the ensemble of socioeconomic and political-cultural relations. The "state" now becomes the "integral State," where the latter is defined as "dictatorship + hegemony," and as "political society + civil society" (Gramsci 1975: 763-64, 801, 1020). A sociopolitical order is therefore formed by the interpenetration of these two analytically separate, but intimately interwoven, spheres.

Thus Gramsci offers two notions of the state, closely related, one narrow, the other more broad. The first is reminiscent of what the classical liberals and neo-liberals understand by state: the administrative, juridical, and military organization of the governmental apparatus, the guarantor of peace, security, and order. This limited state is opposed to civil society, where the two together (state and society, dictatorship and hegemony) constitute what he calls the integral State.

In a note in the *Prison Notebooks*, Gramsci says that differences in sociopolitical structures between Russia and the West require different revolutionary strategies. He writes: "In Russia the State was everything, civil society was primordial and gelatinous; in the West there was a proper relation between the State and civil society, and when the State trembled a sturdy structure of civil society was at once revealed. The State was only an outer ditch, behind which there stood a powerful system of fortresses and earthworks" (Gramsci 1971: 238). The reference to the nature of the state in Russia means that the governmental apparatus, especially the coercive organs, is so pervasive that it overwhelms social and political life. It means, moreover, that the practices and norms specific to "political society" (the culture and way of life specific to bureaucracy and administrative organizations) become prevalent and are generalized throughout the society. At the same time, to say that civil society is "primordial" and "gelatinous" is to say that civil society does not, or barely, exists. Social, cultural, and economic activity is not autonomous, and it is permeated with the culture of the state apparatus. On the other hand, in the West there is a "proper relation" between state and society. "Proper" here would mean not only that the two spheres cannot exist separately from each other, but that the state is (1) limited and circumscribed and (2) responsive and subordinate to civil society. While a state may exist in the East without a civil society, in the West it is impossible to have one without the other. Thus Lenin was able to launch a direct attack on the state and seize power successfully: once the tsarist state fell, there were no sociopolitical institutions sufficiently autonomous and sufficiently resilient to withstand the Bolshevik party organizations. Such a direct assault Gramsci calls the "war of movement," evidently possible only in countries politically and economically less advanced. In the West, however, the strength, resilience, and persistence of civil society account for the failure of revolution, and thus require a radically different method of struggle, the "war of position."

What the "proper relation" between state and civil society implies is shown in a passage where Gramsci discusses the radical and revolutionary nature of the bourgeoisie, and its difference from all other previous social classes. It is a passage which also reveals Gramsci's fundamentally Hegelian perspective. He writes:

> The previous ruling classes were essentially conservative in the sense that they did not tend to construct an organic passage from the other classes to their own, i.e. to enlarge their class sphere "technically" and ideologically: their conception was that of a closed caste. The bourgeois class poses itself as an organism in continuous movement, capable of absorbing the entire society, assimilating it to its own cultural and economic level. The entire function of the State has been transformed; the State has become an "educator," etc. (Gramsci 1971: 260).

The notion of the state as educator harks back through Hegel, Rousseau, and Vico to ancient constructions of politics and the state in Plato and Aristotle. These assert that cultural and moral/intellectual life is made possible by, and can only occur within, the polis or the state. This conception is central to Gramsci, who notes: "The relationship of hegemony is necessarily an educational relationship," and

> the relationship between teacher and pupil is active and reciprocal so that every teacher is always a pupil and every pupil a teacher. . . . [Such a relationship] exists between intellectual and nonintellectual sections of the population, between rulers and the ruled, *élites* and their followers, leaders and led, the vanguard and the body of the army (Gramsci 1971: 350).

Thus an educational relation is hegemonic, and is also political. Modern or Western civil society is the product of the cultural, economic and political activity of the liberal bourgeoisie, and the state as educator means that the state acts as the bearer of the cultural and sociopolitical values and ruling principles of the dominant groups. As such, force and violence (which are specific to "dictatorship" and to political society) are minimized and delimited (though of course never eliminated), and, correspondingly, consent and persuasion (which are specific to hegemony and civil society) are generated by means of the proliferation and dissemination of moral/intellectual and cultural values and principles. These values may range from the religious to the secular, and the principles may be both ethical ("ideological") and "technical" (that is, rational and scientific, economically productive, and technologically instrumental systems of knowledge). As Gramsci notes, the educative and "formative" role of the state is that "of creating new and higher types of civilization; of adapting the 'civilization' and morality of the broadest popular masses to the necessities of the continuous development of the economic apparatus of production; hence of evolving even physically new types of humanity" (Gramsci 1971: 242).

In effect, the state as educator functions on two related levels. First, on the material level it makes possible economic/technological and scientific technical production by establishing stable and regular (more or less predictable) procedures and structures. In this sense the state here approximates Hobbes' conception of the Leviathan as the ground upon which trade, arts and sciences, and "commodious" living emerge and develop (Hobbes 1968: ch. 13). And second, the state presents itself as a cultural, and moral and intellectual *hegemon*—that is to say, it presents itself as exercising leadership in the ancient Greek sense of power based on a persuasive and rational discourse. It exercises power by presenting itself as "ethico-political," as the representative of universal moral values and as the carrier of rational and objective principles independent of narrow socioeconomic and sociocultural interests. The state as educator, and as ethico-political, transcends the narrow liberal conception of the night-watchman, and returns to the Hegelian idea of the state that attempts to realize reason and liberty by encompassing within its sphere all the activities within civil society. At the same time it is reminiscent of Hobbes, who calls the state the "mortal God," a striking phrase that combines the material, cultural (moral/intellectual), and political functions of the modern state (Hobbes 1968: ch. 17). In the same way that the immortal God is the ground for the objective continuity of universal reality and the standard for the determination of value, so too the state is the founder and generator of sociopolitical and sociocultural reality as well as the standard for the determination of meaning in space and time.

As noted above, such a mortal God Gramsci calls the "integral State" and is described by the unity of political society and civil society, dictatorship and hegemony. The dyads depict the state as the embodiment of an ethical/cultural life reinforced by force and coercion. Or, alternatively, they represent the rationalization of power, or the enculturation of power. The state is no longer brute force, nor is it any longer brute interest or narrow appetite.

Hegemony and Civil Society

It is precisely the "proper relation" between state and civil society, and between dictatorship and hegemony, that enables the state to appear as educator and as ethico-political (that is, precisely as rational and as hegemonic). The state, rather than imposing itself on society, emerges and gathers its cultural force from it. State power (dictatorship and force) issues from civil society (most especially from the economic/technical and the cultural/scientific apparatuses embedded within civil society), and, at the same time, civil society maintains its coherence and stability through the rational authority of the state.

All of which brings us back to hegemony, and to civil society as the space within which hegemony emerges and within which it is socially and politically defined and concretized. We should remember that to Gramsci modern society (which, for him, is fundamentally liberal and bourgeois) is structurally constituted by a multiplicity of independent secondary associations and by a plurality of autonomous sociopolitical and sociocultural groups (these are political, economic, cultural, educational, religious, or social). And, at the same time, civil society is characterized by a plurality of ideological/cultural conceptions and moral/intellectual systems of knowledge. It is here that the "war of position" assumes importance. As Gramsci notes:

> [t]he massive structures of modern democracies, both as State organizations, and as complexes of associations in civil society, constitute for the art of politics as it were the "trenches" and the permanent fortifications of the front in the war of position: they render merely "partial" the element of movement which before used to be "the whole" of war. . . . (Gramsci 1971: 243).

The war of position is a cultural conflict involving ideology, religion, forms of knowledge, and value systems. It occurs within civil society, which is itself a "complex" of highly articulated, multilayered associations and voluntary groups. But the complexity and sophistication of sociopolitical life extends beyond the civil sphere. They encompass the "State organizations" themselves. In effect, the level of articulation and complexity within civil society is mirrored within political society. For the state organizations, while juridically and analytically distinct from those of civil society, are nevertheless rooted and grounded within civil society, which provides the educational and cultural resources that determine the character of the state organizations. The greater the complexity of civil society, the more sophisticated the scientific/technical apparatus of the associations within society, the more complex and the more articulated will be the state institutions. There is a direct link between the complex articulated structures of civil society and the structural differentiation and political/constitutional specialization of the modern state. Referring specifically to parliamentary forms of government Gramsci writes that "hegemony . . . is characterised by the combination of force and consent, which balance each other reciprocally, without force predominating too greatly over consent" (Gramsci 1975: 762-63; 1971: 170). Only a modern and democratic state has the resources (technological and cultural) to develop systems of mass persuasion and mass mobilization "to ensure that force will appear to be based on the consent of the majority, expressed by the so-called organs of public opinion—newspapers and associations. . . ." (Gramsci 1975: 762-63; 1971: 170). Referring specifically to public opinion and its relation to the consensual basis of state power, Gramsci (1971: II: 7, pp. 914-915) writes:

> What is called "public opinion" is closely linked to political hegemony, that is, it is the point of contact between "civil society" and "political society," between consent and force. The State, when it wants to initiate an action that is not too popular, will preventively create the public opinion desired, that is, it organizes and centralizes certain elements within civil society. History of "public opinion:" naturally elements of public opinion have existed even in Asiatic satrapies; but

public opinion as it is understood today was born on the eve of the fall of the absolute states, that is, at the time of the struggle of the new bourgeois class for political hegemony and for the conquest of power. Public opinion is the political content of the public political will, one which is very possibly discordant and contradictory: thus there is the struggle for the monopoly of the organs of public opinion: newspapers, parties, parliament, in such a way that only one force models opinion and thus the national political will, reducing opposition to atomistic and disorganized dissent.

What connects state and civil society is "public opinion" (Fontana 2006) Gramsci sees that the formation and organization of opinion within the sphere of civil society are central to the generation of both hegemony and an opposing hegemonic movement. Thus public opinion can both legitimate and delegitimate state power.

Civil society is the sphere where a continual process of conflict and community, dissent and consent, is generated. It is here that the dialectic between conflict and consensus, factional strife over particularistic ends and the generation of common goals is conducted. Gramsci contrasts what he calls the economic-corporative to the political. Such an opposition occurs, and is ultimately resolved, within civil society. The economic-corporative refers to particular, purely economic goods, utilities specific to the interests of a given group; and the political refers to goods that transcend the purely economic and particular, goods that are universal to the extent that they encompass the interests of other multiple groups. The movement from the particular to the universal, from the economic to the political, is precisely a hegemonic movement, where a multiplicity of groups is established and where moral and intellectual leadership is exercised. Consent is generated by such leadership because the interests of the federated or associated groups are aggregated. But such consent is generated within the alliance of groups in competition with an antagonistic alliance of opposing groups.

Hegemony and civil society have generally been associated with consent and community, and rightly so. Yet it is important to note that in Gramsci civil society, while representing and denoting the sphere of liberty and consensus, is at the same time the sphere in which competition, conflict, and factional strife occur. On the one hand, it is the sphere where different systems of belief and of knowledge, different conceptions of the world, oppose each other and vie for the favor of the people. In the process consent is manufactured; consensus is mobilized; and popular support is attained. The mobilization and deployment of the people are achieved through the mediation of ideological and cultural prisms. Moreover, civil society is the locus wherein the state (and its various political organs and functions) generates support and consent for itself—both through electoral competitive mechanisms and through its ability to accumulate and to distribute immense sums in the form of socioeconomic and social welfare measures. The electoral competition and the economic programs mutually reinforce each other and thus strengthen the authority and legitimacy of the state. In this sense, the state and the political order in general are deemed legitimate (that is, consent is generated) to the extent that it is able to penetrate (and, in turn, be penetrated by) the multifarious associations that together form

civil society. This interpenetration contrasts starkly to liberal and neoliberal doctrine, which states that there is a distinct separation between the state and civil
society. However, while there is certainly a legal and juridical distinction between
the two, on the political, social, and economic level the distinction is purely analytical and formal. For the material and moral strength of the state depends precisely
upon its ability to assimilate the cultural and ideological (electoral, educational,
political, economic, even religious) activity taking place within civil society in
order to transform it into legitimating support.

At the same time, it is important to realize the close link between the cul-
tural/ideological and the material/economic. The relationship, within the space
formed by civil society, between the economic reality and the construction of ideological, cultural, and moral/intellectual ways of thinking constitutes an important
factor in Gramsci's hegemony. Thus, in a note entitled "Cultural Themes. Material
and Ideological," Gramsci proposes to analyze the theoretical and ideological bases
of the power of the dominant groups: "A study of how the ideological structure of
a dominant class is actually organized: that is to say, material organization understood as maintaining, defending, and developing the theoretical and ideological
'front.'" (Gramsci 1975: 332-33). This amounts to an inquiry into hegemony, how
it is expressed, how it is institutionalized, and how it functions concretely within
civil society. His analysis focuses on "the most dynamic part of the ideological
structure," which comprises

> publishing houses (which implicitly and explicitly have a political program and
> which base themselves on a given orientation), political newspapers, journals of
> every type— scientific, literary, philological, mass market, etc.— various periodi-
> cals including local and parochial bulletins and gazettes (Gramsci 1975: 332-
> 33).

Gramsci looks at institutions such as schools, libraries, voluntary associations and
various clubs, religious groups (especially the Catholic Church), universities and
colleges, and other groups that pluralist theorists today would call interest or pressure groups. His analysis intends to be thoroughgoing and encompasses even the
physico-spatial and the urban-architectural structure of civil society, such as build-
ings, streets and boulevards, as well as their names. All these institutions, structures,
and sociocultural practices are precisely what Gramsci means by the "powerful
system of earthworks" that make up civil society: the "formidable complex of
trenches and fortifications of the dominant class" (Gramsci 1975: 332-33). These
are the ideological and cultural, and thus hegemonic, apparatuses of civil society.
At the same time they are economic and material. Newspapers, journals, magazines
(the mass media in general), educational and scientific institutions, publishing
houses—the whole complex system devised to construct and generate, to communicate, store, and retrieve, knowledge and information—rests on an economic, technological and material base. Such a complex network, moreover, parallels, and is
dependent upon, a market that desires access to it. Such a market extends in pro-

gressively ever widening concentric circles from narrow, specialized and technical groups of intellectuals (with their specialized languages) to popular and mass audiences. In all cases these markets must be intellectually and economically capable of generating demand (both in terms of literacy and in terms of disposable income). Thus the instruments of hegemonic persuasion cannot emerge or function without a material foundation, at once spatial, physical, technological, and economic. And it is this base which makes possible the generation and manufacture of permanent consent, that is, hegemony. It is indicative that, during and after the three great revolutions of the West that inaugurated modern mass politics and eventually culminated in the modern world generally—namely, the English, the American, and the French—their respective societies underwent a rapid and profound growth in the proliferation and dissemination of ideas by means of the print media (newspapers, pamphlets, broadsides, etc.). At the same time, such a growth was accompanied by an expansion in the manufacture and in the marketing of printed materials (Starr 2004).

On the other hand, precisely because civil society is the sphere of liberty and competition, such legitimating activity is counterbalanced by forces and groups antagonistic and hostile to the prevailing group and to its system of values and beliefs. These forces (what Gramsci calls the "subaltern classes") (Gramsci 1975: 2283-2289) may exist at various stages of development, some merely embryonic, some more mature, some barely politically conscious, others more coherent ideologically and thus better organized. In other words, it is here, in the sphere defined by civil society, that the war of position takes place. As the term implies, the war of position presupposes consensus within the cultural/political and organizational body of the protagonists, and conflict and strife among and between them. The war of position is therefore preeminently a series of moral and intellectual battles whose goal is the construction of social and political reality. In a note on "'Language,' Languages, and Common Sense," Gramsci says that "philosophy is a conception of the world and philosophical activity is not to be conceived solely as the 'individual' elaboration of systematically coherent concepts, but also and above all as a cultural battle to transform the popular 'mentality' and to diffuse the philosophical innovations which will demonstrate themselves to be 'historically true' to the extent that they become concretely—i.e. historically and socially—universal" (Gramsci 1975: 1330; 1971: 348). What he says about philosophy can also be said about morality, ethics, knowledge, and culture in general. The generation and organization of consent is a competitive struggle, that is, the exercise of moral and intellectual leadership in a "battle" (Gramsci 1975: 1236, 1493) whose purpose is to generate, proliferate, and disseminate a given conception of the world, such that it becomes "historically true," which, in turn, means its transformation into the "common sense" of the people. The exercise of intellectual and moral leadership is simultaneously the transformation of philosophy and knowledge into the common sense of the people; in turn, such a transformation is simultaneously the organization and proliferation of consent. And all this occurs within civil society, and by means of a "battle," through conflict and strife.

Counterhegemony and Political Action

The notion of a battle between and among opposing conceptions of the world or *Weltanschauungen* is central to Gramsci's notion of hegemony and underpins his entire political and theoretical enterprise. It is crucial because it captures on several levels Gramsci's understanding of hegemony and the manner in which it operates both within political society (state in the narrow sense) and civil society.

In the first place, the battle of hegemonies underlines Gramsci's original purpose in developing his political theory: to understand the failure of socialism, and to identify social groups within bourgeois modern society capable of challenging morally and intellectually the supremacy of the dominant groups. To Gramsci a subordinate group, or the "subaltern," would not be equal to ruling unless it developed internally what he calls a "critical understanding of self" (Gramsci 1971: 333). Internally (in terms of consciousness) and externally (in terms of organization) the subaltern to Gramsci exhibits, and is characterized by, incoherence, fragmentation, and disintegration. As such the subaltern groups are subject to the action and initiative of the dominant groups (Gramsci 1975: 2283-2290). As Gramsci notes, "the subaltern classes . . . are not unified and cannot unite unless they are able to become a 'State;' their history is thus interwoven with that of civil society, it is a functionally 'disaggregated' and discontinuous part of the history of civil society. . . ." (Gramsci 1975: 2288). Thus it is necessary to identify instances of subaltern autonomous activity that indicate opposition, either cultural or political, to the established system of beliefs and structures of power. It is only when the subaltern begins to know itself that it begins the process of becoming hegemonic (or counterhegemonic). Gramsci notes that "[t]o know oneself means to be oneself, to be master of oneself, to free oneself from a state of chaos, to exist as an element of order—but of one's own order and one's own discipline in striving for an ideal" (Gramsci 1975a: 75; 1977: 13). What is the process by which the popular masses attain critical awareness and political coherence?

In a note in the *Notebooks* on the "passage from knowing to understanding to feeling and vice versa" Gramsci makes an important analytical distinction between those who "know"—intellectuals—and those who do not know but merely "feel," the "people-nation." Intellectuals may possess knowledge but not necessarily feeling or understanding, and the people may possess feeling or understanding but not knowledge. To know something politically and socially, as opposed to abstractly or purely intellectually, is to understand it with feeling and with passion. Gramsci says:

> The intellectual's error consists in believing that one can know without understanding or even more without feeling and being impassioned (not only for knowledge in itself but also for the object of knowledge; in other words that the intellectual can be an intellectual (and not a pure pedant) if distinct and separate from the people-nation, that is, without feeling the elementary passions of the people, understanding them and therefore explaining and justifying them in the particular

historical situation and connecting them dialectically to the laws of history and to a superior conception of the world, scientifically and coherently elaborated—i.e. knowledge. One cannot make politics-history without this passion, without this sentimental connection between intellectuals and people-nation (Gramsci 1971: 418).

The knowledge of intellectuals becomes life and politics only when linked to the feeling/passion of the people. The synthesis intellectual/people and knowledge/passion is what provides the motive force for political and historical activity. Such a synthesis, in turn, is what transforms a fragmented and disorganized subordinate group into an actor capable of questioning the established system and capable of presenting a viable alternative to it. Such a process is necessarily hegemonic, and it involves a reflexive and conscious movement, from passive acceptance of the given reality to active engagement with it, as well as a movement from fragmentation to integration. Active engagement presupposes a condition of conflict and strife, such that the subaltern group understands itself and realizes itself in opposition to the dominant groups. Thus: "[c]ritical understanding of self takes place . . . through a struggle of political 'hegemonies' and of opposing directions, first in the ethical field and then in that of politics proper, in order to arrive at the working out at a higher level of one's own conception of reality" (Gramsci 1971: 333). This hegemonic process is precisely the formation of a "personality," the manufacture of a social and political subject capable of acting in history. In Gramsci's words, it is the giving of a "personality to the amorphous mass element" (Gramsci 1971: 340).

The above passage points to Gramsci's critique of positivism, scientism, and evolutionary economism. Gramsci tries to disencumber Marxism of its positivist and deterministic encrustations, and presents a theory of knowledge in which the relation between the subject that knows and the object of knowledge is active and dynamic. For Gramsci, to know is to master, and to know is to construct material and social reality by giving form and structure to it. To know, therefore, is to "creare il reale" (Gramsci 1975: 1485-86;1971: 345-46). Knowing is not simply an abstract activity, it is a conscious engagement with reality, such that the very act of knowing gives form, meaning, and "personality" to the object. Thus reality is not passively perceived, but it is actively and passionately seized, captured, and possessed by the subject. In this sense Gramsci is fundamentally Vichian. Gramsci, like Vico, understands knowledge in terms of doing and making: *verum et factum convertuntur*. According to Vico, "[t]he criterion of the truth is to have made it" (Vico 1988: 45-46). Man knows truly and fully only what he has made. Indeed, "facts" exist, and are perceived as such, precisely because they come into being as *facta*, as the products of man's historical and political activity. The battle of hegemonies, in this sense, is the battle to transform reality, which involves the battle to create alternative *facta*.

Yet, to act in history also means to speak as a political actor in society: thus the importance of language in Gramsci. Since hegemony is intimately related to the development and proliferation of opposing conceptions of the world and of differing structures of knowledge, the nature and type of languages are crucial to hegemony. The transition from subaltern to hegemonic, therefore, equally means the transformation of a subaltern language (such as a dialect) into a hegemonic language. The language, in other words, must be equal to the constitution of a knowledge and a conception of the world that both capture and construct a particular reality. Language and knowledge mutually presuppose each other. Therefore language, like knowledge, does not passively represent reality, and does not merely describe a preexistent world; rather, language actively structures and constructs the world, and subjects it to the ends and values established by the speaker/knower.[3]

Such an understanding of knowledge explodes the positivist distinction between subjective knowledge and objective reality, and simultaneously undermines the Marxist dichotomy between structure (material objectivity) and superstructure (cultural and moral/intellectual subjectivity). Thus for Gramsci the problem of revolution is no longer the "scientific" analysis and identification of the objective (material/economic) conditions. These had been present in the West since the end of the nineteenth century and the beginning of the twentieth. The question, in the modern bourgeois world, is the formation and development of the subjective conditions. As Gramsci says, "men become conscious of fundamental conflicts on the level of ideology. . . ." (Gramsci 1971: 164). And further, he notes in "Utopia," one of his early pre-prison essays: "it is not the economic structure that directly determines political action, but rather the interpretation given to it and to the so-called laws that govern its development" (Gramsci 1958: 281-282). A strictly abstract and scientific analysis of the material economic conditions, though obviously necessary for understanding social reality, is not sufficient. What is required is the formation of a self-disciplined "personality" (collective and institutional) which is politically and morally determined to act. And political action in turn presupposes both consciousness and will. These latter recall Gramsci's syntheses of knowledge and passion, and of intellectuals and people. Nietzsche famously asserted that there are no moral phenomena, only moral interpretations of phenomena (Nietzsche 1966: 85). Gramsci may be said to perform a similar operation on knowledge and its relation to what is known. Thus, structural and material reality is not merely perceived through ideological and cultural prisms, but these prisms condition and transform the reality itself.

Summary

To sum up: Gramsci's hegemony is a complex and highly articulated notion, defined by means of interlinked yet distinct polarities. It is to be understood as an element within the duality force/consent and violence/persuasion that to Gramsci characterizes the nature of power. It acquires concrete structure and specific content particularly during those periods in history in which the people or the masses either form the ground of political action or have become a force in politics.

In the manner of the ancient Greek dichotomy between political (constitutional) and despotic (dominating) rule hegemony may be seen as an alliance or association of groups that share similar interests, a consensual alliance under the leadership of a group pursuing the interest of the associated groups. Conceptually this is expressed by the dyad "domination/leadership." A group exercises "leadership" over "allied" groups, and exercises "domination" ("even with armed force") over antagonistic groups. In this case, hegemony is opposed to dictatorship, where the latter represents domination and force, and the former represents consent/persuasion/opinion. Underlying such a notion is the reciprocal relation between force and consent, such that hegemony may also delineate a balanced "equilibrium" between force and consent, where force does not prevail "too greatly" over consent. Alliance formation based on consent and on the autonomy of the constituent coalition partners requires the formation of a political-social group that is able to transcend narrow, particular interests (of a class, nation or other social group) to more general universal ones. Thus hegemony describes a movement from the economic to the political.

In addition, hegemony understood as the generation and organization of consent is directly related to the mechanisms and processes by which knowledge and beliefs are first, produced, and second, disseminated. Here the crux is the formation of a "conception of the world" and its dissemination throughout the people. A conception of the world (an "ideology" or a system of beliefs) is always opposed to different conceptions of the world. Thus these are constantly in conflict, in a "battle" against each other, and the hegemonic conception is one which has become the "common sense" of the people. But a counterconception is constantly generated, even if only embryonically, to challenge the prevailing common sense.

In effect, to be hegemonic is to be political both at the level of consciousness (subjective and intersubjective) and at the level of rule (power), such that to be political is to be hegemonic (or to strive towards hegemony, that is to be counter-hegemonic). For every hegemony presupposes a counterhegemony.

If this is the case, that is, if hegemonic = political = ruling, then the issue is the formation of a group or a subject capable of rule: thus, as Gramsci says, a hegemonic relationship is a pedagogic relationship, that is, the development of what Gramsci calls a "personality" that is conscious, active, and autonomous—autonomous understood as self-governing and self-ruling. Hegemony operates at two levels: first, internally, the formation within the social group of self-discipline and self-government, that is, the self-constitution of the group into a coherent and active political actor, and second, externally, the extension and dissemination of the group's conception of the world throughout the society.

We conclude by recalling the centaur, for Machiavelli and for Gramsci the metaphor that embodies the dual nature of power: force and consent, violence and persuasion. Both elements define political action. The question is to identify the "proper" balance or proportion in the dyadic relation. For Gramsci, as for Machiavelli, the exercise of power (or the relation between ruler and ruled) rests (or should rest) on an inverse relationship between force and consent, which, in turn, depends upon the generation of consent. The more weight consent acquires, the less force is necessary. To Gramsci the power and resilience of a sociopolitical order (the "State") is defined by the individuation of consent and persuasion within concrete political and social structures. Hegemony is the institutionalization of consent and persuasion within both civil society and the state. Yet the element of force and domination, as the balancing and limiting pole of the dyad, cannot be eliminated. Machiavelli, Sheldon Wolin wrote, tried to establish a politics characterized by an "economy of violence." Hegemony represents Gramsci's attempt in the modern world simultaneously to delineate and to construct such an economy.

Notes

1. Thucydides 2002 uses the term hegemony in various senses, such as military leadership (I, 128; II, 11; III, 105, 107), power (I, 94, 130; IV, 91; V, 7; VII, 15), and political leadership (I, 4, 25, 38, 76, 95-96; III, 10; V, 16, 47, 69; VI, 76, 82; VII, 56).

2. Anderson 1976-77 renders *autoritá* as "domination." While Gramsci directly opposes *dominio* (domination) to moral and intellectual leadership, in this case Gramsci opposes "authority" to hegemony because he want to stress the nonvoluntary, binding, and coercive character of this particular type of authority. Here it must be understood as a legal command enforced by legal sanctions. Thus, in the case of hegemony dissent or disobedience carries no legal penalties, whereas in the case of authority disobedience is a violation of the law and penalized by the coercive force of the state.

3. Gramsci's writings on language (1971: 38-43, 323-25, 348-51), its relation to knowledge and thought, and the manner in which it informs the politics and the socioeconomic position of contending factions are crucially related to his epistemology and to his understanding of revolutionary activity. The relation Gramsci establishes between hegemony and language is another important point of contact between his hegemony and that of the ancients. See LoPiparo 1979. For an excellent analysis see also Ives 2004.

Chapter 3

Power and Hegemony in Social Theory

Mark Haugaard

While the concepts of power and hegemony are inextricably and mutually constitutive, it is a curious fact that there is remarkably little literature which theo-
rizes both concepts. Gramsci, for instance, never theorized power and in one of
the most influential postmodern theorizations of hegemony, *Hegemony and Socialist Strategy* (2001), Laclau and Mouffe problematize the concept of hegemony without any substantive analysis of power. In contrast, in this paper I propose to deepen our understanding of hegemony by theorizing it as a specific instance of power. However, by way of introduction, so that we know what hegemony is, I shall analyze the concept of hegemony in the writings of Gramsci and
of Laclau and Mouffe. This will be followed by an account of "power to,"
"power over," and their relationship to hegemony.

Hegemony in the Writings of Gramsci and of Laclau and Mouffe

In the writings of Gramsci, hegemony is used as a master concept to explain the
ability of the bourgeoisie to dominate modern capitalist society and, from that, to
construct a socialist strategy of proletariat counterhegemony—socialism or communism. Gramsci argued that the bourgeoisie occupied the position of a
hegemon because they managed to present their particular interests as universal
for society as a whole. Through the language of universality they gained support
from other classes and, in this manner, effectively organizationally outflanked
potential proletariat opposition.[1] As argued in Chapter 1, the bourgeoisie were
responsible for a generalized consensus superseding class—in the case of
Gramsci's Italy, the bourgeoisie had the support of the peasantry and local petit
bourgeoisie. In contrast, the proletariat failed to gain power because of their inability to present their particular interests as other than their own. One of the
reasons for this was the (mistaken) view held by Marxists that the realization of

class-consciousness by the proletariat would automatically lead to a revolutionary situation in which they would gain power—the transformation of a class-in-
itself to a class-for-itself. This misperception entailed that part of socialist strategy had been the development of proletariat self-consciousness, with the unintended consequence of making the proletariat focus upon their uniqueness.
Through class-consciousness they become essentially inward-looking and inca-
pable of forming alliances with others. Consequently, in the event that the proletariat was to realize full class-consciousness (become a class-for-itself), they
would constitute a single class confronting a bourgeoisie at the center of a hegemonic web of class alliances. According to Gramsci, the key to the proletariat
developing a counterhegemonic strategy should be their ability to present their
interests as universal, thus they would attract other classes and groups, including
peasantry, professionals, and petit bourgeoisie.

The Gramscian concept of hegemony presupposes that power over others is
not reducible either to physical coercion or to economic resources. Neither the
control of the state's coercive resources nor control of the means of production is
sufficient to explain bourgeois domination. The corollary of this is that even if
the proletariat were to gain control of the means of violence through bloody revolution and confiscate the means of production, they would be unable to initiate
real social change if they did not institute new hegemonic practices. While hegemony comes from the Ancient Greek idea of leadership of a military alliance,
Gramsci viewed hegemony as much more complex than control of resources
gained through strategic alliances. Hegemony is a tacit phenomenon rooted in
the social practices that constitute everyday life. Prior to a coercive revolution
the proletariat should wage a "war of position" whereby they out-maneuver the
bourgeoisie so that they could place themselves at the center of a new set hegemonic practices. Hegemony is not only the key to bourgeois power; equally it is
the master concept for proletariat power. It is not sufficient simply to gain control over material coercive resources or economic assets; power is equally located in nonmaterial resources. Contrary to most Marxist usage of the base-su-
perstructure distinction, for Gramsci the coercive resources of the state were part
of the base. In keeping with Gramsci's desire to move away from simple economic determinism, the surplus power (which is over and above economic and
coercive resources) entailed by hegemony is attributable to the superstructure.

The key orienting phenomenon within the superstructure, which facilitates
hegemony, is ideology. In the writings of Marx, ideology is largely conceived in
terms of confusion between appearance and reality. This is a process whereby,
for instance, the proletariat willingly reproduce the capitalist system because of
an unawareness that they are the creators of capital and hence slaves to their own
creation. To the "politically immature" proletariat capital appears as something
alien, created through profit by astute capitalists operating market mechanisms.
In reality, capital is embodied profit created through exploitation. Once this is
understood, the proletariat comes to perceive capital as illegitimately acquired.
This ideology is theorized as "false consciousness" in the writings of Lukâcs
(1971) and later, of Lukes (1974), as three-dimensional power. In this perspec-

tive ideology is linked to "falsity" and is inherently normatively negative. However, in Gramsci the strength of ideology does not lie so much in the obscuring of truth (although that element is still present) but is located in the capacity of a set of ideas and consciousness to tie together divergent interests into a singular hegemonic interpretative horizon. In this sense, ideology is tied to leadership, in the Classical view. This unity takes place through the ability of intellectuals (organic intellectuals) to universalize the consciousness of a particular class (Gramsci 1971: 375-77). This coming together takes place through ideas, perceptions, and shared morality. As argued by Fontana (1993; Chapter 2) and Ives (2004), this shared consensus derives from the ability of social agents to create new meanings. This is not only Vicean but prefigures many postmodern debates and is the fertile soil in which Laclau and Mouffe anchor their analysis.

In Gramsci a "common will" is created between the hegemonic and the other classes whereby the power of the hegemon is built upon the consent of the supporting classes. This coming together of ideology, common will, and material resources (coercive and economic) totalizes into, what Gramsci referred to as, a "historic bloc." Because such a historic bloc is not simply held together coercively but also has a common will, ideas, and morals, it constitutes a powerful force of domination which is substantially greater than the sum of its material resources (Gramsci 1971: 125-33). Consequently, the overthrow of the hegemony of the bourgeoisie is not simply a matter of gaining control of their resources (and those of the other classes which support them), it means removing the consensual base of their support and relocating it to the proletariat. Establishing a new hegemony entails the creation of a new interpretative horizon which replaces the old ideology. Thus the interests of the working classes become universalized, and in so doing other classes consent to the creation of a new counterhegemonic order.

In the work of Laclau and Mouffe, the language of discourse largely replaces the concept of ideology. Just like Gramsci they wish to replace one form of hegemony with another—rather than moving beyond hegemony. Because the concept of ideology is so frequently linked to the idea of "false consciousness" (although not primarily so in the writings of Gramsci), they do not wish to make these kind of "truth claims" for their own vision of "radical democratic" politics as a new counterhegemonic practice. Hegemony is derived from "discourse" which is not linked to these kinds of ideological truth claims. As we have seen, Gramsci had already moved fairly far from economic determinism; in Laclau and Mouffe this move is completed and any residual essentialist claims to the effect that the economic base determines the superstructure are dropped.

The concept of discourse is derived from Foucault and from a form of meaning holism developed by de Saussure (1960). Words do not derive their meaning from any direct relationship between signifier and signified (word and object referred to) but, instead, from a set of relations and differences between words. If one takes chess as a (relatively) self-contained language game, the word "knight" is not constituted through its link to a wood or ivory horse (the latter can be replaced by a bottle top) but derives its meaning from its relations of difference and similarity to the other pieces in the game—imagine explaining the meaning of the word without reference to the other pieces (it is impossible). Similarly, the concept of bourgeoisie only makes sense relative to that of proletariat, feudal aristocracy, peasantry, and so forth. In de Saussure's work this theorization of meaning has no normative connotations, nor is it in any way linked to domination. In Foucault's genealogy the analysis of language is extended to cover the reproduction of meaning as a historically constituted set of categories which enable us to make sense of the world. This enlarged interpretative horizon is termed "discourse" and covers the entirety of social life to the extent to which all social action entails the reproduction of meaning. Once social life becomes discursively constituted (in archaeology there are discursive and nondiscursive realms but not in genealogy), the distinction between economic base and superstructure disappears. There is no nondiscursive base which determines the realm of ideas (superstructure)—the economic is discursive. The conflicts which Marxism attributed to contradictions within the base become conflicts over meaning. Because systems of meaning (discourses) constitute themselves self-referentially this is a source of continual potential instability. Any system of thought is potentially continually subject to collapse as a contingently constituted system of conventionality. Within this system truth performs a special stabilizing function. If a discourse is "true" it is relatively stable. Truth therefore becomes a site of struggle as a disguised "will to power." There are two types of power conflict: conflict within a discourse, which reproduces the rules of the game, and there are deeper conflicts over meaning itself. In the latter, discourses have the potential to become destabilized. It is these "deep" conflicts which Foucault analyzes in his histories and considers significant as sources of possible resistance and social critique.

In their theorization of hegemony, Laclau and Mouffe add to the Focualdian analysis an emphasis upon the workings of exclusion. In Foucault exclusion is largely considered in terms of the direct confrontation between discourses (Renaissance, Classical, and modern discourse formations). Laclau and Mouffe emphasize that there is a continual process of exclusion at work in the constitution of meaning whereby the relational essence of any meaning entails the exclusion of potential other meanings. As is in Chapters 9 and 10 below, there is a continually excluded surplus of meaning, which is the source of "local" everyday resistance. This exclusion does not simply come in the form of a direct challenge from a different discourse but is inherent in the constitution of meaning as a moment of exclusion of surplus. If we make sense of the world by imposing categories of thought upon it, this entails the exclusion of modes of interpretation that, in turn, become a constitutive outside which continually threatens to destabilize the symbolic world. As interpretative beings this exclusion is not only external to ourselves but also internal because the interpretative horizon, which enables us to make sense of the world, constitutes our identity. The excluded outside is internal to us as a repression. It is outside of meaning, as a lack which the self continually tries to repress in order to maintain security of self. This lack, which is repressed internally and excluded externally, Lacan terms the "real." This is, of course, not "real" in the empiricist sense of the word, quite the contrary. Rather than the "thing-in-itself" and "true human essence" (or "species being" [Marx]), it is the opposite of these—their impossibility. Thus it performs a disruptive function. However, the disruption is not through the exposure of the falsity by truth but takes place through a continual process of destabilization because of the impossibility of closure, which is a continually sought after moment of stability. The illusion of the conquest of the excluded outside gives discourses a totalizing effect which silences critical democratic dialogue. In the terminology of Laclau and Mouffe, a discourse tries to maintain its dominance through "suturing." As there is no substantive outside (only a lack) upon which to anchor a discourse formation, specific signifiers perform the function of stabilization from within the discourse. These are known as "quilting points." Because the real threat to discourse dominance is from an essential lack, these "quilting points" themselves internalize this lack of meaning. They are empty signifiers. Democracy and "the nation" are typical; they are continually drawn upon to fix or suture, specific meanings while, simultaneously, remaining devoid of positive content—or so it is claimed by Laclau and Mouffe.

Hegemony is maintained through the capacity of a discourse formation to unite people into a shared mode of interpretation that reinforces particular relations of domination. A discourse becomes systematized through an internal logic whereby quilting points form a unity. In Thatcher's Britain, quilting points included: "market forces," "the nanny state," "spongers," "traditional values," and put "the Great back into Great Britain."

While Laclau and Mouffe criticize the use of discourse by the right to form a hegemonic bloc, like Gramsci they do not wish to transcend hegemony. Rather, they wish to constitute hegemony of the Left. In fact, they would view the idea of transcending hegemony with suspicion—as an attempted act of exclusion—in much the same way that Foucault regarded any claim to truth as a disguised will to power.

In her works on democratic theory, Mouffe (2000) argues that one of the keys to developing counterhegemony is from within the logic of existing hegemony 2000). She argues that the most effective strategy of counterhegemony is to radicalize the logic of some of the quilting points of democratic liberalism. If the Left uses existing quilting points from a hegemonic discourse, the radicalized discourse will take with it a significant sector of the support base of the current hegemonic bloc and, in so doing, create a new hegemony. In the discourse of liberal democracy the concepts of equality and liberty are two quilting points which, if extended sufficiently, will invariably destabilize the current neoliberal hegemony. Current hegemony is premised upon the containment of the logic of equality to the "political sphere" and that of liberty to freedom of expression and economic liberty. This containment is not intrinsic to the meaning of these signifiers. If equality were extended to the personal and economic spheres this would entail a different hegemonic social order. However, I would argue that, implicit in this strategy is the claim that these signifiers have an essential logic, or telos, that can be used to construct a counterhegemonic strategy. Hence, these particular quilting points are not quite *empty* signifiers as is presupposed by postmodern theory.

Power and Hegemony

Central to Gramsci's view of hegemony is that it embodies some level of consent that is not derived from coercion. Hypothetical proletarian hegemony is relatively easy to understand in that consent is both sociological and normative. If all agree upon their collective goals (normative consent) it is not mysterious that social interaction generally will be consensual. However, in the case of bourgeois hegemony, what is theoretically interesting is that one can have consensus at the sociological level (empirically) without normative consensus. Such a hypothesis is both interesting and significant, especially if, as I do, one regards the idea of proletarian hegemony as envisaged by Gramsci entirely utopian. If we take hegemony as a specific form of power, what we wish to theorize is how power has a consensual aspect that facilitates relations of domination.

One of most frequently made errors concerning power is to assume that it is negative, oppressive, and coercive. There are two types of power, "power to" and "power over." The former corresponds to the ability to act in concert (Arendt 1970) while the latter entails an unequal power relationship in which one actor within the relationship will be able to make another do something which they would not otherwise—Weber and Dahl.[2] Consensual power is a joint capacity for action directed towards commonly desired outcomes. Even though hegemony presupposes consensus we must not make the error of including consensual power within hegemony. For Gramsci and his postmodern interpreters, hegemony is clearly a phenomenon of domination not consensual power. Our theoretical problem is to explain the consensus between the dominated and dominators in acts of "power over" and also in the reproduction of relations of domination. However, in order to understand "power over" it is necessary to make a brief excursion on the subject of "power to."

"Power to"

The image of "power to" is captured by Barnes in his comparison of natural and social power (Barnes 1988: 3). Our knowledge of natural phenomena gives us a capacity for action; similarly our knowledge of social phenomena gives us a capacity by allowing us to harness the power of others. We know when we boil water it expands as it turns to steam. If held inside a container this pressure will drive an engine. Similarly, our knowledge of predictability of others gives social agents a capacity for collaborative endeavor.

"Power to" derives from social order as a shared system of predictability. If actors A know with relative certainty how actors B will behave (the conceptual equivalent of water turning to steam) they have the capacity to act collectively in concert. The source of this predictability is social structure. If an action is structured, as opposed to random, it is predictable. What makes it ordered are mutual understandings based upon consensus on meaning. At its most basic, an action is structured if it is meaningful to others. An action that is only "privately" meaningful is not predictable in the eyes of others and consequently useless for the purposes of collective endeavor. Structural reproduction takes place when actors engage in acts of structuration which are recognized as meaningful by others. It is not the case, as argued by Giddens (1984), that social structures are reproduced by individual social actors structuring their action. That is a necessary but not sufficient condition. Socially "deviant" actors structure their actions (engage in acts of structuration), but what distinguishes the outcome is that others either fail to understand the meaning of their action or they reject the act of structuration as illegitimate or inappropriate. It is others who define their "deviancy" and in so doing, exclude their actions from the social system by blocking structural reproduction. Of course, it has to be accepted that what is defined as "deviant" in one context may be legitimate in another. However, what are termed deviant subcultures by the dominant groups are structured systems in their own right and from the sociological perspective constitute structured systems of order. The recognition of an act of structuration as legitimate by others I have termed an act of confirming-structuration (Haugaard 1997, 2002). The reproduction of social order presupposes a continual set of acts of structuration and confirming-structuration. In contrast, the deliberate rejection of structuration by others is "destructuration." Destructuration is an act of exclusion which leaves the structuring author speaking a "private language."

Wittgenstein begins *Philosophical Investigations* with a simple description of two actors engaged in building a wall. One gives the other a "brick" when asked. This collective endeavor is premised upon the reproduction of the meaning "brick" which, as Wittgenstein argued, does not exist as private meaning for either actor. Each act of asking for a brick is an act of structuration, while the giving of the brick is confirming-structuration. The unintended consequence of these acts is both the reproduction of the structures of the English language and the structuredness of the working practices of the bricklayers. The joint capacity for action which they gain from these structures is "power to."

While we have been focusing upon the interactive agent-centered aspect of structural reproduction, at a systemic level the meaning of the word "brick" does not exist singly either but is systemically constituted. As argued by de Saussure (1960), it is constituted through membership of a language where the meaning of each word is constituted through difference from and similarity to other words within the linguistic system: "brick" it is similar to, but different from, a "block," a "stone," a "lump of clay," etc. Simultaneously, on the interactive level this meaning is reproduced through acts of structuration and confirming-structuration. The combination tells us that both actors have broadly similar internal systems of meaning in order to have "power to." Obviously with "bricks" there is unlikely to be divergence, but with respect more political concepts the potential for divergence can be significant, and structural reproduction may not

be routine. When the reproduction of meaning is a political act yet entails collaborative endeavor (structuration and confirming structuration), it should never be
taken for granted.

While the system of meaning that gives meaning to a "brick" does not necessarily entail relations of empowerment and disempowerment, this is not the
case for many signifiers. Domination refers to structured relations of empowerment and disempowerment, and many signifiers are explicitly tied to specific
relations of domination even if they are obviously "political" (democracy and
rights would be political signifiers) in any obvious way. To take an example
from Marx, a coat exists as "use value" both in capitalism and in traditional society. However, it is only within capitalism that it also has meaning as "exchange
value"; the latter is a "social hieroglyphic" (to use Marx's phrase) which is
branded onto it under capitalism. Take "time"; while we may agree with Kant
that time is a universal category of mind, its particular manifestation as "clock-
time" is far from universal (as is forcefully argued by Heidegger in *Being and
Time* (1962). Clock-time is particular to modernity in the same way that "walk-
about-time" is particular to the Australian aboriginal social system or "cyclical
time" to the Algerian Kabyle (Bourdieu 1970). However, industrial production is
only possible with "clock-time"—how else can one buy labor power by the
hour? Similarly, industrial production presupposes measured abstract space—an
aboriginal sense of space would be entirely useless for most of the processes of
modernity. The idea of individual ownership is also particular to modernity and
one of the premises of industrial capitalism. Money does not simply exist "out
there" but is a signifier particular to modernity. Hence, exchange value, clock
time, measured space, ownership, and money are all signifiers central to capitalist relations of domination. These signifiers enable us to act in concert. However,
they also preclude other forms of action. Actors wishing to return to a pre-capi-
talist social form may wish to form a commune in which private property does
not exist and become fishermen in the morning, carpenters in the afternoon and
poets in the evening. However, I would argue that such a move should also exclude "clock-time," "linear space," and "exchange value" for it to be a true return to this lost Arcadia. Consequently, the "power to" of capitalism is premised
upon a duality of consensus on meaning (structuration and confirming-
structuration) and exclusion of a massive number of alternative meanings
(destructuration).

Political signifiers are the more obvious signifiers which entail specific relations of domination. The word democracy means something very different to a
follower of Hayek than it does to a radical feminist. Consequently, meaningful
dialogue, of the kind envisaged by Habermas, in which it is possible for one actor to recognize when the other puts forward a compelling argument, can become impossibility. Once the signifiers themselves become contested an ideal
speech situation is difficult to construct as acts of structuration will constantly be
met with destructuration. Consequently, the structural base of "power to" will be
lost.

"Power over"

"Power over" is not qualitatively distinct from "power to," in the sense that it also presupposes a given system of meaning. When a person is placed in a position of power, that position is meaning given and confers "power over" others. This is most obviously seen in the case of institutionalized authority. In a traditional "Gerontocracy" (Weber 1968: 346), the authority of the "elder" is derived from what it means to be an "elder." To the extent to which their power is legitimate it has to be consonant with that meaning. When an individual exceeds this meaning their power becomes illegitimate and those to whom a command is issued are likely to destructure. Within modernity, authority is frequently constituted through either meritocratic principles or by election, and the office is tied to specific structures of meaning that define the scope of power in question. In this case if someone occupies such a position but comes to it without election or the correct qualification or if they attempt to exercise power outside of the intended scope, their authoritative power will decrease. Offices like "manager" and "president" are signifiers which give the actors who occupy these positions "power over" the rest of the population. As long as they behave appropriately relative to the shared meaning of this position they will hold "power over" others. If they are particularly effective, or possess charismatic qualities, they may try to change the meaning of their position but this change will be successful only if the surrounding population will confirm-structure the new meaning. If they destructure, any such exercises of power will decrease their "power over." Hence, authoritative power is non-zero sum. That is to say, unlike a cake that is about to be divided up (which is zero sum), one person's gain is not necessarily at the expense of another.

In his account of the advance of modernity, Giddens correctly insists that capitalism is premised upon advances in *both* economic and authoritative resources. For a factory to function it presupposes both the means of production (the steam engine) and the ability of the manager to control the exact movements of workers in time and space. This entails not only clock-time and measured space but also the "right" to command another to situate themselves in a certain way in time and space—authoritative power. If any of the three elements (clock-time, measured space and managerial authority) were removed, the system would collapse. For instance, it is an observed fact that in traditional societies, which do not use clock-time, industrial production invariably fails. Similarly, in a traditional society in which authority is based upon the sanctity of tradition and filial obligations, democracy is outside the conditions of possibility—a lesson the process of decolonization has amply demonstrated and the West is slowly learning in Iraq at present (2005). Resistance to meaning through destructuration is one of the most effective methods of undermining a system of domination and the sociological explanation for the success of Gandhi's technique of "passive resistance."

A system of meaning gives us a capacity for action ("power to") and facilitates the creation of hierarchies of power ("power over"). However, these mean-

ings exclude other meanings. We have many actual and potential systems with
different mutually relating logic of meaning, each of which can create "power
to" and "power over." One aspect of hegemony is the process whereby one system of meaning facilitates the creation of certain forms of power and precludes
others. The consensus, which Gramsci observes is central to hegemony, is a consensus upon meaning. The exclusions which Laclau and Mouffe write about are
the excluded meanings that have the potential to destabilize a particular set of
relations of domination. Since meaning is essentially arbitrary it is possible to
construct reality, hence relations of domination, differently. We can understand
why an elite might resist meaning that destabilizes existing reality, but what is
more complex is why do the dominated or subaltern continue to reproduce
meanings that are central to the reproduction of the power of dominators? Why
don't they simply destructure? Answering this question is the key to understanding hegemony.

We are going deliberately, methodologically to bracket coercion in our
analysis because Gramsci argued that hegemony was not based upon coercion.
However, as it is frequently used to as a basis for "power over," we will make a
brief mention of it. Coercion is necessary to make up for a deficit in consensus
upon meaning. Coercion is a way of gaining compliance from actors who do not
willingly confirm-structure existing structural practices. Because they do not
confirm structure they are a threat to the existing system of domination. Coercion can either take the form of a threat of violence or it can derive from a threat
of material deprivation. When coercion fails, then violence as pure physical
power becomes the ultimate source of compliance. In the limiting case of pure
violence meaning need not be involved. Violence of this kind does not presuppose social order. Consequently, I would argue that it is subset of "natural
power" rather than "social power." If the other is reduced to her physical body
social order is not reproduced. However, most cases of coercive power are not of
this kind, they presuppose social order. The need for threats are there "to induce"
the other to confirm-structure. However, as Gramsci was careful to emphasize,
hegemony is not based upon coercion. For our purposes, the question is why
relatively powerless actors confirm-structure hegemonic relations of domination
without being coerced into doing so? Hence, we are going to methodologically
bracket coercion for the moment.

Hegemony, "power over," and domination

The most obvious and straightforward reason for actors to confirm-structure relations domination, in which they are not dominant, is that social order gives
actors both "power to" and "power over." For those who are relatively powerless, who have little "power over," the "power to" which they gain from consenting to the reproduction of existing social structures gives them obvious benefits.
This is essentially Giddens' point when he argues that domination always presupposes relations of mutual autonomy and dependence (1982: 38-9). If a person
sells his labor power for so much an hour to the owner of the means of produc-

tion, the former does gain some advantage from the relationship—although it may be less than the latter. Because the owner of the means of production needs the labor power of those selling it, they are also dependent upon him, and, as a consequence, there is the potential for the seller of labor power to bargain. If those in a position of domination feel that destructuration by those who are less powerful (but upon whom they are nonetheless dependent) is likely, they can increase the quantity of "power to" which the dominated gain from the relationship. As power is non-zero sum, it is quite possible that a system with high levels of domination (power over) may actually deliver more "power to" than a more egalitarian system. If this is the case, the dominated may consider it to be in their interest to reproduce their own domination—the commonly held view that capitalism is more efficient than socialism would be one such instance. In this instance the dominated fully understand the consequences of their consent, and it is a rational one according to means-ends calculation. This type of pragmatic reason for the reproduction of relations of domination does not in any way imply domination through the manipulation of meaning or consent.

In everyday social interaction the knowledge which social actors have of meaning is largely tacit knowledge. It is a "practical consciousness" knowledge (Giddens 1984—*habitus* in the work of Bourdieu and Elias) which enables them to "go on" in social life. This tacit knowledge is overlaid by discursive consciousness knowledge—knowledge that we can put into words. Because everyday social interaction is a complex layering of meaning, most of the knowledge use remains practical consciousness knowledge. Hence, it is not open to social critique. Most actors in modern society use clock-time to order their interactions without ever reflecting upon time as a discursive phenomenon. Consequently, the first source of systemic stability is the tacitness of meaning/structure. The structuredness of social life is encountered with the same "natural attitude" (Schutz 1971) which actors use to get out of bed in the morning. After all, authoritative power and allocative resources are reproduced through meaning and, consequently, gain stability from the fact that the human mind is so constituted that it can process masses of meaning nearly as reflex. This is reinforced by the fact that the number of structures implicated in relations of domination are extensive in nature and many of them implicated in an indirect way. When we see a table set for dinner, we see forks, knives, spoons, etc., not pieces of metal and wonder what they are for. A reflection along the following lines would be highly improbable:

"In Western society we have the local custom of using a 'fork,' which is a tool used for lifting food to the mouth. The first user of a fork was a 14th century princess who married into the family of the Venetian Doge. She considered herself a lady of 'refinement' and developed, to what contemporaries seemed, the quaint practice of using a two-pronged gold fork to lift food to her mouth. She died young because she was too delicate to live (or, so it was reputed at the time). However, the habit of using a fork spread through the royal families and aristocracies of Europe over the next two centuries. By the late 15th century the aristocratic habit of eating with a fork was a mark of 'civilization' that distinguished the aristocracy from the rest—especially bourgeoisie. Over the next couple of centuries, the bourgeoisie adopted the fork as a marker of their coming civilization and by the 19th century the Western working classes were adopting the fork in everyday use—again copying the class above them. As Western societies generally used forks, the internal class distinction between the 'civilized' and 'uncivilized' classes became externalized toward the rest of the world as a signifier of the opposition between civilization and 'savagery.' In particular, eating with your hands became a mark of the 'uncivilized' nature of the African continent, which reinforced the racist view that some of the African races were lower on the evolutionary scale, thus providing legitimacy for the slave trade. Consequently, this pronged metal object, which I see in front of me, is only a fork by convention—it could have been otherwise—and is bound up with exclusion, domination and ultimately the slave trade." (This imaginary account is based upon Elias 1994.)

What is obvious in the above thought experiment is the impossibility of carrying on routine social action if every signifier were subjected to this form of radical reflexivity. Hence, most social action reproduces meanings, many of which legitimate relations of domination (including the humble fork) at a totally unreflective level. What is also apparent is the real difficulty in not "seeing" the fork as a fork. The reason for this is that meaning is not external to us. Unlike the Cartesian view of the self as struggling to get in touch with the world-out-there, we are not separate from external reality. The world-out-there exists only through meaning, and the latter is imposed by our minds upon the sense data as we receive them—our historical *a priori*. Hence, the world as we see it is inextricably bound up with our "being-in-it." Our existence as interpretative beings is a form of "presencing" in which both the world and our being-in-the-world are recreated. When we ask ourselves to see the fork as other than a fork, this does not simply concern the fork but is tied into the reproduction of our very being-in-the-world. The act of limiting the world by excluding other meanings is not something which we accomplish simply in order to preserve existing systems of meaning but entails the "presencing" of self. The idea of the "real" as an excluded meaning is not solely a "will to power" but is necessary for the continuity of our being-in-the-world. This is why Garfinkel's experiments with trust elicited such strong reactions.[3] This was not simply an attack upon the "world out there" but upon the *self*. For this reason actors will invariably tend toward conservative social action and more than likely destructure new meaning. Structuration practices which elicit destructuring reactions from others are not simply disputes over arbitrary signifiers; they are conflicts over the constitution of self—deep ontological conflicts. Within a given social order, authority and what counts as material resources are, of course, constituted through meaning. However, the ontological being-in-the-world (ontological security) of *both* the dominated and dominators are inextricably tied up with the reproduction of meaning. Both parties have an extrinsic interest in hegemonic stability. Let's not forget, properly understood, a counterhegemonic strategy should not simply entail replacing the personnel of specific relations of domination. The world itself has to change. If actors continue to see time as clock time, commodities as exchange value and consequently "time as money" or "wasted time," nothing has changed. Because agents are inseparable from their tacit interpretative horizons, dominated social actors have deep ontological reasons for giving consent to existing relations of domination. Return to Foucault's concept of deep and shallow conflict: replacing the personnel in an existing system of meaning is a shallow conflict that, viewed from a systemic level, reproduces relations of domination, while a deep power conflict replaces a world ordering reality—an "order of things." The former reproduces hegemony (but with an illusion of change brought about by the circulation of elites), while the latter is genuinely counterhegemonic. The former is the conceptual equivalent of the working classes replacing the personnel of the bourgeoisie or, to use Gramsci's language, taking over the "political sphere" but leaving "civil society" intact. When Marx described the transition form feudal to capitalist society in those famous words from the Communist Manifesto, "All that is solid melts into air, all that is holy is profaned ...," he was arguing that this was a genuine transformation in world ordering reality. Capitalism was a counterhegemonic move relative to feudalism because what was "solid" to the feudal mind melted into air. Consequently, the overthrow of capitalism presupposes the same kind of "deep" change.

While actors do not have the capacity to move into the absence of cognitive order, they can imagine alternative orders of being-in-the-world. Consequently, ontology only contributes to hegemonic stability but it does not preclude social change entirely. The ability to understand alternative interpretative horizons is demonstrated, for instance, in *our ability to understand* Foucault's description of the Renaissance idea of the world mirroring and folding upon itself. It *makes sense* (even if we may consider it odd and mistaken) to argue that a walnut mirrors the human head and that this is God's signature which tells us that walnuts are good for the brain. Contrast this with the Chinese Encyclopedia:

> in which it is written that "animals are divided into: (a) belonging to the emperor, (b) embalmed, (c) tame, (d) suckling pigs, (d) sirens, (f) fabulous, (g) stray dogs, (h) included in the present classification, (I) frenzied, (j) innumerable, (k) drawn with a very fine camel hair brush, (l) *et cetera*, (m) having just broken the water pitcher, (n) that from a long way off look like flies" (Foucault 1970: xv)

We do not know what it means to think like that, we cannot make the epistemic jump—it makes no sense. Hence, it comes as no surprise to learn (in fact it is a relief) that the encyclopedia never existed—it was actually an invention by Borges, even if Foucault mistakenly thought to the contrary. In everyday life we constantly make switches of interpretative horizon—which is why we can switch to the Renaissance system of thought, even if we consider it erroneous.

The ability to change interpretative horizon is central to everyday life and exemplified in the praxis of bureaucratic authority with its close affinity with instrumental rationality. At 9:30 a.m. hypothetical officials "see" others as "numbers" and "cases" to be administered, but at 5:30 p.m., as they leave the office, loosen their ties, or change out of black patent high heels (symbolic acts which signify a change of interpretative horizon), interacting agents become "individuals." As has been argued by Bauman (1989), it is the ability of actors when in bureaucratic mode to administer people as "things" which made events like the Holocaust possible—it did not require a nation of dedicated anti-Semites, just a few in charge of the instruments of bureaucracy. If those officials had chosen not to be "good bureaucrats," switched interpretative horizons while at work, and seen the Jews as people (and indeed a small exceptional minority did and resigned or subverted the system), then the Holocaust would not have been possible.

Actors cannot combat meaning with the absence of meaning. They cannot replace meaning with lack of meaning, but they can replace it with alternative meanings. Because meaning is relationally constituted these alternative meanings cannot exist in a vacuum—the Chinese encyclopedia was such a vacuum. Hence, actors can resist meaning if they wish to do so—destructuring where they might normally have confirm-structure. Derrida is mistaken in thinking that we cannot escape the meanings in which we find ourselves. It is just that we cannot move into nowhere. As long as there exist possible alternative orders, the social actor can maintain ontological security.

Mouffe's idea of a counterhegemonic strategy of radicalizing concepts such as freedom and equality, presupposes an exercise of maintaining ontological security while unfolding the inherent logic of these signifiers and, in so doing, giving them new meaning. However if, as she is suggesting, we use their already implicit logic, it could be argued that this suggestion is not sufficiently radical to qualify as a counterhegemonic strategy.

Actors can change meaning either within an interpretative horizon through the exploration of an existing system of meaning or, more radically, propose alternative interpretative horizons. The latter is what lies at the heart of Kuhn's interpretation of scientific revolutions. From our perspective, the important way to interpret a paradigm is not as a method of problem-solving which has an inherent logic (the usual interpretation of Kuhn); a paradigm is a self-referential system of meaning. This is the significance of Kuhn's use of gestalt pictures. The point of a gestalt picture is that the substance remains the same (the sense data) but the thing itself changes depending upon the interpretation placed upon it. A scientific revolution is where familiar sense data are fundamentally changed by an alternative interpretative horizon. These new interpretative horizons are acts of imagination which reflect the capacity of social agents to transcend the system of meaning into which they have been socialized. Of course, what distinguishes a scientific revolution from the ramblings of a "madman" is not in the gift of the originator of that interpretative horizon, it is in the gift of others. What distinguishes Napoleon from the "napoleons" frequenting psychiatric institutions is not their structuration practices but the reaction of others—confirming-structuration to the former but destructuration to the latter. In this instance structural constraint does not come from within but from others—the need to interact. What makes the "madman" a "madman" is the absence of confirming-structuring other actors. Destructuration leaves him in a solipsistic "social world" (which is not social), speaking a "private language" (which is not a language). The "genius" on the other hand finds his novel structuration practices confirm-structured, consequently his act of imagination is no longer personal to him—he is not speaking a "private language" even if his action is novel. In this sense Foucault's claim concerning the "death of the author" and Derrida's assertion that it is the reader, not the writer, who creates the meaning of a text, are half correct. The confirm-structurer is the real Hobbesian sovereign who has the power to let the lone social agent in from the "state of nature." The destructuring sovereign on the other hand casts excluded meanings into the abyss of the state of nature. The structurer is cast into a condition which is solitary and, even worse than physical insecurity, is a perpetual state of ontological insecurity. Consequently, it can be argued that destructuration is a form of domination through ontological insecurity.

What strategies other than a fear of ontological insecurity are available to those wishing to maintain the hegemony of a particular order of things? The most obvious is the denial of the arbitrariness of the sign. While it seems self-evident that meaning is mere convention, most social actors are resistant to this idea.[4] Part of this comes from the fear of ontological insecurity (which we have just discussed), but another aspect comes from strategies which are routinely used to argue that meaning is *not* a cultural construct. I would argue that these strategies are central to hegemony.

There are endless ways of arguing that certain interpretative horizons and meanings are "beyond" culture. The most common source of such epistemic stability was God, but with the death of God in the late 18th century (in some Western societies) that position became usurped by science. This is the link which Foucault observes between power and truth. By power, of course, he really means a system of meaning which produces both "power to" and "power over." These systems of meaning are fought for by linking them to truth—by claiming that they are not mere conventions. For instance, Pierre Riviere (Foucault 1975) ran out into the street swinging a bloody axe shouting that he had killed his mother and two sisters. Immediately a whole posse of "experts" came to the scene and compiled endless information on the fellow. Why did they do so? It was not necessary for his conviction? No, his guilt was beyond doubt. The experts were establishing the absolute existence of the "pathological" and "dangerous individual"—a being who had yet to be created at that time. Once created this object of knowledge existed as a "quilting point" for the modern social sciences, criminology, and psychology. The pathological individual is no "arbitrary signifier," no object of "mere convention," no "act of God": he is a product of scientific "discovery." As "all we moderns know," a scientific fact is true irrespective of culture; it is a rock of certainty surrounded by the endless flux of human societies that are like the waves of the sea, thrown here and there by the contingencies of chance, the imperfections of the human mind, the frailty of the human spirit, the distortions of human emotion, the weight of opinion, the suffocation of tradition, the blight of superstition and above all else the cognitive inability of humans to speak the pure language of mathematical symbols.

As observed by Foucault (1980: 85), when Marx argued that his theories were scientific, this was no mere statement of method. It was a claim to the effect that his ideas were not "his creation" but reflected an external reality that transcended the perspective of the interpreter. It was a counterhegemonic move whereby that which is contingent became certain.

There are of course other ways of deconventionalizing social order in order to maintain hegemonic consent. In the literature on nationalism, Gellner often expressed surprise at the fact that nationalists find the idea that nationalism is a Western invention associated with the advent of modernity deeply disturbing. However, imagine for a moment someone giving her life for an arbitrary convention which in most instances is barely 200 years old (although, English and a couple of other manifestations may be slightly older). It is inconceivable. The willingness of many nationalists to die for their nations (without being coerced into it) is a startling instance of the effectiveness of reification. They believe that people are "naturally" divided into nations and that their particular nation extends into the "mists of time." In some instances the nation may appear to have died but, in reality, he or she (usually) is waiting to be reborn—which is why most nations have a past hero slumbering, waiting to be awoken, if the memory of the nation is in jeopardy (in the Irish case *Cuchulain* and in the Danish *"Holger Danske"*).

The belief in the naturalness of nations is also, of course, central to current immigration policy. In terms of internal logic liberal democracy is cosmopolitan. Yet, these rights, which citizens have within democratic nation-states, are denied to those of different nationality—who, in many instances, can be deported. However, there is nothing in liberal or democratic political theory that defines the "demos" in terms of nations. The latter is an entirely arbitrary signifier of exclusion which is extraneously inserted into it. Yet, the majority of citizens in Western democracies take for granted that nationality rather than, for instance, having a "need" define citizenship.

An appeal to nature has always been considered a way of transcending the arbitrariness of convention. When Aristotle asked himself whether slavery was justified (Aristotle 1940: 1130-31) his answer was that it is justified if there are "naturally" born slaves but not if slavery is by "convention" only—he concluded that there are naturally born slaves but, in his will, freed his personal slaves. Similarly, patriarchy has traditionally been legitimated by an appeal to the biological differences between men and women.

One of the premises that legitimizes capitalism is the idea that people are *naturally* competitive. Yet, our society spends huge amounts of resources in developing this supposedly "innate" predisposition. Not only is nationalism contemporaneous with modernity; both coincided with a massive revival of competitive sport. As argued by Gellner (1983), capitalism presupposes a large mobile workforce. In traditional society, socialization and education were a local affair. However, mass industrialization is premised upon objective credentials, which an employer can examine in order to ascertain precisely what skills a person has. The common curriculum also ensures that workers do not speak some obscure local language or dialect that renders them unpredictable employees. Furthermore, education entails training of the body and the internalization of restraint. Irregular movements are eliminated and part of that elimination process is physical training.

National sports organizations became built upon pyramidal structures in which local loyalties became channeled into national events. So, local allegiances that might, in the natural course of events, run contrary to the "imagined community" of the nation, became functional to nationalism—the local team could win the national cup. Traditional local sports were invented and projected into the mists of time when the nation was born. So the nation was born as a collective identity transcending class, ensuring that Marx would be mistaken in his prediction that class identity would emerge as a consequence of the advance of capitalism. In fact, in an ironic twist of fate, in most Western societies those most willing (or likely) to die for the nation are the poor. Yearly ritualized warfare on the sports field ensured the reproduction of the imagined community of "them" and "us." The heroes of the nation are those who compete and win. Emulating their national sports heroes, children internalize the desire for competition, which makes it appear innate. Competition can be further reified by an appeal to Darwinian notions of the survival of the fittest. All species are by nature competitive, so why should the human species be any different? Capitalism is really the "natural condition of mankind," the working through of the natural laws of evolution, the "end of history." This kind of Darwinian argument is implicit in many of the justifications for neoliberalism.

The class interests of those who dominate capitalism (by now more the managerial class rather than the traditional bourgeoisie) do so by naturalizing and scientizing the order of things. They do not hold their share of the cake purely for their own benefit. There is a collective consciousness, a common will, through the nation which benefits collectively from their "skills." An unfathomable greed becomes reified as a naturally competitive urge and becomes transmogrified into something which even the poorest in the nation identify with—something that makes them "proud" to be part of whatever nation they believe their identity to be part of.

For a group that is excluded through the reification of sport, this provides alternative paths that illustrate the workings of hegemony. People with physical disabilities are such an excluded group who have two alternative paths to power one that reproduces hegemony and the other that is genuinely counterhegemonic. The counterhegemonic move would be to deconstruct the significance of sport —it is after all only an arbitrary convention of recent date; it is exclusionary and reinforces a competitive urge which is normatively reprehensible because it contributes to inequality. Since this is directly contrary to some of the legitimating principles of capitalism (the doctrine of natural competitiveness), such a move would stand the greatest chance of success if allied with other anti-capitalist social movements. The other move is to argue for "special" sports events—a strategy that has culminated in events such as the Special Olympics. While this move gives certain individuals with disabilities the opportunity to compete and defeat fellow individuals with disabilities, it comes at the cost of reinforcing and legitimating the spirit of competition that excluded them in the first place. It also comes at the cost of reinforcing the idea that there is such a group as "disabled people" who share an identity, rather than individuals who are the same as everyone else but who, through sheer chance, happen to have a specific "disability" relative to the (constructed) norms concerning "ability" of society. What distinguishes the counterhegemonic move from the hegemonic one is the fact that the former constitutes a fundamental attack upon the existing order of things (an act of destructuration), while the latter reproduces the existing social structure (confirming-structuration).

The counterhegemonic move is, in fact, highly unlikely because the majority of people with disabilities have internalized the reifications which exclude them. Like everyone else, their knowledge of social life would be largely tacit—although experience of discrimination might make it more discursive than usual. It is also obvious that the counterhegemonic move will meet with substantially more resistance (destructuration) than the hegemonic one and is, consequently, likely to create ontological insecurity. Furthermore, by reinforcing hegemony social actors do gain "power to" in the short term.

Hegemony, Power and Violence

Following Gramsci, I have made the case that hegemony is essentially rooted in meaning and social knowledge, not coercive resources. It is a position which is consistent with Foucault's view and the ideas of Arendt (1970). However, in international politics the idea that hegemony and power are reducible to coercive resources is a commonly held one that informs much of "realist" policymaking. Consequently, I would like to reflect upon the relationship between physical coercion and hegemonic social power. I would argue that it is an inverse one. In the final instance, physical coercion means treating the other as a physical object. You inflict pain or threaten the body of the other to make him compliant. However, once the other is no longer a social actor reproducing structures willingly he iscontrollable only in a limited way.

The image of the Panopticon springs to mind. Sovereign punishment represents physical coercion in its pure form. This is the execution of Damiens which Foucault contrasts with timetable (Foucault 1979: 3-7). The Panopticon on the other hand is a resocialization machine. As such it failed, but the idea behind it was based upon a correct social intuition. Power comes from the predictability of the actions of others—from the certainty that structuration will meet with confirming-structuration. In the cure of the insane, Tuke liberated the mad from their chains and took them to tea parties instead (Foucault 1971: 249). Each one was told to observe others closely for any signs of anomalous behavior and report it. Slowly the mad came to internalize the predictability of "reason." Tuke understood that true power over an individual is not created through the strength and hardness of chains but through the soft tissues of the mind. Because social structures are arbitrary it is in fact counterproductive to coerce others into them as this exposes their arbitrariness.

If this is the case, why is the world's hegemon at the moment engaged in massive military adventure? The answer lies in the false and mistaken belief that power is essentially coercive. The facts of the US-led invasion of Iraq confirm this. The US (with the assistance of Britain) had the physical resources to invade Iraq, but it *does not* have the power to govern it. Compare this for a moment to Britain at the height of Empire when it effectively governed one-third the landmass of the globe and a population over twenty times that of Britain. In contrast, the US is unable to govern a country which is substantially smaller than one of the larger states of the Union. Where is the difference? I would suggest that it lies in the realm of social knowledge. During the 19th century, nationalism was confined to Europe and the Americas. Outside these areas social actors did not consider it in any way irregular or odd that those that governed were of a different cultural group than those they governed (Gellner 1983). After all in India, for instance, the caste system was based precisely upon the idea that the governed and governing were culturally distinct. In the early 19th century over 80 percent of the 291,000 imperial troops in India were Indian and even after the 1857 mutiny (caused by British insensitivity to the soldier's dietary needs—incompetent practical consciousness knowledge) two-thirds of the imperial army was Indian. During World War I, 130,000 Indian troops fought for Britain. None of this suggests that coercive resources were the main source of Britain's ability to control India. However, the point is even more forcefully made if we compare Iraq with Northern Rhodesia (now Zambia). Both are of a similar territorial area, yet as late as 1912, Britain could govern the latter effectively (collecting taxes, etc.) with the minimal coercive resources of one battalion comprising 750 *African* troops who were commanded by 26 British officers (all figures from Mann 2003: 26). Were these people (Zambians did not as yet exist) governed purely by coercion? I think not. At the same time, much closer to Britain, a potential nation state a quarter the size, Ireland, was becoming ungovernable. What was the difference? The discourse of nationalism and modernity had arrived in Ireland. Local peasants were becoming "Irishmen" at a time when the locals in that part of Africa had yet to discover the national essence that lay dormant in the depth of their souls. To return to the case of India, it is interesting to note that what really undermined British rule was not military rebellion but Gandhi's policy of passive resistance. This was counterhegemonic strategy in the true sense of the term, whereby the objective was to undermine British authority by refusing to reproduce the structures of the system—a policy of destructuration.

As argued by Parsons (1963) power is non-zero sum and decreases through the use of violence. It is interesting to note that the more coercion Israel uses against the Palestinians the more uncontrollable their territories become, and I predict that the more coercion the US uses against the Iraqis the more ungovernable Iraq will become. To repeat the words of Arendt, "It is insufficient to say that power and violence are not the same. Power and violence are opposites; where the one rules absolutely the other is absent. Violence appears where power is in jeopardy, but left to its own course it ends in power's disappearance" (Arendt 1970: 56).

The US may wish to make Iraq governable, but the failure of the Bush administration to understand that power and violence are opposites will lead to failure. It is a depressing thought, but I predict that the common and mistaken view that hegemonic power is based upon coercion will in all probability lead us into a world in which social order will be ever more contingent and arbitrary. Hegemony will be replaced by the state of nature—a condition that will be characterized by physical force and increasing ontological insecurity. The reaction of most actors will be to seek security in the certainties of foundational beliefs, thus increasing physical conflict and insecurity because "power to" and "power over" decrease as convergence of interpretative horizons diminishs. If Elias' (1994 [1939]) "civilizing process" is interpreted as a process of increased restraint and consequent exclusion of violence to the hidden margins of society, it may be that, while modernity was characterized by an increasing civilizing process, postmodernity will be characterized by a decivilizing process whereby violence becomes privatized and part of everyday life.

Notes

1. The concept of "organizational outflanking" comes from Mann (1986) and Clegg (1989). It is not a Gramscian term but a highly felicitous way of describing how a hegemon attains and maintains dominance.

2. Weber's definition of power was "Power is the probability that one actor within a social relationship will be in a position to carry out his own will despite resistance, regardless of the basis on which this probability rests." (Weber 1964: 152). Dahl (1957, 1968) defined power as a causal relationship in which A causes B's behavior.

3. In a series of experiments Garfinkel instructed students to interpret everyday interaction slightly differently than normally but in a manner that was comprehensible. So, for instance, they were instructed to interpret "Hello, how are you?" as a literal request concerning another's well-being. The reaction was strong considering that all that was involved was minor change of social convention (Garfinkel 1984).

4. The author is acquainted with this from the reaction of students when teaching social theory, and William Labov has observed the same phenomenon when teaching linguistics (personal conversation). By and large, students find the conventionality of meaning counterintuitive.

Hegemony and Power in International

Relations and Political Life

Chapter 4

Dilemmas of Operationalizing Hegemony

Philip G. Cerny

Hegemony in international politics is not "all of a piece." Rather, it denotes a highly complex phenomenon which exists at a number of asymmetric levels and across a number of different dimensions. Indeed, the term itself can be considered an "essentially contested concept" (Gallie, 1955-56). The very definition of hegemony is contested. Thus any analyst's use of the term will inevitably be value-loaded in terms of both a choice of definition and the methodological implications of applying it to particular empirical phenomena. Furthermore, hegemony is not a homogeneous or holistic phenomenon. It is made up of a range of component parts, and any hypothetical synthesis with predictable implications for real-world behavior is historically educated guesswork. Its application to the complex contemporary world is fraught with hazard. Any attempt to pursue hegemony as a policy, therefore, is open to political and bureaucratic maneuvering, ideological manipulation, serious miscalculations, and potential opportunity costs. Finally, there is no such thing as perfect hegemony; hegemony is always contested by challenges from those who are left out of the hegemonic project or placed in a subordinate position (Haugaard and Newman, this volume). In the contemporary world, both the use of the term hegemony in current international relations theory and analysis, on the one hand, and attempts to operationalize it in foreign policymaking, on the other, are likely to expose the inherent contradictions of hegemony and lead to instability and opportunistic behavior.

Analytical Complexities

The problem starts with the definition of hegemony (Jones 2001a: 659-73; Cohn 2000: 66-73; Fontana, Haugaard and Lentner, this volume). The word derives from the Greek, where it originally meant domination or rule in general; Barry Jones (2001b: 669) defines it as "the occupation of a dominant position in any system."

Indeed, some analysts simply use hegemony in a system of states as a synonym for dominance or disproportionately preponderant power (e.g., Leffler 1992). However, in Ancient Greece, the concept of hegemony evolved into a more specific form meaning a relatively consensual form of leadership within an alliance of quasi-independent political units (Fontana, this volume; Lentner 2005). It connoted leadership, authority, and legitimacy, in contrast to domination by force or coercion (despotism and empire). The tension and ambiguity between domination in general and consensual leadership lie at the heart of International Relations today.

However, hegemony also has two further dimensions at the international level that are relevant to both this chapter and this book in general. The first is a structural dimension. Hegemony is not merely the fact of holding a disproportionately powerful position, but one where that dominant position is firmly embedded in, and indeed generated through, a wider system which gives it its very meaning and effectiveness. Hegemony thus represents a structural space or level that is only significant insofar as it gives rise to, stabilizes, manages, shapes, expands, and/or controls the wider system in which it is embedded. Hegemony is a state or condition of the system itself, and *not a property belonging to the hegemon*. The systemic role of the hegemon (i.e., hegemony) in turn constrains as well as empowers the hegemon in quite specific ways. Being located in a hegemonic position either (or both) permits and/or compels the hegemon to act in a *systemically rational* fashion rather than merely in a self-interested manner.

For collective action theorists, hegemony is merely the most rational way of providing public goods in an anarchic system where defection is the "default" rationality and other actors are most likely to be "free-riders" (cf. Waltz 1979; Krasner 1976). In contrast to free-riders, the hegemonic state, precisely because its disproportionately preponderant power only exists and is utilizable *relative to* the systemic context in which it is embedded, is more likely to rationally equate its self-interests (in a stable system, in particular) with the general welfare of the system as a whole. The essential role of the hegemon is to *assume the costs of providing certain key public goods in a system in which other actors lack either the resources or the system-level identity required to do so* (Krasner 1976).

In his seminal work on collective action, Mancur Olson outlined various ways that public goods could be provided in a system where no authoritative "government" existed and therefore where incentives for free-riding and defection were dominant strategies (Olson 1971). This set of conditions is mainly applicable to international relations. In neorealist theory, in particular, relative gains (who's up, who's down, in relation to the others) outweigh absolute gains to the actors in the system generally (as in, for example, positive-sum or Pareto-optimal terms) with regard to providing actor incentives in an anarchic system. Where one actor or unit possesses disproportionately more resources than others, it is possible for that single actor to pay the most vital costs of providing key public goods unilaterally. Providing that actor has a sufficiently strong interest in the maintenance of the system as a whole—as liberal hegemonic actors are seen to have done in an international capitalist system (Britain in the 19th century, the United States in the 20th)—it is rational for that actor, *in its own interests*, to bear disproportionately the costs of the provision of those key public goods.

In a capitalist international system with a liberal hegemon, such public goods may include stability, openness, property rights, monitoring and other transaction costs, establishing and enforcing rules for free trade, providing and underpinning a stable international currency regime, promoting the overall economic growth of the system, crisis prevention, and the like. These goods may be provided either by the hegemon itself, if its resources and will are sufficient, or through the hegemon's support for cooperative institutions and practices, including international regimes, "global governance," or various forms of multilevel governance and webs of bilateral and "minilateral" agreements. Bilateral agreements are agreements between two countries; minilateral agreements are between a very small number of countries; and multilateral agreements are between the large majority of countries. Bilateral and minilateral agreements are easier to make, but may create "closed" cartels and are widely seen as destabilizing by excluding others. Since World War II, the international norm has been to make trade and other regimes as multilateral as possible, and the United States in general has used its hegemonic power to support multilateralization. However, that approach has been under pressure from the George W. Bush Administration's support for "competitive liberalization" through bilateral and minilateral trade agreements such as the Central American Free Trade Area while negotiations over the World Trade Organization's Doha Development Agenda ("Doha Round") stagnate. Bilateral and minilateral agreements therefore sometimes represent a move away from hegemonically-supported multilateralism, although sometimes they are in contrast seen to add up to a kind of *de facto* multilateralism, as with the U.S. Reciprocal Trade Agreements Act in the 1930s.

Thus hegemony ought to have more than a whiff of international systemic legitimacy about it (Ferguson 2003). A genuinely hegemonic actor, in pursuing its own interests, should be rationally led to pursue the public or general interests of the system as a whole, or else the hegemon turns in on itself and becomes not only systemically destructive but also self-destructive—to the extent that its own self-interests are bound up in the maintenance of the wider system. In this sense, hegemony begins to approach "authority," in the sense that the latter is used in political theory (Lukes 1974: 18, 23). Indeed, in neo-Gramscian theory as well as both some realist and some liberal theory (especially liberal institutionalism: cf. Keohane 1984), hegemony implies a significant degree of consensus. Thus hegemony loses its last claim to be an empirical phenomenon and is unveiled as an essentially normative one.

The second additional dimension of hegemony at the international level is found in International Political Economy. The use of the concept of hegemony in contemporary debates began with the economic historian Charles P. Kindleberger, who revived the term and applied it to the capacity of the leading economic power of a particular period to provide key economic public goods (Kindleberger 1973). Kindleberger's use of the term did not, of course, eliminate its ambiguity—capitalist hegemons in the modern world have needed military power too. But it highlighted the relationship between international hegemony and domestic relations of forces of the kind stressed by Antonio Gramsci (Fontana, this volume), such as economic actors and social groups, both dominant and "subaltern." It further blurred the distinction between the international and domestic levels, and led to the emergence of a neo-Gramscian school of international political economy that has brought Gramscian notions of hegemony into IPE and IR too (Cox 1996; Gill 1990).

Hegemony and the Role of the United States

American hegemony exhibits all of these features. Given (a) that the distribution of power capabilities and economic resources in the world enables the U.S. to play the role of hegemon, (b) that the same distribution means that "hegemony" is a systemic requirement if key public goods are to be provided (in other words, that there are no other actors capable of and willing to supply those public goods either individually or in concert), and (c) that the U.S., as a "liberal hegemon," seeks to externalize a kind of national interest that supports the spread of liberal capitalism, hegemonic stability theorists would posit that there is likely to exist a fundamental congruity between American national interests, on the one hand, and the structural imperatives (normative and empirical) of the international system—especially the international economy—on the other. This supposed congruity—if not identity—of American national interests with the provision of international order thereby resolves the paradox of international anarchy.

For liberals, American hegemony does not simply concern the provision of international order as such but rather the effect of American agency in institutionalizing liberal mechanisms—from the spread of market institutions and practices around the globe, to (liberal) democratization, and to the strengthening of what might be called "arm's-length" hegemony through the development of international institutions. For historical political economists, hegemony is about economic stabilization and expansion, i.e., the promotion of free trade and the provision of an international monetary system through a reserve currency, among other things (Kindleberger 1973), with military power seen more as a facilitating variable—something achieved by Britain in the 19th century and the United States in the 20th. For neo-Gramscians, hegemony is not "American" hegemony as such, but the domination of a transnational capitalist class through inclusive strategies—to a large extent rooted nonetheless in the agency of the United States Government and/or American elites – that enable cross-class coalition-building, and incorporate subaltern groups into the dominant consensus (Cox 1996; Gill 1990; van der Pijl 1998). And to certain American policymakers—those whom Daalder and Lindsay indeed call "hegemonists"—hegemony means "that America's immense power and the willingness to wield it, even over the objections of others, is the key to securing America's interests in the world" (Daalder and Lindsay 2003: 40-41).

Historically, the concept of American hegemony has always had a number of subspecies, reflecting the ambiguity of the U.S.'s trajectory from isolationism to interventionism and ultimately to "unipolar superpower" status. Washington's Farewell Address is the classic statement of the need for self-imposed limits on the use of American power, in order to avoid entanglement in the corrupt power games of the Old World. But while hegemony seems to imply a denial of traditional isolationism, it also reflects the famous lines of John Winthrop in 1630: "We must consider that we shall be a city upon a hill; the eyes of all people are on us ..." Even American isolationism was seen to be an example to the rest of humanity, reflecting universal values and not mere American self-interest. It did not logically entail dominance, force, or coercion but aspired to leading by example. In the long and painful transition from isolationism to interventionism, from the 1930s onward —especially in the light of the breakdown of the fragile post-World War I settlement—American foreign policy involved a growing understanding that American security could not be assured unless international security (the core international public good) were provided also (Yergin 1977). No nation alone could do that, in the eyes especially of the "internationalist" faction in the Franklin D. Roosevelt Administration, *other than* the United States itself (Gardner 1971; Penrose 1953). Thus the Roosevelt Administration pursued not dominance but "reluctant leadership," promising that American interventionism and foreign policy goals would precisely *not* entail narrowly self-interested American coercive dominance. Later, the Cold War enabled the United States to have its cake and eat it too—to exercise dominance, but palpably in the interests of the international system, as seen through Western lenses.

Today, without a clear systemic enemy or state-based revolutionary power to contend with, except the disparate forces grouped around terror tactics (Cerny 2005)—and therefore without the alliance cement that comes from a common external foe—the post-Cold War era has once again revealed the fault lines in the American role. American dominance in the 21st century is inextricably intertwined with the legacies of reluctant leadership. Both genuinely Wilsonian liberals and supposedly Wilsonian neoconservatives ostensibly wish not to pursue narrow American self-interests, but rather to promote and institutionalize international and transnational systemic structures and processes around American-style values that go far beyond the provision of public goods as such. American "hegemonists" therefore not only misunderstand the nature of American hegemony but also prescribe policy goals that exacerbate the fault lines within it. Four particular fault lines stand out:

- the disparity between the requirements of hegemony in different issue-areas;
- the problem of institutionalization;
- the different "faces" of hegemony, following Steven Lukes's notion of the "three faces of power" (Lukes 1974); and
- the potential consequences that flow from the divergence between the hegemon's "interests" and those of the international system *qua* system.

Of course, there are other fault lines in American hegemony. One of them is the fault line between the functional/geographical center and the periphery of the world system, leading to an underestimation of the problems and dysfunctions of the latter when the former tries to absorb and mold it to its own values and practices. Another, which partly converges with the previous one, is the fault line between the insiders and the outsiders of the hegemonic project. In both these cases, the reaction of geographically, economically, and socially peripheral actors and "outsiders" would seem, rationally, to be one of rejection of the norms of the center and the "insiders." However, many elites and subaltern groups in the periphery are indeed drawn into effective partnership with the norms and practices of the core as defined by the hegemon—what I will define below as "infrastructural hegemony." Hegemony is not just the preponderance of power; it also entails some sense of authority, so that hegemony must achieve a relatively high degree of consensus among its constituents and *must deliver either or both tangible and/or ideational benefits to the latter*, both predominant and subaltern. Those constituents are varied, and, as neo-Gramscian theory posits, they are not merely domestic but increasingly international and transnational in nature; hegemony reaches out beyond the borders of the U.S. and has an impact on many levels and pockets of global society.

Each of these fault lines therefore manifests different degrees of cooptation into and/or support for hegemony. They involve the consent and support of those states, transnational actors, and domestic groups that might otherwise have been seen as relatively powerless. Active consent and support can be expected at the hegemonic core, but in the functional and geographical peripheries, support and consent is weaker. Sometimes the best the hegemon can expect is passive acquiescence. Among countries allied to the U.S. some are important constituents of the hegemonic system and some are outsiders. This is true also of different social, political, and economic interest groups *within* those countries, cutting across supposedly national societies. Within the center countries in the capitalist world, the proportion of active constituents and of those who are coopted is bigger, but in the peripheries hegemony is weaker, though certainly not nonexistent. Thus one fault line can be drawn between the center, consisting of the active pro-hegemonic alliances of social forces, and the peripheries or the "recipients" of hegemony. In addition, there is another crosscutting fault line between those who are inside the "historic bloc" of social forces and those who are left out of it, whether in the center or in the periphery. The complexity of world society makes the use of coercion, especially through military force, highly problematic and potentially counterproductive, as it cannot be targeted against outsiders to the extent they are spread geographically and sociologically, leading to resistance and backlashes in a range of niches partly insulated and partly linked in archipelago fashion (cf. Pøkiæ 1997; Brenner 2004).

Infrastructural hegemony ultimately depends upon what is perceived by *subaltern* as well as dominant groups as "good" hegemony. Such hegemony gains normative traction through active support and/or passive acquiescence from "peripheral" actors. It involves the isolation, containment, and eventually socialization and incorporatation of those who are marginalized within or even outside of the hegemonic order into internalizing the values of that order. *American* hegemony, with all its warts—the hegemony of "America" as a way of life and as a set of socioeconomic arrangements, not just U.S. state-centered global dominance—can only be effective if it is underpinned and proactively spread by others. However, the fault lines listed above ensure that attempts to create new forms of top-down American hegemony, whether "democratic imperialist" or "assertive nationalist" (Daalder and Lindsay 2003) are likely to run into quicksand. Because of the difficulty of operationalizing hegemony in a homogeneous and effective fashion, hegemony, however much it may reflect the disproportionate preponderance of American power in the international system, has serious opportunity costs in a globalizing world in terms of increased opposition, instability, and opportunistic behavior that in the long run—even in the short run—can undermine the real existing cultural hegemony (reinforced, paradoxically, by the random violence of terrorism and extremism) of American *ways of doing things*.

Opportunistic behavior, in particular—which is analogous to monopolistic behavior in economic theory—leads to a perversion of hegemony, enabling the United States to extract "rents" from the system, sometimes called "predatory hegemony." As Lord Acton famously said in 1887: "All power tends to corrupt. Absolute power corrupts absolutely." Thus the pursuit of coercive hegemony or mere preponderance of power can indeed be counterproductive, undermining the systemic rationality that gives it whatever legitimacy it may possess. Any *effective* American hegemony—whether seen as normatively good or not—requires not so much the pursuit of "hegemony from above," but rather a kind of *"hegemony from below,"* rooted in globalization, or rather in the internalization of globalizing practices and not in the exercise of relational or even structural power by the United States Government as such. "Real" American hegemony, I argue, does not derive from preponderant U.S. military power nor from unilateralism in foreign policy. Rather it comes from globalization itself—from the spread of American-style economic, social, and political practices across transnational space, their acceptance and internalization by an ever-widening range of *non*-American actors, and their growing embeddedness in local, national, translocal, transnational and international institutions and processes around the world, whether we see those practices as normatively good or not.

The Disparity Among Issue-Areas

The first "fault line" in understanding hegemony concerns the disparity among issue-areas. These are highly stylized categories: military-strategic; political, in the sense of political institutions and processes, particularly with regard to democratization; and socioeconomic. Hegemony has different meanings and different, sometimes mutually contradictory, implications for each category. The pursuit of hegemony as a political objective requires actors to choose to privilege particular issue-areas, sometimes downgrading and even undermining hegemony in other issue-areas.

Military-strategic hegemony

Military-strategic hegemony requires a disproportionate preponderance of effective military power compared to other states—and nonstate actors too, including, for example, criminal gangs and terrorists as well as multinational firms and NGOs. However, in today's complex world, the buildup of military power can have two types of counterproductive effects. In the first place, as is well known (strategic thinkers since Thucydides have wrestled with this problem), the application of military power is notoriously vulnerable to events, strategic and technological change, battlefield conditions, the psychological state of political and military leaders, etc. The advent of nuclear weapons over several decades seemed to narrow down these problems to highly technical questions of deterrence such as targeting, technological improvements, formal models of escalation, etc. Nevertheless, nuclear weapons and nuclear warfare systems, however much they may have represented the organizational core of the Cold War international system, were never used after 1945 and their development became more and more abstracted and cut off from the real world of international politics—what Mary Kaldor famously called the "baroque arsenal" (Kaldor 1982).

Actual conflicts, in contrast, have since Korea in the early 1950s been either border skirmishes or, increasingly, "low-intensity warfare" of various kinds. The nature of the warfare had long shifted toward "new wars" (Kaldor 1999). Vietnam (for the United States) and Afghanistan (for the Soviet Union) became quagmires where the nuclear system became increasingly irrelevant to outcomes on the ground. Indeed, the very perception that nuclear deterrence effectively *prevented* direct inter-superpower challenges helped shift the key determinants of those outcomes. Attempts to assert hegemonic power in military terms have not been deemed to be rational and/or persuasive enough for America's allies. Today, the rise of "new wars" and the "Revolution in Military Affairs" have prompted the development of a new baroque arsenal, including ballistic missile defenses and high-tech "virtual" warfare, often untested and, so far, much more potentially costly than foreseen. Thus military-strategic hegemony is itself full of pitfalls, including ones that are difficult or impossible to predict. The fact that many of these pitfalls are today glossed over by labeling threats as a generalized "Global War on Terror"—a nebulous and misleading term that mistakes superficial symptoms for complex underlying social and political dynamics—merely illustrates how the pursuit of military-strategic hegemony can be misguided and counterproductive. Recent mixed signals from the Bush Administration over whether the Global War on Terror (G.W.O.T.) should be restyled the "Global Struggle Against Extremist Violence" (G-SAVE), with the President ostentatiously reemphasizing his preference for the former despite Defense Secretary Donald Rumsfeld's attempt to introduce the latter, merely demonstrates the confusion over what the current military-strategic dimension of hegemony requires.

However, the main problems with pursuing military-strategic hegemony do not so much concern the endogenous aspects of the military-strategic issue-area itself, but rather its *interaction* with other issue-areas. First, military-strategic power necessarily involves several economic dimensions. Perhaps the best-known category here is what Kennedy (1987) called "imperial overstretch"—the calculus of how much power projection can be afforded in the ostensible hegemon's national budget, especially where popular support for the use of such power is weak or declining and competes with other priorities. Defense spending competes with domestic spending, especially social spending and economic policy, and, as the 1992 Clinton presidential strategy posited, except in clear-cut cases of national emergency: "It's the economy, stupid." During the Cold War, the role of the military-industrial complex in promoting a form of Keynesian economic growth reconciled military-strategic hegemony with economic policy goals for a time, but this identity broke down in the 1970s and has never been really reinstated, despite the ill-fated attempt by the Reagan Administration in the 1980s to do just that and the current Bush Administration's willingness to expand expenditure on the War in Iraq.

Furthermore, in liberal democracies, the additional defense spending required for the pursuit of hegemony comes up against a range of political as well as purely budgetary constraints. The problems of imperial overstretch in Vietnam are well-known and the subsequent significance of the "Vietnam Syndrome" in American foreign policy is clear if somewhat episodic—today back in the spotlight in the wake of the invasion and occupation of Iraq, with all its various consequences for the domestic politics of the United States as well as foreign policy disputes with France, Germany, the United Nations Security Council, etc. The 2004 U.S. presidential election campaign highlighted this revival. Military-strategic hegemony seems more and more difficult to operationalize even in purely military terms in 21st century conditions, just as the current Bush Administration seeks to emphasize and rest its legitimacy upon it.

Democracy, democratization, and socioeconomic issues

Moreover, military-strategic power can also clash with other potential hegemonic priorities. American foreign policy has notably been faced throughout the 19th, 20th, and 21st centuries with the problem of democracy and democratization. The projection of hegemonic power has often required support for (and from) nondemocratic regimes. The current emphasis put by the George W. Bush Administration on spreading American-style democracy—as exemplified by the President's inaugural address in January 2005—implies not merely the need for military-strategic hegemony to spread democratization, but also requires considerable ongoing political, economic, and social investment in parts of the world *without* embedded democratic traditions and engagement with local power configurations that over the years have positioned major social and economic groupings and coalitions in *opposition* to ostensibly stable, American-style democracy in various ways. Democratization from above (Cohen 1987) is highly problematic and frequently either crumbles or results in the imposition of pro-American authoritarian elites and regimes (Robinson 1996). It also alienates independent-minded groups and actors that value their autonomy above American-style democracy, often seen by subaltern groups as collaborating with repressive and avaricious domestic elites. The pursuit of military-strategic hegemony has therefore been notoriously counterproductive in terms of democratization unless it has been connected with some sort of spontaneous democratization from below, as in post-World War II Western Europe and post-Cold War Central and Eastern Europe. Local desires for independence and autonomy usually position actors in opposition to American military-strategic control *per se*. The current experiments in Iraq and Afghanistan merely illustrate the dilemmas. Only in the context of fully-fledged American occupation, as in post-World War II Europe and Japan, where alliances with strong local pro-democracy political and economic forces and a prewar experience of at least partial democratization existed, could liberal democratic institutions and practices be built up over time in a context of economic reconstruction and the development of a more open world capitalist system (the Marshall Plan in Europe and economic democratization, the "Dodge Line" and the "Korean War boom" in the case of Japan).

Much the same could be said for a range of other social and economic issues, such as the provision of welfare states, the problem of economic and social development more generally, and, indeed, the spread of American or Western values in societies where other traditions are deeply culturally rooted and practiced. Much is made of the hegemony of American or Western cultural or social values in a world of more rapid information flows, market practices, Western media domination, and the like, but such values cannot become embedded if imposed top-down. The fact that such values are indeed spreading rapidly and being internalized around the world is not due to the military-strategic preponderance of the United States but rather to the much more horizontal and bottom-up processes of globalization.

It is worth mentioning again at this stage that much discussion of hegemony in the academic literature has not been in terms of military-strategic hegemony. It has concerned economic hegemony, especially, as noted earlier, the role of the hegemon in providing public goods to the international system. Stephen Krasner (1976) argues that genuine hegemons are liberal hegemons—the Netherlands, Britain, and the United States in successive centuries being the select sample—precisely because their first priority was spreading free trade and a stable international monetary system rather than military dominance as such. Angus Maddison (1982) indeed prefers to refer to what others have called "hegemons" as "leading economies." And most specifically, Charles Kindleberger (1973), often cited as the first author to systematically analyze the notion of hegemony in recent debates, expressly considered only economic criteria to identify that phenomenon, in particular:

- the maintenance of a large open market to absorb surplus production elsewhere in case of an international economic downturn;
- the provision of a stable and liquid reserve currency for foreign market participants;
- willingness to act as a lender of last resort in financial crises to bail out systemically significant players;

- support for moves to institutionalize free trading and other liberal international arrangements; and
- readiness to inject Keynesian reflationary liquidity into the international economic system at key times.

In this perspective, military-strategic and political measures are only significant—only genuinely *hegemonic*—where they promote and facilitate these functions, as exemplified by Cordell Hull's approach to foreign policy in the Roosevelt Administration before and during World War II (Gardner 1971). American economic war aims, reflected in the postwar Bretton Woods Agreements, are perhaps the paradigmatic exemplar of this relationship (Gardner 1980; Penrose 1953). Thus to the extent that the pursuit of military-strategic preponderance detracts from achieving these aims—in particular, by reducing economic cooperation with other actors—hegemony is undermined, not achieved. This set of circumstances gives rise to what analysts have called "predatory hegemony," which is not genuine hegemony but one in which narrow self-interest undermines the systemic rational of hegemony itself. United States administrations have frequently been accused of acting in this fashion, whether in President Richard M. Nixon's "closing the gold window" in 1971 (Gowa 1983) or in trade negotiations and disputes in the 1990s and 2000s, especially now that the originally American-sponsored World Trade Organization is increasingly being utilized against U.S. protectionist practices.

Attempts to pursue American hegemony through military unilateralism have generally—and increasingly—come up against a range of barriers from unanticipated military-strategic consequences, along with the lack of resources and/or will to deal with those consequences, undermining of the capability of the United States to act in an economically effective hegemonic fashion. The American pursuit of military preponderance in an unaccountable manner has bred instability rather than stability. In trying to ride several horses at the same time, American policymakers have too often assumed that American national interests and the interests of systemic stability and prosperity were identical, leading them to behave like opportunists in a political marketplace where competitive conditions—especially, paradoxically, American-style globalization—make monopoly increasingly difficult to achieve and interdependence more constraining even in military terms (Nye 2001), a theme to which I will return at the end of this chapter.

The Problem of Institutionalization

The second "fault line" in the pursuit of hegemony is the issue of how and whether hegemony is institutionalized. A key difference between hegemony as a systemic attribute and hegemony as a disproportionate preponderance of power is that genuine hegemony needs to be embedded into the practices of a wide range of systemic actors, otherwise systemic rationality is likely to be lost. There are a number of ways that hegemony can be embedded in this way, but an increasingly significant mode of embedding, especially since World War II, is through the establishment of formal institutions that can develop a certain limited structural autonomy as well as the entrenching of informal structural practices. During the Cold War, for example, the combination of

- American ideological leadership at the level of state action,
- domestic support for anti-Communism,
- the key role of nuclear deterrence and stalemate,
- the system of alliances,
- U.S. sponsorship of the postwar system of international institutions (Foot, McFarlane, and Mastanduno 2003), and
- American economic support for "embedded liberalism" in the capitalist world (Ruggie 1982),

jointly constituted a broad and flexible framework that knitted together the formal and the informal networks of institutions in clear systemic fashion. Since the end of the Cold War, however, each of those dimensions has been in transition and alternative institutional frameworks have fragmented. Hegemony in this context is being pursued despite this institutional decay, with the result again being instability, counterproductive outcomes, and the resulting tendency for the U.S. to engage in opportunism and monopolistic behavior in an unfavorable competitive environment.

In the first place, American ideological leadership is increasingly precarious in terms of the capacity of the American state to exercise sufficient relational or coercive power to get other actors to act in ways they would not otherwise have done (Dahl's [1957] definition of power)—except in very limited circumstances in which direct U.S. military power is applied, as in Iraq and Afghanistan, and even that capacity is extremely limited on the ground. For example, although the rhetoric of antiterrorism has to some extent been successfully applied as a generic rationale for American interventionism, terrorism itself is an exceedingly hard-to-grasp phenomenon. Hegemonists in the George W. Bush Administration have in common the realist belief that "self-interested nation-states are [still] the key actors in world politics," and that

> Whenever they mentioned terrorism, they almost always applied it to rogue re-
> gimes and hostile powers. The assumption was that terrorists were the creatures
> of states, and they would wither without state support (Daalder and Lindsay 2003:
> 42).

Terrorism is not primarily state-based but essentially a combined substate and cross-state phenomenon that is more compatible with neomedievalism than with a realist, state-centric analysis (Cerny 2000 and 2005; Berzins and Cullen 2003). In particular, it is a set of methods employed by a range of quite different groups with different social, political, and economic objectives—and has been throughout history. Thus the use of the label "War on Terror" targets a highly intangible and fungible phenomenon with very different and even contradictory ideological characteristics. It is whatever anyone wants to use to label their opponents in a way that delegitimates them. To the Israelis, Palestinian militants (or potentially all Palestinians?) are the terrorists; in a mirror image, to Palestinians, it is rather the Israeli government and its military machine who are the terrorists. What is lacking is an analytical frame that (a) clearly identifies achievable goals for a hegemonic state, (b) identifies the enemy or the groups over whom hegemonic sway must consistently be exercised, and (c) creates a genuine consensus from below that the goals of that enemy are illegitimate—and that the goals of the U.S. government, in particular, are legitimate

Disenchantment among Asians in a range of different countries with the American "obsession" with terrorism, for example, has been seen to undermine American credibility in a region increasingly concerned with economic growth and prosperity. This weakening of subaltern support for the U.S. hegemonic project, it has been argued, has augmented the influence of China, seen as increasingly concerned with economic issues (*The New York Times*, December 3, 2003) rather than with coercive dominance—with the partial exception of the issue of Taiwan, where both economic carrots and military sticks are being employed. Certainly, China's image in Asia is rapidly changing. China is now a leading player in creating a system of free trade areas between ASEAN (the Association of South-East Asian Nations) and China. There was a fear among ASEAN countries just after the Asian currency and financial crisis of 1997 that their economies and the Chinese economy were not complementary and that the infant industries which finally they could foster were fast losing out to their Chinese competitors. Now those countries are finding that their own and the Chinese economies are mutually complementary, leading to a growing consensus that China should be stably anchored in the regional system. These changing tides are the main reasons that the Japanese government is desperately trying to find partners for new free trade agreements; indeed, it has been very active in creating regional cooperation mechanisms for coping with possible future financial crises in Asia. Thus regional interdependence in Asia has advanced notably advancing in recent years. It is interesting that the high-profile unilateralism of the United States is paradoxically prompting regional multilateralism in Asia and other parts of the world.

In addition to the weakness of the concept of the War on Terror in providing a credible ideological basis for American leadership, the domestic public in the U.S., while horrified by the destruction of the World Trade Center in New York City on September 11, 2001, is faced with contradictory information, challenges, and doubts about what American hegemony requires, and is increasingly disillusioned with the military adventurism of the current Bush Administration, as opinion surveys have shown since the invasion of Iraq. The rapid dissolution of the bipartisan consensus on the American war in Iraq has brought back the Vietnam Syndrome, i.e., public reluctance to engage in interventionist policies overseas except where quick victories and low costs in both economic and human terms can be guaranteed. Whether the debate over the lack of weapons of mass destruction in Iraq; or the lack of links between the Saddam Hussein regime and Al Qaeda (until recently a majority of opinion poll respondents believed that Saddam Hussein was responsible for the events of September 11); or the increased internal security measures and their impact on civil and individual rights; or the continuing violence and deaths of American soldiers (not to mention the increasingly noted loss of civilian Iraqi lives, estimated in mid-2005 at around 25,000); or the failure to capture Osama bin Laden; or the focusing of the recent presidential election campaign on what happened to the two candidates during the Vietnam War itself, the response of American public opinion is not so much to support wider American hegemony but rather to return increasingly to the "new isolationism" of the post-Vietnam period.

Defense policy and spending too are no longer elements of domestic or international hegemonic consensus. Although the War on Terror for a time created a base of support for reversing what was seen as a neglect of defense during the Clinton Administration (the search for a "peace dividend"), the "Revolution in Military Affairs" championed by Secretary Rumsfeld is proving too fragmented to create the basis of a new consensus. Despite the public talk of the neglect of the defense spending during the Clinton years, the defense budget of the U.S. started to increase rapidly during the second Clinton Administration, with somewhat reluctant leadership by the President himself and strong initiatives by the Congress (Greider 1997). Although the deployment of technological developments such as unmanned drones and Global Positioning Systems alongside more mobile forms of deployment of military personnel could be seen as rational responses to the changing nature of warfare, other projects such as expensive national ballistic missile defense systems and the militarization of space may be seen to pave the way for a revived perception of useless "Star Wars" or of a new "baroque arsenal," but this time without any coherent strategy to hold the whole defense posture together in the way that the doctrine of nuclear deterrence succeeded in doing during the Cold War. It will be increasingly difficult to mobilize domestic support for military-strategic spending in such circumstances. In terms of international support, the strains on the alliance structures caused by the war in Iraq, the doctrine of preemptive war, and divisions over the role of the United Nations have still to be resolved. Alliances themselves are increasingly problematic, as the North Atlantic Treaty Organization has yet to find a role in a post-Cold War world and alliances in other parts of the world, especially Asia, are coming under strain. The Japanese government led by Junichiro Koizumi seems to be the exception, given the fact that Japan sent supply gunships to the Indian Ocean to support activities of the U.S., the U.K., and Australian navies and also some troops on the ground to Iraq. Thus the sort of consensual and partly institutionalized defense institutions and practices of the Cold War are displaying increasing Humpty-Dumpty-like tendencies.

Perhaps the most important point of fragmentation and conflict, however, concerns the development of a range of old and new formal international institutions. I have already touched on conflicts over the role of the United Nations, long seen in an unfavorable light by the American conservative right. Nevertheless, the withdrawal of the George W. Bush Administration from the Kyoto Protocol on control of climate change, its refusal to participate in the International Criminal Court and the Ottawa Convention on the banning of antipersonnel land mines, abrogation of the 1972 Anti-Ballistic Missile Treaty, and nonparticipation in a range of other international institutions and agreements, has even more strikingly undermined the perceived legitimacy of the U.S. role in what until recently was an expanding web of international regimes and processes. Even in the economic field, where American support for the postwar system of embedded liberalism was crucial to the development of international economic institutions, American policy appears to be increasingly at odds with the very aspects of the working of those institutions that previously were instituted ostensibly in order to achieve U.S. objectives. In particular, the dispute settlement mechanism of the World Trade Organization is increasingly being used not by the United States to pressure and/or persuade other countries to lower their trade barriers, but by the European Union, Japan, and developing countries to pressure the United States to lower its own trade barriers, some of them quite new, and to comply with WTO rules. The United States is finding itself more and more isolated from those very institutions which have been designed and set up, often at U.S. initiative, precisely to institutionalize and embed American values at an international level. The United States is deinstitutionalizing its own hegemony, thereby undermining its wider legitimacy and systemic rationale.

The Three Faces of Hegemony: "Hegemony from Above" *versus* "Hegemony from Below"

The third "fault line" in understanding hegemony is that between different kinds of power. Hegemony is a particular type of power—the power of a disproportionately preponderant actor within a wider system. But, as Steven Lukes has argued in a seminal work (Lukes 1974 and 2005), power itself is not a homogeneous phenomenon. While theories of power focus on a number of different typological distinctions (Haugaard 1997; Goverde, Cerny, Haugaard, and Lentner 2000), Lukes's threefold typology has stood the test of time as a starting point for power analysis. Lukes identifies three different overlapping and interacting types of power that will here be labeled relational power, structural power, and infrastructural power. Relational power, first, concerns the traditional image of power, as employed by analysts such as Robert Dahl, as "something like this: A has power over B to the extent that he can get B to do something that B would not otherwise do" (Dahl 1957; Lukes 1974: 11-15). Structural power, second, does not require the direct exercise of power, but rather the embedding of asymmetric power positions in certain "rules of the game," in institutional structures, and in selecting in certain kinds of issues and decision outcomes and selecting out others (the "mobilization of bias" and the ubiquitous presence of "nondecisions"), while simultaneously reinforcing the existing distribution of power and resources in society (Lukes 1974: 16-20; Bachrach and Baratz 1962, 1963 and 1970).

Infrastructural power, derived from Lukes's "third face of power," is concerned not with the exercise of power as such nor even the mobilization of bias, but with the internalization of power in the understandings, world views, habits, attitudes and behaviors of those systematically subjected to the exercise and disciplines of power in such a way as to systemically reinforce the influence of the norms of the powerful upon the powerless—to incorporate the latter into the processes of their own subjection (Gaventa 1980). It is not simply about structuring the playing field or the rules of the game (cf. Clegg, 1989), which is still the property of the hegemon as power-exerciser, however indirectly it may be refracted through the system. Rather it is the property of those who *lack* relative power; it is something created, however inadvertently, from the "bottom up." Such infrastructural subjection may involve, for example:

- the *internalization* from below of values that legitimate the distribution and exercise of power in the current system;
- the *adoption* from below, especially where this is done proactively, of behavior patterns that embed that power structure in everyday life, such as active support for the norms of the system; and
- the spread and *convergence* of such patterns across social and political cleavages and boundaries so as to form a "common sense" of how the world works, again from below.

Indeed, Lukes himself suggests that hegemony is found within the third face of power.

Therefore genuine, effective hegemony cannot be based on the exercise of relational power alone—compare, for example, the concept of "soft power" as developed by Nye (1990; 2004), the notion of structural power as developed by Strange (1988), and the neo-Gramscian conception of hegemony as developed by Cox (1996). Neither, however, can it be found in structural power, which does not in and of itself create the necessary basis for consent. It is still too infused with top-down elements to succeed. Although some degree of relational power and structural power may be necessary conditions for hegemony, neither is sufficient on its own, *nor* are both sufficient taken together, to generate and ensure the ideational and material conditions for effective, durable hegemony. Systemically rational hegemony, I argue, must ultimately be rooted in an infrastructural "hegemony from below" if it is to be fully systemically rational. It is here that the exercise of both relational power and structural power—hard power and soft power—*conflicts* with the imperatives of embedding infrastructural hegemony in a globalizing world.

American hegemony has broadly developed in three ways since the 1930s. In the first place, as traditional analysts of the "rise to globalism" (Ambrose 1971) have emphasized, U.S. military-strategic power and the ability of the United States to use economic expansion to fund its role as a "world policeman" have not only far overshadowed the capabilities of its enemies but also those of its allies. American intervention transformed the battlefield and balance of forces in two world wars and American economic clout in the post-World War II period shaped the international economic system despite partial challenges. In the Cold War, the United States not only led the way but also, along with its allies, so outperformed the Soviet Union and its allies in both economic and military terms—despite occasional claims of "missile gaps," "windows of vulnerability," or rapid economic catch-up by the Soviet Union at least until the late 1960s—that it is widely seen to have "won" that conflict without having to go to war. Where the U.S. did go to war, it was not with the direct enemy, the U.S.S.R., and it was frequently unsuccessful.

However, despite the continuing and indeed increasingly disproportionate preponderance of U.S. military power in the post-Cold War period, the capacity of U.S.
policymakers to *translate* that preponderance into systemic hegemony is increasingly being challenged.

Second, of course, American structural power is crucial (Strange 1987), if
insufficient, and goes well beyond the purview of the state and state actors. This
structural power is materialized in the ability of U.S.-based multinational corporations, international investors, and U.S.-sponsored international economic institutions implementing the so-called "Washington Consensus" (Williamson 1990). This
structural power is not simply based on the United States as nation-state "unit actor" in realist terms; indeed, it is partly and in some ways significantly transnational
in nature. However, its significance in systemic terms puts the United States as
what might be called a "national state/economy complex" in the driving seat when
it comes to the mobilization of bias in the international system and the international
political economy in particular. It is this structural power that is the main concern
of U.S. foreign economic policymakers and businesspeople alike; it is also the main
target of policymakers and interest groups in other countries who believe that their
vital "national economic sovereignty" is being undermined, sometimes illegitimately, by American structural hegemony. And it is, of course, the main target too
of antiglobalization and alternative globalization protest movements. American
relational and structural power therefore stand in an uneasy systemic relationship
with each other. The exercise of military and political power does not simply stabilize the current system but also creates offsetting and even destabilizing perceptions
of threat. This threat makes other countries less willing to accept American political
hegemony except in immediate emergencies. At the same time, American structural
power creates images of exploitation and dependency that are highly vulnerable to
antiglobalization appeals, protectionist responses, and the alienation of groups who
perceive themselves as "losers."

Most important, then, is the way both relational and structural hegemony *interact*
with infrastructural hegemony. Four particular dimensions of infrastructural hegemony are critical to hegemony more widely:

1. the spread and inculcation of liberal (neoliberal?) market values and practices
    informally in society in general;
2. regulatory reform and the formal institutionalization of market practices,
    property rights, etc.;
3. the increased pluralization of interest groups, both old new, and the genera-
    tion of new patterns of positive-sum coalition and competition among them
    to replace zero-sum conflict among social forces; and
4. the embedding of these liberal and pluralist patterns of behavior in some
    form of liberal democratization or quasi-democratization.

American ideology and political culture—the ostensible rationale for hege-mony
among both American domestic elites and mass publics—is rooted in a belief in the
superiority of the American "way of life" as the ultimate justification for the pursuit
of hegemony, not merely U.S. national interests. At the same time, for other actors,

the perceived desirability of imitating the American way of life is also the most important justification for voluntary compliance with American-style norms, the convergence of political and economic institutions and practices, and an emphasis on capturing the benefits of globalization for the purposes of domestic coalition-building. Just as European nationalism was the inspiration for national liberation movements in the mid-20th century—the belief that progress was unattainable without copying the institutions and practices of the core states of European empires—so the American mix of liberal democracy and liberal economics, what Francis Fukuyama (1989) saw as leading to "the end of history," has become the inspiration for developmental elites and popular groups seeking to assert greater clout within a pluralizing sociopolitical framework. Without infrastructural hegemony, the underpinnings of American hegemony would gain neither practical support nor normative acquiescence from those actors whose cooperation is essential to the success of the hegemonic project.

However, infrastructural hegemony—hegemony "from below"—and relational and structural hegemony—both forms of hegemony "from above"—sit uneasily together in terms of all four of the dimensions listed above. Liberal and neoliberal market practices and values are rooted in an individualistic conception of society and take as perhaps their most basic premise that social and economic organization must be developed endogenously—and indigenously—from the bottom up. The combination of individual rights and economic entrepreneurship that form the core of the "American dream" is essentially antistatist. Nevertheless, in the international arena, the top-down role of the U.S. state apparatus and of the American national state-economy complex, while often externalized directly by American political and military intervention and/or by American firms and investors, has also been widely mediated through local elites whose power bases are rooted in clan, ethnic, feudal, or authoritarian structures. American power and economic influence are widely perceived as limiting the autonomy and potential success of the very sort of domestic actors seeking empowerment *against* these elites. It has been part of the ideology of capitalism since Adam Smith that the role of the state should not simply be limited in and of itself but also directed against those feudal structures and practices that restrain trade and spontaneous, market-rational economic activity. But the political, military, and economic requirements of hegemony often demand a kind of control that further privileges the already privileged. Indeed, the increased pluralization of groups in a society without embedded liberal pluralist institutions and practices often leads to violent conflict rather than to stability and peaceful, competitive pluralization of the sort that represents the ideal-type American way of life.

Furthermore, the embedding of these liberal and pluralist patterns of behavior in some form of liberal democratization or quasi-democratization frequently has unanticipated consequences. Such institutions are easily captured, in a context of conflict-based pluralization, by the very elites and/or anti-American popular forces they were meant to constrain. This problem has bedeviled development theory throughout the 20th and 21st centuries. Furthermore, supposedly pro-market forms of regulation, corporate governance, and Keynesian interventionism have often been introduced, and subverted, by highly politicized predatory elites—what has come to be known as "crony capitalism." Indeed, aid programs from both developed states and international economic institutions usually end up captured by host country elites, unless forced by extreme crisis to restructure elements of the domestic economy despite attempts by the U.S. or international economic institutions to impose conditionality. In many cases, on the contrary, strong conditionality punishes those who are suffering most, and public resentment against that conditionality results in anti-government protests and conflicts over scarce resources. These conflicts can open the way for state failure. In addition, suffering at the bottom leads to the resentment against the I.M.F. or the World Bank and their main sponsor, the U.S.A. The good intentions of liberalization and democratization can result in institutional decay and the loss of legitimacy of hegemony itself.

In these ways, both relational and structural hegemony, even in their "American Dream" manifestation, involve imperatives of control that hinder and even undermine the kind of pluralization, regulatory reform, and ideological change that the genuine hegemony of American-style practices and attitudes is intended to foster and which would result in a world modeled on American values. Infrastructural hegemony is often sacrificed to control from above either by the U.S. state acting as a "world policeman" or U.S.-based multinational firms and investors working through the articulation of American economic interests with local "*comprador* elites." Even where American intentions are explicitly to undermine such elites and inculcate American-style liberalization and democratization, as in Iraq and Afghanistan, the result is necessarily a compromise with warlords, tribal leaders, religious authorities, and military or paramilitary hierarchies that can ostensibly provide "order" at the cost of progress toward infrastructural hegemony. If the U.S. stops supporting the corrupt elements and backs out of those areas, the most likely possibility is institutional decay and disorder. "Bottom-up" hegemony loses both ways. In a world where there is as yet no development of an apparent Gramscian counterhegemony, bottom-up hegemony may provide the best chance for subaltern groups to benefit from globalization (de Soto 2000).

Consequences: The Contradiction Between the Hegemon's National Interests and the Systemic Rationale of Hegemony

The fourth and final "fault line" is that between the national interests of the hegemon, on the one hand, and its own systemically rational interests, on the other. Of course, national interests are notoriously hard to define. In classical geopolitical realism, it seemed possible hypothetically to identify certain "permanent interests" of a particular state. Britain as an island long had different concerns from Germany as a land power, with borders vulnerable to invasion, and from France, which was both a sea power and a land power and often failed to keep both balls in the air at the same time. Halford Mackinder's identification in 1904 of control of the "Heartland" and the "World Island" as the central determinant of national interests is often still seen as an important factor today. Nevertheless, governments and other actors have always identified other kinds of objectives as constituting essential national

interests too, objectives that are not so ostensibly self-evident, historically or structurally. Current controversies over the role of oil in the Middle East belie the assumption that control of that area's oil resources are somehow indispensable; however, such control tends to serve particular special interests within the United States
and other countries, whether oil consumers or oil producers, rather than some
immutable or long-term national interest. Perhaps even more important is the tendency to assert that particular national interests need protection from unfair competition, whether originating in domestic interest groups like the U.S. steel, cotton-
producing, and textile industries, or the interests of American firms operating
multinationally.

American interests are ostensibly embedded in an increasingly open world.
Nevertheless, American policymakers are divided between those who favor increasing the openness of that world systemically through the provision of the sort of
public goods discussed earlier, and those who seek to protect American national
interests in the plural, i.e., those manifold self-interests that are rooted in domestic
interests or in the interests of American actors operating internationally. This conflict is of particular significance for an ostensible hegemon, whose position of
dominance within a structure does at least involve the imperative of operating
according to some sort of systemically-rooted rationality. Different, often conflicting interests not only create divisions within the United States as to the meaning
and significance of hegemony but also exacerbate each of the three other fault lines
analyzed earlier.

Hegemony as such, therefore, is a chimera. Indeed, perhaps what is most
important about it is its "lack" in the Lacanian sense and the consequent felt need
to fill the void, even if that can only ever be partly successful (Newman, this volume). Most theories of international relations that employ the concept of hegemony
in a central way—realist, liberal, and neo-Gramscian alike—assert or assume that
hegemony is a relatively homogeneous, really existing phenomenon. Hard core
realists and neorealists like Waltz (1979) do this by assuming that hegemony results
from the character of the nation-state within the enfolding structure of the international system, i.e., by assuming that (a) states as such are the most important, indeed the only significant, actors in the international system, and (b) that states
possessing disproportionately preponderant power within that system will rationally
decide to provide stability, mainly of a military-strategic nature (but with economic
capabilities in a supporting role). More liberal (or mixed neorealist/liberal) hegemonic stability theorists like Krasner (1976) also see the provision of public goods
as a systemically rational, relatively homogeneous project, although only operational in tandem with the projection of military-strategic power. Liberal
institutionalists like Keohane (1984), furthermore, seem to assume not only that
hegemony is a relatively homogeneous phenomenon, but also that it primarily
concerns economic and social policy issues and can therefore be transferred to
civilian international regimes—something the current George W. Bush Administration's approach would appear to contradict. Meanwhile, neo-Gramscians like Cox
(1996) see the emergence of hegemony as an historically and politically constructed
"historic bloc." But although neo-Gramscian approaches appear to be more sophis-

ticated than neorealist and liberal institutionalist perspectives at analyzing the internal divisions and generic cleavages within this historic bloc, they nevertheless overemphasize the mutually reinforcing mechanisms and overlook their inherent limits and contradictions of hegemonic projects. This tendency becomes most explicit and vulnerable especially when structural hegemony is being translated into operation through concepts like the "transnational capitalist class" (e.g., van der Pijl 1998).

In contrast, I argue that hegemony is not only complex but *inherently incomplete*. It contains several varieties of seeds of internal contradiction—the incongruity of, and potential points of conflict between, different issue-areas, the problematic nature of institutionalization, the way the pursuit of relational and even structural hegemony can erode and undermine infrastructural hegemony, and the perennial incompatibility between different types of national interests the systemically rational interests of the purported hegemon. No matter how disproportionately preponderant the hegemon's power and capabilities, it cannot escape from these internal tensions and contradictions except in exceptional and temporary circumstances—normally a war or a relatively highly controlled state of quasi-war in the system like the Cold War. In peacetime, when absolute gains, economic prosperity, and peace itself are more prioritized as values and objectives by both elites and mass publics, the hegemon cannot pursue its hegemonic project without making choices as to which dimensions to prioritize and which to neglect, leading to backlashes and instability on the one hand, and the temptation to predatory hegemony —monopolistic, even corrupt, self-seeking behavior—on the other.

Finally, the internally contradictory nature of hegemony not only leads to instability, self-destructive behavior, and opportunism, but in the case of the United States today, undermines the most important dimension of genuine hegemony—i.e., infrastructural hegemony, or the global dissemination and internalization of American values and practices, the American way of life. This leads not only to the tragedy of American hegemony but also to the tragedies of many people at the bottom of the scale who are not in a position to support "hegemony from below" but have no real alternative.

Acknowledgements

Earlier versions this chapter were presented at the Annual Convention of the International Studies Association, Montreal, 17-20 March 2004, and the Interim Workshop of Research Committee No. 36 (Political Power) of the International Political Science Association, New York, 10-12 June 2004. I am particularly grateful to Seiji Endo for his detailed comments and suggestions, as well as to Mark Haugaard and Howard Lentner.

Chapter 5

Hegemony and Power in International Politics

Howard H. Lentner

Hegemony and power are both conventional concepts in the analysis of international politics. The former has been employed less widely than the latter, and hegemony has never been carefully defined or thoroughly analyzed. As in political science as a whole, international politics studies treat power as a central analytical concept. Moreover, the field includes quite sharply defined debates over the meaning and usefulness of the concept of power and its relationship to broader theories that seek to explain phenomena in international relations. Although these debates do not fully encompass or parallel the more focused disputes within the general literature on power, they do refer to aspects of that literature, most commonly to the views of Robert Dahl but to the interpretations of others as well. At the same time, without invoking the general literature about political power, international politics scholars employ such concepts as domination and resistance, structural power, and other notions that resonate with theoretical and conceptual power analysis. I take up the issue of whether an interchange might prove beneficial to both camps. Before reaching that point, this paper proceeds as follows.

Overall, the paper offers a survey of the meaning and uses of the two concepts in the international politics literature, placing the debates in broad conceptual context. First, I will define hegemony and power and the relationship between them. Second, I provide a brief survey of the main theoretical treatments of them in the international politics literature. This survey treats as a central divide in the literature the contest between those embracing diffusion of power and those emphasizing concentration of power. Another intellectual cleavage occurs between those who emphasize capabilities (means) and those who stress outcomes (effects). The review includes recent new debates stemming from sociology and from policy concerns. The presence of uncertainty and of unwilled consequences shapes many debates in international politics in a way that is not characteristic of treatments in the theoretical and conceptual literature about power. Furthermore, despite the characteristic of inequality, power tends to be distributed more nearly equally among states in international politics than between governments and citizens within states, thus differentiating the two realms. Although military resources are not generally regarded as prominent instruments for exercising power in the general power analysis literature, they feature centrally in the analysis of international politics. In addition, debates in international politics tend to be affected importantly by events and shifting circumstances in the world during the period in which writers are situated. I conclude with an assessment and suggestions for moving the debate forward.

Hegemony and Power

Hegemony in the international politics literature has two separate though related meanings: leadership and dominance. The term itself comes from the Greek word for leadership. In his *History of the Pelepponesian War* Thucydides thought that hegemony was a stage on the way to empire but he nevertheless included matters such as prestige and respect, not just material power, as characteristics of the hegemon (Wickersham 1994: 43-71). In the modern period, hegemony did not form a central concept in diplomatic and military history, memoirs of statesmen, international law, or peace movements—the antecedent disciplines of international politics. Nevertheless, the idea behind the term was employed implicitly not to characterize leadership but rather to designate dominance and to express fear of preponderance. Knorr (1973: 27) distinguishes between hegemony, "which . . . means supremacy in an area that the hegemonical state controls fundamentally by coercive power" and leadership. He writes, "Noncoercive influence . . . can bring about leadership but not hegemonical supremacy." Writers on balance of power were the most frequent users of this idea; in these cases, it referred to a single state that might assume a position of preponderance in the international system (Luard 1992, esp. Part Three; Bull 1977). The term does not appear in the indexes of the leading books in international politics in the post-World War II period (Morgenthau 1973; Waltz 1979).

In a curious development, hegemony was brought prominently into the vocabulary of international politics in a context in which scholars regarded the United States, conceptualized as the post-1945 hegemon, to be in decline. The two most prominent analysts in this mode regarded themselves to be writing in a era of change, which they sought to understand, and they concerned themselves primarily with political economy. The first, Robert Gilpin (1981, 1987, 2001), invoked the Greek meaning of hegemony as leadership, whereas the second, Robert Keohane (1984), treated hegemony mostly as dominance, although both meanings emerge in their analyses. Both drew on Marxist thought as well as on formulations from economics. Gilpin (1981: 29) treated hegemony as a structure of the international system in which a single state dominated or controlled others and laid down the rules under which the system operated; he equated a hegemonic system with an empire, and he contrasted such a structure with two alternatives, a bipolar structure and balance of power one. That is to say, Gilpin offers a typology of international systems that varies by the concentration and diffusion of power among its units. He draws on Trotsky specifically to explain change resulting from uneven growth (Gilpin 1981: 179).

Keohane (1984: 32) presents a "theory of hegemonic stability" in which hegemony is "defined as preponderance of material resources," especially "control over raw materials, control over sources of capital, control over markets, and competitive advantages in the production of highly valued goods." However, he also brings in Gramsci's "conception of ideological hegemony" to supplement materialist arguments, emphasizing the value of ideology for the continuance of international political economic regimes in a period of hegemonic decline. In his invocation of Gramsci, however, Keohane shows little appreciation for the rich analysis done by scholars such as Fontana (2004) and others. Both Gilpin and Keohane confine their concerns to the periods of British and American hegemonic reigns over the international political economy. Furthermore, neither conceives hegemony as preponderance, for other great powers continue to exist in the systems that they treat. There is also a good deal of ambiguity in both analyses. Even though Gilpin equates hegemony with empire, he clearly does not think that either Britain or the United States was the sole major power in its respective era of hegemony. Despite Keohane's equating hegemony with a preponderance of material resources, he apparently means by preponderance merely the possession of more control over resources than others.

In contrast, Mearsheimer (2001: 40) expands hegemony to encompass military power, and he provides this definition: "A hegemon is a state that is so powerful that it dominates all the states in the system. . . . In essence, a hegemon is the only great power in the system." Moreover, he specifically refutes the view that Britain was a hegemon in the nineteenth century. Furthermore, he maintains that no state has global hegemony, and he distinguishes regional hegemons, the only one in the modern period being the United States, which is a hegemon within the western hemisphere (Mearsheimer 2001: 41). He contends that it is unlikely that any state will attain global hegemony but that, nevertheless, great powers strive to prevent others from rising to the position even of regional hegemon.

One cannot derive a precise synthetic definition of hegemony from this literature. Despite the absence of power as an entry in the index of a recent survey of international relations that gives extensive space to British hegemony (Elman and Elman 2001), most treatments of hegemony do reflect a broader debate about power, and they agree that the concept of hegemony lies near one end of a continuum from high concentration to wide diffusion of power.

Power is the central concept in the international politics literature of the post-World War II period. The foremost writer in the early part of that era was Hans Morgenthau (1973: 28-29), who defined power as "a psychological relationship" of control of an exerciser and the one controlled. He distinguished between political power, which includes the threat to use physical violence, and the actual application of force, "which substitutes for the psychological relation between two minds." He regarded all politics as a struggle for power, whether conducted in circumstances of family, group, political organization, or among states. His general approach treated the struggle as one between agents supporting the status quo and those advocating change. Morgenthau laid great stress on the limitations placed on national power, especially checking or balancing by others, but also morality and public opinion, and law; nonetheless, he claimed that power is always the defining consideration for analysis. He regarded a "tendency to dominate . . . [as] an element of all human associations" (Morgenthau 1973: 35).

Reflecting a tendency during the Cold War to emphasize military aspects of the struggle for power, Claude (1962: 6) defines the term power as "essentially military capability—the elements which contribute directly or indirectly to the capacity to coerce, kill, and destroy." Knorr (1973) focuses on military capacity but he also discusses noncoercive influence. He defines coercive influence as power in the widely-understood sense of Dahl's definition, but he also distinguishes between capabilities (means) and outcomes (effects), devising the terms "putative power" for the first and "actualized power" for the second. Drawing on Lasswell and Kaplan (1950), he differentiates power along dimensions of weight, scope, and domain. Knorr also draws on Schelling (1960, 1966) to note reciprocal influence between stronger and weaker parties and resistance by weaker ones (Knorr 1973: 23).

In an early post-World War II work, the Sprouts (Sprout 1951: 40) ran capabilities and control together in their definition: " national power means the total capabilities of a state to gain desired ends vis-à-vis other states. This definition rests upon three basic concepts: (1) the tools and techniques of statecraft, (2) the intensity of effort . . ., and (3) the relativity of all political power." Of course, Dahl (1957) separated these elements and came down on the side of control in defining power.

Waltz (1979: 191-92) explicitly disputes Dahl by distinguishing between power and control:

> To use power is to apply one's capabilities in an attempt to change someone else's behavior in certain ways. Whether A, in applying its capabilities, gains the wanted compliance of B depends on A's capabilities and strategy, on B's capabilities and counterstrategy, and on all of these factors as they are affected by the situation at hand. Power is one cause among others, from which it cannot be isolated. The common relational definition of power omits consideration of how acts and relations are affected by the structure of action. To measure power by compliance rules unintended effects out of consideration, and that takes much of the politics out of politics.

Waltz (1979: 192) actually fails to provide a definition, but he argues, "What, then, can be substituted for the practically and logically untenable definition? I offer the old and simple notion that an agent is powerful to the extent that he affects others more than they affect him." His argument against Dahl forms one of the points he employs to distinguish military power and political control: "Conquering and governing are different processes (Waltz 1979: 191)." Apparently having in mind his considerable pondering about the effectiveness of nuclear weapons, he contends that force is "useful . . . for upholding a status quo, though not for changing it" (Waltz 1979: 191). Implicit in Waltz's analysis is a definition of power as an aggregated fund of material capabilities.

Mearsheimer (2001: 60) continues this assault on Dahl's definition by distinguishing between power and control: "one of the interesting aspects of international relations is how power, which is a means, affects political outcomes, which are ends. But there is little to say about the matter if power and outcomes are indistinguishable; there would be no difference between means and ends. We are then left with a circular argument." In providing a definition of power, Mearsheimer (2001: 55 and 43) describes two kinds of power, latent, consisting of wealth and population, and military. Furthermore, his view of "actualized power" emphasizes armies "because they are the principal instruments for conquering and controlling territory," with sea and air forces providing support for land forces. In this respect, Mearsheimer sharply differs with long-cycle theorists (e.g., Modelski 1987) who stress the centrality of sea power.

Keohane and Nye (1989: 11) draw a distinction between potential and actual influence, thus incorporating both capabilities and control, but they essentially accept rather than reject Dahl's definition of power. On the other hand, their position on uses of power turns out to be remarkably similar to that of Waltz. In a section on "power in complex interdependence," they argue: "Measurable power resources are not automatically translated into effective power over outcomes. Translation occurs by way of a political bargaining process in which skill, commitment, and coherence can . . . belie predictions based on the distribution of power resources" (Keohane and Nye 1989: 225). On the other hand, they disaggregate power into military and economic components, and they bring in perceptions of threat which shape structural power arrangements (Keohane and Nye 1989: 47).

Baldwin (2002: 178-86) draws a sharp distinction between an "elements of power" approach and a "relational power" approach, tracing the latter to Lasswell and Kaplan (1950). He takes a very critical stance with regard to treating power as capabilities, and his criticism includes charges that Waltz is nonspecific, contradictory, and confused. He downplays military power but he also opposes Nye's attempt to expand the elements of power to include "soft power."

In these debates over definitions of power, both those clinging to the meaning of material capabilities and those adhering to the denotation of control over outcomes recognize that the use of power involves the deployment of resources for shaping the behavior of others and that outcomes do not flow directly from the existence of capabilities. Debates continue between those who treat capabilities in the aggregate and those who disaggregate them. To some extent, it depends upon how the different treatments use the conceptions. For example, analyses of balance of power require aggregation, and treatments of international political economy lend themselves to disaggregation. As Nye (1990: 108) has warned, however, analysts who focus on economics often exaggerate power, for they neglect military and political power. For example, the claim by political economists that the United States was a hegemon in the post-World War II period overlooks the fact that in military terms that was never so; thus, "The United States never enjoyed a general hegemony after the war, so hegemony can be neither lost nor regained in the future."

In regard to disaggregation, disagreements continue between those who believe that military capabilities remain at least as important for wielding power as they ever were (Waltz 1979, 1993; Mearsheimer 2001) and those who think that military power has diminished in efficacy (Keohane and Nye 1989; Mueller 1989, 1995; Nye 1990). Furthermore, this debate and the one over aggregation are closely related to another concerning the concentration and diffusion of power. For realists, those writers who emphasize power in their analyses, the distribution of power is highly concentrated. They focus on the most powerful states in the world and they emphasize the unequal distribution of power. On the other hand, for liberals, writers who emphasize liberal aspirations, human will, and ideas in their analyses, power is considerably diffused and disaggregated. They emphasize both economic power and nongovernmental institutions and groups. For example, Nye (2002: 39) uses the metaphor of chess to describe the world as three dimensional, with military unipolarity, economic multipolarity, and diffuse transnational relations outside government control. These views are synthesized by Lentner (2004), but it is unlikely that the synthesis will resolve the debate.

A final contribution to the debate involves structure. Although it may be the most important contribution of the last fifty years to the international politics literature, the concept of structure is not well understood by opponents who stand on the other side of this set of related disputes over the conception of power. Waltz (1979) formulated the concept most clearly, but it has been taken up by other realist writers such as Mearsheimer (2001). Structure is the positional relationship of units in a system; in international politics, which is characterized by the organizing principle of anarchy, the structure may be defined solely by the distribution of power across the units. Because of inequality, the essential characteristic is the number of major powers in which capabilities are concentrated. If one, the system is unipolar; if two, bipolar, and, if three or more, multipolar. There are a few advantages of this structural analysis, but among the most significant is that it provides a means for exploring why unintended consequences occur. Another significant advantage is that it helps to explain latent power which works its effects without any intention or specific act of will on the part of the more powerful actor in an ongoing relationship.

Last, structural analysis brings together power and hegemony by providing an explanation of why a very small number of great powers, one or two, have increased incentives for managing the international system. (Waltz 1979: 195) writes, "great power gives its possessors a big stake in their system and the ability to act for its sake. For them management becomes both worthwhile and possible." When there is only one major power, its primary incentive is to keep its position in the international system, that is to say, to protect the status quo, and that requires management of others, which is to say, leadership or hegemony. Obviously, balance of power considerations enter, for, if the single major power attempts to dominate, to push others around in objectionable ways, they will tend to coalesce as an opposition designed to check the superpower.

With these definitional matters unresolved but definitely in play, scholars have devised a number of prominent theoretical treatments of international politics. These form the subject of the next section of this paper.

Main Theoretical Treatments in International Politics

The central theoretical concerns that shape the study of international politics revolve around the units that participate in and compose a system, the causes of war and conditions of peace, the prerequisites of order and cooperation, the dynamics of strategic interaction, and the consequences of actions (cf. Holsti 1985). Suffusing all is a search for identifying and explaining the operations of power. Debates abound with regard to every one of these concerns. Different conceptions of power and distinct views about its nature and its effects contribute to the disagreements on other matters.

As noted in the previous section, scholars differ about concentration and diffusion of power, about aggregation and disaggregation of power, about definitions—capabilities versus control of outcomes, about power resources and the fungibility of power, about the underlying reasons and motivations for seeking power, and with respect to conscious use of instruments, in contrast to structural power which does not rely upon discrete conscious acts to work its effects.

Despite severe limitations and well-deserved criticisms, the best theory available in international politics is balance of power theory. Much has been written, and a variety of understandings and interpretations characterize the literature. Nonetheless, the central notion of balance of power theory holds that power is dispersed among major political units which counteract or check one another and that balances of power are recurring phenomena in international politics. Disagreements abound with regard to whether a balance of power maintains peace or contributes to war, but a wide range of scholars agree that it assures the maintenance of a system of independent units, for the absence of checking results in a single unit's assuming a position of preponderance, with the threat of establishing an empire. At the same time that balance of power theory is built on the assumption that power is dispersed across a system, it also assumes that power is concentrated within the units. Thus, both empire and the proliferation of nonstate centers of power threaten the fundamental assumptions of balance of power theory.

Among the important implications of structural theory, Waltz's (1979) variant of balance of power thinking, is that it provides a place to look for explanations of unintended consequences. That implication emerges from defining power as capabilities rather than outcomes, for explanation must be sought in the distribution of capabilities across the units of the system. For example, in the aftermath of World War II neither the Soviet Union nor the United States intended that Germany would remain divided until 1990, for both brought their military forces to bear against a unified state in the expectation that the state, after defeat, would continue to exist. As it turned out, however, the superpowers established, respectively, East Germany and West Germany as separate states, with Berlin under continued occupation by the victors. One cannot claim that this state of affairs resulted from the exercise of power of one actor over another in the direction of the will of the former. The establishment of the German Democratic People's Republic fits the conventional power formula, for the Soviet Union exercised power over the land and people of East Germany. A parallel argument applies to the Federal Republic Germany. However, the overall pattern in Central Europe resulted not from the application of power resources to achieve someone's will; instead, it resulted from the distribution of power in the bipolar international system in which the superpowers checked each other to a stalemate. Even in the long run in which Germany was united, the result cannot be understood entirely as the triumph of American, allied, or German will, even though many aspects of the Cold War settlement provide evidence for a Weberian or Dahlian formulation.

An implication of balance of power theory involves survival of the units as a nearly routine consideration. Seldom in the course of politics within states does survival enter into the calculations of participants. In Dahl's New Haven, for example, power resources may be distributed unevenly and may be invoked at the discretion of participants, but the physical survival of the player and the nature of the polity within which he exists do not enter into consideration. Furthermore, the protagonists of New Haven do not need to arm themselves in order to protect their physical and cultural survival, for they live within conditions of security and social formation that, on the whole, do not come under attack.

In less established contexts, in Rwanda or Sierra Leone or Sudan for example, security situations more nearly resemble international politics than the urban politics of New Haven. But these are not the conditions envisaged by authors in the general analytical literature on power. They fall outside conventional thinking about international politics as well, but the insecurity that characterizes them more nearly resembles international war than it does contention over city planning.

Neither does balance of power theory fit Foucault's (1977) prison metaphor that has been employed by so many writers on power or Clegg's (1989) circuits of power. Both of these deal with the reproduction of power relationships in which a system of domination reproduces itself by the compliance of subjects with the framework of power shaped by authorities. In balance of power theory, protagonists check one another in a standoff, and, in general, the power that strives to achieve preponderance tends to be defeated not by power and resistance but by violence in major power war. Frequently, outcomes are the unintended result of the conflict among very powerful antagonists, none of which can prevail entirely.

Whereas balance of power theory treats circumstances characterized by the diffusion of power, part of the literature of international politics also deals with conditions of power concentration. There are four variants of this theme: concert of power, power transition theory, hegemonic stability theory, and long cycle theory.

Concert of power arose as a formulation of the international situation in Europe following the Napoleonic wars when the powers formed a dominant coalition designed to restore and uphold legitimacy in the face of the challenge of democratic revolution. In this realm dealing with a clash of ideas and principles, analysis in the international politics literature tends to be underdeveloped. Hardly recognized as such, the situation seems to represent a struggle between hegemony and counterhegemony, as described in Fontana's chapter (2004). The powers also sought to resolve their differences through concerted diplomacy. The concept has been carried forward to apply to situations following the wars ending in 1918, 1945, and 1989, in which the victors attempt to establish a new order (Ikenberry 2001). Another recent book presents a policy-oriented analysis that aims to consolidate a new order in the contemporary world (Rosecrance 2001). At the present moment, Americans are engaged in a mighty debate about how to preserve and spread the domination of the United States. The literature is immense and growing, but a few recent examples are: Boot 2002; Brzezinski 2004; Ferguson 2004; Kagan 2003; Mead 2004; Nye 2002, 2004. But this is more a quarrel over diagnosis of contemporary world conditions and diverse preferences over a course of action than a scholarly analysis of international politics, even though it includes elements of the latter. For the most part, there is an agreement that concerts of power are not long-lasting, representing as they do victorious coalitions that tend to disintegrate into balances as the respective competing interests of the states within the concert are revealed over time. Indeed, the attention devoted to a post-1945 order focuses only on the coalition led by the United States and overlooks the balance between it and the bloc led by the Soviet Union.

The other three schools of thought that emphasize concentration rather than diffusion of power represent variations on the theme that preponderant power is desirable because it brings order, stability, and peace. Instead of checking, others cooperate with the hegemon until a challenger arises to overthrow it and replace the extant order with a new one. Most of these approaches tend to emphasize some single factor that shapes international relations, and, more often than not, each tends to cast its gaze upon part of the international system rather than the whole of it. Organski (1968: 361) brings a greater breadth of approach than others, but he mostly deals with the post-World War II period, which he characterizes as an era of American preponderance, by which he means "the single most powerful nation on earth heads an international order that includes some other major powers of secondary importance and some minor nations and dependencies as well." In his view, change emanates from within countries, with industrialization and moderniza-tion providing the most important dynamics. For Organski (1968: 376), wars tend to occur when preponderance is lost and balances occur. In his view, the Soviet

Union did not balance against the United States during the Cold War, although he does speculate that the United States might someday adjust to a loss of power (Organski 1968: 490).

Gilpin (1981) regards as a hegemon the power that single-handedly provides public goods to establish and maintain an international order. Over time, uneven growth leads to relative gains by others until eventually a challenger to the hegemon arises. At that point, war appears likely, for the hegemon will initiate it in order to preserve its position or the challenger will start it with a view to defeating the hegemon and replacing it. Despite the logic of his argument, Gilpin backs off from his conclusion by developing the notion of a benign hegemon which will either rule without much friction or will step aside gracefully to make way for a successor. Gilpin's optimism was also fueled by the stability of the bipolar balance and by the relative internal stability of both superpowers. This rather benign view of international power transitions forms the thesis of a more recent speculative study (Kupchan et al 2001) which adds to the traditional types of states, status quo and revisionist, a third type, "benign states." Furthermore, the authors estimate that the United States is not a predatory hegemon that would provoke a challenger and that it "is likely to cede leadership willingly" (Kupchan et al 2001: 4, 6). Lobell (2003) presents a more nuanced view in which he argues that hegemony is not all of a piece but rather occurs in different regions. A hegemon, in his scheme, has the option to adjust to rising regional challengers, when they are liberal powers, by acceding to their military dominance within regions, while retaining overall control of the rules of the international economy.

Similar to Gilpin, Keohane (1984: 34-35) treats the United States as a hegemon "powerful enough to maintain the essential rules governing interstate relations and willing to do so," but his viewpoint leaves aside the central strategic relationship in the world between the United States and the Soviet Union. Moreover, Keohane (1984: 37) conflates several distinct relationships when he writes, "America's economic partners—over whom its hegemony was exercised . . .—were also its military allies . . ." Most writers regard economic partnership, hegemony, and alliance as distinct categories of relationship. Keohane largely restricts his view to economic hegemony and invokes military power as germane only insofar as it is necessary to prevent others from denying the hegemon access to major areas in which it is economically active (Keohane 1984: 39-40). Despite having mentioned Gramscian ideological hegemony, Keohane 1984: 45-46) also draws attention to the fact that the powerful ideology of nationalism is not available to a hegemon and may even be employed by the weak against it.

In presenting long-cycle theory, Modelski (1987) introduces the idea of a global political system which he treats not as an arena for a power struggle, although he does include that, but rather as a forum for collective action. He stresses "global learning" and the "'production' of leadership" of expectant members (Modelski 1987: 7-8). At the same time, he puts forward an analytical scheme in which a dominant country possesses sufficient seapower to maintain ocean supremacy. He holds that seapower is the "yardstick separating global powers from others" (Modelski 1987: 10). Coexisting with such a country are a challenger and other contenders, but together these form a network (Modelski 1987: 8).

In addition to but to some extent within this debate about the effects of concentration versus diffusion of power, disputes occur over the question of treating power in the aggregate, on the one hand, or in separate elements or by issue area. Both scholars and practitioners have generally understood that states employ a wide range of instruments to achieve a panoply of objectives in their relations with other states. Traditionally, international politics has occurred in an arena characterized by insecurity, so military instruments have always been regarded as the final means to use when economic and diplomatic routes have not been able to achieve vital objectives. In the post-World War II period, as security has become abundant in certain circumstances, some observers have chosen to stress the disaggregation of power into different elements as they are used within defined issue areas (Keohane and Nye 1989). More recently, Nye (1990, 2002) has stressed the utility of adding what he calls "soft power" to the elements that at least the leading power can bring to bear in its relations with others. Soft power means framing the debate and coopting others so that one can shape their behavior without applying material rewards and punishments in influencing them.

Another important debate with respect to disaggregating the instruments of power, though seldom invoked by the advocates of disaggregation, involves nuclear weapons. A number of writers have held that nuclear weapons compose a distinctive power resource (Brodie 1946, 1965, 1973; Schelling 1960, 1966; Waltz 1990; Sagan and Waltz 2003) that effectively provide security for states possessing them but that cannot be used to achieve any realistic political goals. This deterrent capacity of nuclear weapons rests on a conception of power that tends not to be included in general analyses: power includes the ability to retain one's autonomy in the face of force wielded by others. Such a dimension of power tends to be assumed, but, in actuality, it remains problematical for every possessor of power in contention with others and is merely highlighted by the nuclear weapons debate.

Furthermore, this view is held by a relatively small number of analysts. More broadly, nuclear weapons are regarded not as belonging to a distinctive class but are regarded rather as simply more powerful than others. The introduction of nuclear weapons on the world scene in 1945 occurred in a context in which more people died in the fire-bombing of Tokyo than died in Hiroshima under the nuclear explosion. Furthermore, without the conceptual apparatus of deterrence, there is little basis for regarding nuclear weapons as unique. In recent years, new developments have tended to erode the distinction between nuclear weapons and others. Among these developments is the fairly recent conceptualization of weapons of mass destruction, a notion that runs together nuclear, chemical, and biological weapons. Recent pressures emanating from the American military to engineer small nuclear weapons that can be used to penetrate caves and deep earthworks represent another development that erodes the distinction, and the arming of ordinary bombs with fissile material does the same thing.

Debates over aggregation and disaggregation of power may not be resolved easily, although nearly every analyst holds a complex view of power and applies aggregated or disaggregated conceptions depending upon the circumstances and uses to which the notion of power is applied. Possibly, the importation into international politics analysis of Wittgenstein's (1968; Haugaard 2002) treatment of power as "a family resemblance concept" might prove useful. There nevertheless remains a tendency by some analysts to insist upon a hierarchical arrangement of the elements of power, with military force topping the list.

Another debate involves a disagreement over the sources and motivations that drive the quest for power in international relations. Mearsheimer (2002: 19-22) classifies realist thought into three categories representing different understandings of motivations for seeking power: human nature, defensive, and offensive. Morgenthau (1973), for example, argues that human beings by nature seek to dominate others and that states, as human institutions, endlessly quest for power. In contrast, Waltz (1979) argues that states may at a minimum wish to survive but that their ambitions may go so far as to seek preponderance. At the same time, he thinks that major powers largely aim to maintain their positions in the international system. Thus, there can be satisfied or status quo powers. Mearsheimer labels these writers respectively as human nature and defensive realists. His position is one of offensive realism in which he argues that the structure induces states to gain power in order to survive and the striving remains endless and states are never satisfied. At bottom, I believe, Mearsheimer's view is that great powers seek power out of fear of others. He discusses the ways in which fear varies depending upon variations in the distribution of power (Mearsheimer 2001: 42-46).

Although much of the literature in international politics concentrates on states as the fundamental units in the international system, in recent years some writers have argued that other entities have acquired sufficient power to be regarded as important actors. These include multinational corporations, intergovernmental organizations, and international nongovernmental organizations. Once an international system structured by states is in place, it makes sense to examine the power and roles of these other entities, all of which operate within a context of constraints established and operated by states (Lentner 2000). Furthermore, the power of most of these nonstate entities is linked closely with states. For example, multinational firms are headquartered and do most of their trade within a home state, and they operate by grants of access and within legal systems of host states. International organizations are the creations and instruments of states. Many nongovernmental organizations operate not only by grants of operational authority of states but often are subsidized by and act as arms of states (Lentner 2004: ch. 9). Some entities, such as drug traffickers and so-called terrorist organizations such as Al Qaeda, possess sufficient power to draw the policy attention and resources of major states which seek to crush their ability to employ means of violence. Except for entities such as these last and other political movements that aim to take over existing states for their own purposes, nonstate entities pretty much operate on the assumptions underlying an international system structured by states.

At the same time, some of the globalization literature portrays the world as one in which power has diffused away from states to intergovernmental and nongovernmental organizations which have accrued such amounts of power that they need to be considered as significant actors in international relations (e.g., Keohane and Nye 1989; Arts 2004; Cerny 2000; Strange 1996). Keohane and Nye present the view that, under conditions of complex interdependence, international relations resemble domestic politics. Thinking along the same lines, Cerny (2000) argues that the state is in the process of losing control over outcomes but that power has not yet become embedded in nonstate institutions and entities, leaving power "disarticulated" and the international system in a transitional stage between stable equilibrium positions. Strange (1996: 4) presents the view that markets have become more powerful than states, and she regards the authority of states to have declined. She (Strange 1996: 17) defines power as "the ability of a person or group of persons so to affect outcomes that their [sic] preferences take precedence over the preferences of others." This is a curious formulation in view of the fact that Strange thinks that the market has gained in power, for it is not an agent; the market is simply the structure that results from the coactions of firms and other agents. To say that the market has a preference confuses matters between agents and unintended results. Similarly, she tends to conflate power and authority. In general, then, this literature does not clarify or advance our understanding of power in international relations. As to whether power has diffused significantly has been responded to by several authors, including Evans (1995, 1997), Lentner (2004), and Weiss (1998), who argue that the powerful state remains central to the globalization process.

Another dimension of the globalization debate takes up an ancient debate with substantial normative overtones. There are different ways of conceptualizing this debate. One formulation casts the matter as between universalism and particularism. Kleinschmidt (2000) traces the universalist theme from early religious thought and St. Augustine's theory of international politics through the attempts in medieval Europe to secularize universalism, which was met by the resistance of territorial rulers. Similarly, a tension has run through western history since the Stoics and Cicero conceived the idea of cosmopolitanism or concern for human beings beyond one's own tribe, city-state, or national polity. Although much has been written in recent years about universal human rights (e.g., Donnelly 1998), the obligation to protect (*The Responsibility to Protect* 2001), and other normative concerns, the vocabulary was formulated in the early nineteenth century. As Kleinschmidt (2000: 153) puts it,

> New words coming into use at the beginning of the nineteenth century betray a concept of the international system that differed from that of the eighteenth century. Among the newly current phrases were 'community of states', 'world state system', 'general concert', 'cultural family', 'society of nations', and 'monarchy of nations'.
>   These words denoted a system that either remained unconfined in terms of its geographical boundaries or explicitly engulfed the entire world. . . . [The

concept] no longer characterized the system as derivative of its member units but, conversely, allowed the member units to appear as dependants of the system as an entity in its own right.

Treating the world as a unit rather than as an international system composed of states or states and other units marks a good deal of the discussion about contemporary affairs. However, the difference in conceptualization between most political analysts and statesmen, on the one hand, and those advocating a universalist conception hinders intellectual engagement and understanding in this debate. In addition to the intellectual divide, the sides explicitly or implicitly hold distinct value preferences;   thus, the debate represents a struggle for domination of the discourse about the subject matter. Generally, those advocating a global or universalist view regard the possibility of a world system dominated by the values they prefer as a dream, whereas those clinging to a state-centered, pluralist system regard such a global system of domination as a totalitarian nightmare.

Another debate grows out of policy concerns for stability or change. For the most part, those who emphasize power in their analyses tend to be conservative and promote stability. In contrast, many visionaries from diverse traditions advocate and use their power on behalf of change; these provide much of the dynamic that moves international politics. Traditionally, revolutionaries and other advocates of change gained control of major states and fomented their doctrines by war, a portion of the debate in contemporary discourse that conceives matters internationally. Napoleon spread the French Revolution by conquest, as did Hitler promote ideas of racial superiority. One of the tensions in American foreign policy debates occurs between those who wish to stand as a model of democracy and those who advocate the use of force to spread democracy. John Quincy Adams and George W. Bush represent, respectively, the sides of this disagreement over means. This duality in policy has been encapsulated in many analyses, from Morgenthau's scheme of status quo and imperial foreign policies, mentioned above, to hegemonic stability theory's notion of a hegemon and a challenger. Balance of power thinking also conceives the matter as one of status quo powers checking the ambitions of a dissatisfied power that aspires to preponderance.

Stability versus change sometimes combines with the arrival of a universalist idealism linked with power. The Cold War pitted Communism against liberal capitalist democracy, both ideologies having universalist ambitions. In the aftermath, liberal ideology has met little resistance, but one manifestation has been displayed by the universalist ambitions of Muslim fundamentalists, even though they have not thus far succeeded in bringing a strong state to bear on behalf of their cause. Another source of resistance to the liberal globalization project has emanated from dissenting groups, including academic analysts (e.g., Cox with Sinclair 1996; Gill 2003) who envision a broad transnational coalition of nongovernmental entities forming a new basis for political organization. With an evident ideological content, these debates would undoubtedly be enriched by drawing on a sophisticated understanding of hegemony (Fontana 2004).

Finally, a new debate has opened within the past number of years spurred by the sociological approach called constructivism and represented most forcefully by Ruggie (1998) and Wendt (1999). These writers displace material power as the central focus for understanding international politics and argue that power is largely constituted by intersubjective understanding of ideas. To this stance, Krasner (1999) has argued that international politics, while employing ideas, continues to be driven by material force, that, for example, the idea of sovereignty has been used from the beginning in a very flexible set of meanings in the service of material power. Nevertheless, the impact of this new approach has led some leading writers (Katzenstein, Keohane, and Krasner 1998) to conclude that the main cleavage of the debates in the field of international politics has shifted from that between realists and liberals, which had been the focus throughout most of the twentieth century, to that between neoutilitarians and constructivists.

This brief survey of the main definitional and theoretical debates indicates that writers in the field of international politics conduct vigorous inquiries about power and treat the concept along many dimensions. Their concerns tend to be quite distinct from those writing in the tradition of the more general power debates in political science and sociology. International politics scholars devote considerably more attention to the distribution of power, and they tend to cast discussions of power in the context of using it for policy purposes and in conjunction with strategic thinking. War and survival of political units tend to be more at risk in international politics than in domestic politics under circumstances considered by power theorists; thus, international politics scholars cast their gaze more immediately and more attentively on threats and uses of military force. Where international relations more nearly resemble ongoing systems of domination—such as in hegemonic stability theory, international institutional analysis, and complex interdependence conditions—scholars do work parallel to that of power theorists, bringing to bear ideas of routine compliance, resistance, and techniques of dissuading partners from defecting from agreements.

As this survey has noted, however, international politics does not possess a single line of orthodoxy that lends itself to easy comparison with the power debate. In its place, there persists a tradition of vigorous contention over how most effectively to move forward research programs that explain how the international dimension of power politics operates. The study of international politics is largely driven by concerns for the causes of war and the conditions of peace. It encompasses attention to international political economy, or the problem of sustaining the conditions for increasing prosperity and other forms of cooperation. Furthermore, the field includes concerns with institutionalization of relations within a system characterized by anarchy, the absence of authority over the relations among states. Perforce, the field also includes analysis of foreign policy and, thus, of strategy and the interactions of competing and cooperating states. Finally, normative matters draw the explicit attention of some analysts and are implicit in the work of all, for certain of the matters that fall within the purview of international politics rank among the most momentous of moral concerns, including mass killing and organized war as well as inequality, injustice, and other difficulties that afflict the human condition.

Potential for Cross-Fertilization and Exchange

In his comprehensive book of readings about power, Haugaard (2002: 4) schematizes the power debate along four dominant dimensions: power of one unit over another despite resistance, power as a general capacity to achieve objectives, conflictful and consensual power, and constitutive power. This scheme provides a framework useful for comparing the analyses of power in international politics with those developed in the general political science and sociological treatments of power. In the course of my analysis, I will supplement Haugaard's dimensions by drawing parallels between the general debate and dimensions treated in the international politics literature. I begin with one such supplementary point.

Both literatures have treated the distribution of power as an important question, even though, because of different normative concerns, each has approached the distribution question in a distinctive way. In American social science in the 1950s, community power theorists (Hunter 1953; Mills 1959) claimed that at both the local and national levels in the United States power was concentrated and consequently undemocratic. Dahl (1957, 1961) confronted this view with his influential analysis that distinguished the possession of power resources from the their employment to exercise influence, and he defined power as the ability to get another to do something that he would not otherwise do. It is clear that this debate was driven by a normative concern for achieving democratic governance.

In contrast, international politics scholars, with a normative concern for achieving stability as a condition of peace, focus on the distribution of power in a very different way, quarreling whether diffusion or concentration of power is more effective. Furthermore, within the research community on balance of power, there has been a debate about which diffusional model—multipolarity or bipolarity—more effectively provides stability. For the most part, the spread of democracy has not entered the international politics power debate, except that Huntington (1991) has put forth the argument that a high concentration of power in a state that aims to spread democracy is a requisite condition, a situation that presents the paradox that only a means antithetical to democracy at the international level offers the possibility of spreading the model to additional states. In the contemporary world, of course, the concentration is and must be in the United States.

Because international politics scholars have been less limited in their focus on distribution, they have gone substantially farther in their empirical studies of the distribution of power than have general power analysts. The latter have largely restricted their vantage point to matters of democracy, where diffusion facilitates it and concentration interferes with it, and of domination and compliance or resistance, where concentration leads to reproduction of power relations. So far as I am aware, there has been no analysis in the general power debates to parallel the theoretical developments in international politics that examine the way in which different structures—that is, distributions of power—shape and constrain behaviors, as Waltz' (1979) theory has done. Giddens' (1984) conception of structure performs some of the same functions, but it is derived from agency and is reproduced through practice. In contrast, Waltz arrives at his conception of structure by abstracting the positional relationship of states from their overall relations, setting aside their interactions as well as their attributes.

Both general power and international politics analyses have manifested Haugaard's first dimension, the power of one unit over another despite resistance. Many studies have employed this conventional understanding of power. At one time, writers (e.g., Wight 1946) in international politics equated the subject with this meaning of power. More interestingly, Waltz and Mearsheimer have contested this interpretation of power by dividing power and politics. To them, politics involves strategic thinking and interactions that include resistance, and power. They define power as a general fund of capabilities, which provides an ingredient but not the whole formulation for understanding politics. Additionally, as structural theorists, Waltz and Mearsheimer also indicate that there exists a dimension of power outside the realm of conscious policy and instrumental choices that is crucial for understanding unintended consequences. This distinction is one that might very well, if incorporated into them, contribute to further development of general debates about power.

Despite a variety of formulations, both the general debates and those within international politics recognize the distinction between power resources and the use of those capabilities in exercising influence. Furthermore, both sets of debate also produce as much confusion as enlightenment in formulating these different phenomena as a single concept, power. The strategy used by Waltz and Mearsheimer to separate power, defined as capabilities, from politics, defined as relational interactions designed to achieve objectives, and from outcomes, promotes a clearer path to analysis. It provides a useful solution to a problem that all power analysts face in separating capabilities, strategies aiming to dominate, strategies aiming to resist or collaborate, outcomes, and distribution of power. Moreover, this course of analytical action provides a way of treating structure that separates it from the actions of agents; this helps to clarify political analysis that often tends to be confused by conflating actions and outcomes with capabilities.

Haugaard's second dimension, a general capacity to achieve objectives, provides a useful formulation, but Waltz (1979: 194-95) has parsed it in a functional way that offers additional insights. He argues that power provides four functions. "First, power provides the means for maintaining one's autonomy in the face of force that others wield." Even within a state that holds a monopoly on the legitimate use of violence, such capabilities as locks, bodyguards, security personnel, and gatekeepers and doormen offer some members of society greater autonomy against predators and armed criminals than slum dwellers and other poor people are able to muster. Similarly, states vary in their capacities to provide effective security to their citizens, a point made by Ayoob (1995) and others.

The second function in Waltz' analysis notes that "greater power permits wider ranges of action, while leaving the outcomes of action uncertain." As Dahl (1961) argued in his study of New Haven politics, participants have the discretion to employ their power resources for different ends, not necessarily as instruments in public policy battles. Nevertheless, those with few resources lack the discretion to engage at all. In neither case does the fund of capabilities make results certain. Even the most powerful units in a political system do not always get their way. At the same time, the most powerful have sufficient capabilities to permit them to engage in quite wide ranges of action.

Waltz' third function includes two facets: in dealing with less powerful units, "the more powerful enjoy wider margins of safety." In international politics, regimes in small countries dealing with large ones are often put at risk, whereas regimes in more powerful countries can afford even to make grand errors without jeopardizing their tenure. Similarly, firms and individuals find themselves in parallel circumstances. The other facet of Waltz' third function has to do with the ability to determine the structure and rules of interactions: which games are to be played and how. Such weak parties as guerrillas and terrorist groups can surely wield substantial influence on structuring certain limited conflicts, but, over the range of activities that compose international politics, major powers do much more to shape the form and modalities of interaction.

Waltz' last function deals with management of the international system, which is performed by those with great power, for they possess "a big stake in their system and the ability to act for its sake." Within states, with their systems of domination, governments manage the system, but they do so by accommodating or repressing elements in the system that press for change or transformation. In either international or domestic political systems, transformation as well as managed stability may occur. Just as international politics has focused on these possibilities, the general power debate might benefit from attention to both power distributions and other conditions for either of these possible paths to be followed.

Haugaard formulates his third dimension as conflictual power and consensual power. In so formulating these categories, Haugaard notes that they are parallel to the "power over" and "power to" conceptions. Conflict and cooperation have long formed fundamental categories of analysis in international politics, with conflict being the predominant emphasis in realist analysis and cooperation providing the greater emphasis in liberal thinking. However, as the strategic literature (Oye 1986; Schelling 1960, 1966; Snyder and Diesing 1977) stresses, there are elements of conflict in every mainly cooperative relationship and elements of cooperation in every mainly conflictful relationship. Indeed, a mixture of cooperation and conflict is essential to the very definition of a bargaining relationship. Thus, the parallels between international relations analysis and general power theory tend to be quite close, if not exact.

The last dimension that Haugaard posits, constitutive power, is reflected in international politics in the constructivist approach. However, this more recent contribution to the debate brings a quite different definition and understanding of power than the one held by most writers in the more established traditions of realism and liberalism. These writers, whom Ruggie (1998: Introduction) designates "neoutilitarians," agree that power rests primarily on material foundations even though they recognize, to varying degrees, that those foundations are organized by and put in the service of ideas. In contrast, moderate constructivists like Wendt (1999) argue that material matters form a minor basis for power, that power must be conceptualized largely as ideas. Secondly, these different perspectives differ on the way in which systems are formed. Realists particularly but also liberals believe that systems result from the coaction of materially powerful units, that the primary source of systemic arrangements is the distribution of material power. In contrast, moderate constructivists claim that systems are brought into existence through intersubjective understandings. Neorealists argue that a system structure in international politics is the unintended result of the interactions of autonomous, self-help units; they draw a clear distinction between the structure of the system and the units composing it. Wendt and others argue that the international system cannot be so segmented, that the system is structured by the agents that make it up even as they are constrained by the structure. This debate separates the antagonists along the dimension of change. For realists, change can only emanate from within the units composing the system. On the other hand, for moderate constructivists, the system structure itself contains a generative capacity for change (Ruggie 1983). Thus, Wendt (1999) foresees the possibility of transforming the international system from one largely conflictful and characterized by a Hobbesian understanding to a more cooperative condition based upon a Lockean or even Kantian set of shared meanings.

In general, it does not seem obvious how these debates can be transferred to the general power debates except to draw attention to the need to concentrate on the mechanisms that generate change and transformation. Ruggie's views draw on Durkheim, and so do Giddens' ideas (Durkheim 1986; Giddens 1987). Perhaps from this common source may be drawn further cross-fertilization of the two literatures. Certainly, both can benefit from attention to change. Perhaps the general power debate needs greater concentration on change, for even the traditional treatments of international politics have attended to explanations of change, the realists focusing on war and uneven growth, the liberals treating ideas and political aspirations. Traditionally, as noted above in discussing Morgenthau, policies with respect to power have been dichotomized as status quo and revisionist. The fundamental concern with change appears to be relatively neglected in the general power literature. To the extent that change and transformation have been introduced into the general literature, it has been brought in by recent attention to globalization, an import partly from the realm of international relations (Goverde et al 2000).

Conclusion

Hegemony has remained a relatively imprecise and underanalyzed concept in both international politics and the general debates about political power. No settled definition provides the basis for ordered debate and the accumulation of knowledge about hegemony. Most recently in the international relations literature, hegemony was introduced in the context of what appears in hindsight to have been a misunderstanding about the decline of the United States. Meanwhile, two basic meanings—domination and leadership—have provided the terms of debate. Scholars have drawn on Greek historians and the twentieth century writer Gramsci for their understanding of hegemony (Lentner 2005), although great benefit might result from drawing on the insights of Gramsci scholars (Fontana 2004).

In contrast, power has remained a central concept in both literatures. Both have developed rich debates and sophisticated understandings of power. Because of their distinctive normative concerns, one with democracy, the other with stability, their debates have branched along different paths. For the general power debate, the path has closed off attention to many of the more unsavory aspects of political power. Aside from that consideration, the international politics literature has paid significant attention to the employment of force in power relations, and it has emphasized strategy in a way that general power analysts have not. By including strategic thinking and differentiating capabilities from outcomes, some international politics scholars have clarified the distinction that all power analysts make between resources and their application to achieve influence. The more nearly equal power distribution among major states has given rise to balance of power thinking, a course of analysis that seldom would offer new knowledge in domestic politics. At the same time, balance of power thinking gives rise to questions of war, change, and transformation that, in somewhat different form, could productively be introduced into the general power debates.

The notion of structure as formulated by Giddens has lately entered the international politics literature through constructivist thinking. However, Waltz' positional relationship conception of structure retains the added advantages of isolating power from perceptions and of contributing to an understanding of unintended consequences. In this, international politics has given more attention to distribution of power than has the general power literature even though the modern debates within it originated with disagreements over the distribution of power within American democracy.

Given the separate orientations of the two streams of thought, it is likely that they will mostly proceed in well-channeled grooves. Nevertheless, there is reason to believe that each would continue to benefit from reading the literature of the other and taking new developments into consideration in its own research programs.

Chapter 6

Mars and Venus in the Atlantic Community:

Power Dynamics Under Hegemony

Henri Goverde

In this chapter which focuses on the dynamics of power in the Atlantic Community, I assume a persistent pattern of European civic integration under military
dominance of the U.S. within a common western value system. Understanding
the dynamics of power within this hegemonic arrangement needs an analysis in a
three-layered way. These layers include power as capacity (espisodic or power
over), as relational (dispositional or power to), and as structural (power balance)
(Goverde et al. 2000) and are distinguished only for analytical reasons; empirically, they are interconnected. Some forms of episodic power enhance
dispositional power, while structural power can be the result of authoritative use
of rules included in dispositional power. Well established structural power supports legitimate episodic exercise of power. Thus, the layers of power are related
cyclically. Power dynamics, then, can be analyzed as a process of iteration. Furthermore, it is underscored here, as Lentner (2005) points out, that the autonomy
of actors is underexposed in the power debate. Indeed, a conception of power is
needed that allows us to acknowledge both the influence of actors on the development of policies, institutions, and regimes in political organizations and networks as well as the impact of the structural context in which the actors operate.
As Clegg (1989: 20) has stated, "power is best approached through a view of
more or less complex organized agents engaged in more or less complex organized games." Haugaard (1997: 144-145) argues that continuity and change of
power occur on the continuum, consensus to conflict, by using specific combina-
tions of agents' goals and specific social constructions. Then, the idea of "power
dynamics" supposes the simultaneous existence of different social constructions.
Structures tend to make different actions seem similar, leading legitimate actors
to take for granted certain practices, for example, acts of superordination or sub-

ordination. At the same time, actors can attempt to obtain their goals by consensus or conflict. By doing so, they can change the rules or even the structure of the game. That is why the concept of power implies dynamism. Theoretically, power dynamics can be regarded in two ways. First, they reflect the power relations caused by the ever-changing forms of social construction such as social capital, political participation, or hegemony. Second, power dynamics reproduce circuits of power as a capacity, power as a relational phenomenon, and power as a structural phenomenon (Goverde et al. 2004: 16). However, the ultimate result of power dynamics is contingent on time and space. Under hegemonic conditions power dynamism may produce a predictable result in the short term. At the same time, however, the position of the hegemon can be sustained or eroded by actors in different spaces and this will have a huge impact on the structure of power in the long term. I will first position power dynamics in the hegemony debate and consider the theoretical consequences for US-European relations during the George W. Bush administration. Second, I will summarize Atlantic Community relations as described in recent essays by Robert Kagan (2002, 2003) and Vaclav Havel's (2002) views about the future of this community. Third, I will explain community developments using a two-fold view of hegemony, domination, and reaction. I explain American dominance by using Janis' theory of "groupthink." I elucidate the reactions of the European states along dimensions of respect for and challenges to the hegemonic leader. I explain the resulting European Divide by the operation of central and peripheral processes in the world-system. I conclude the chapter with some reflections about how power functions under hegemonic conditions. This essay focuses on the period from September 11, 2001, to June 2004, but some references are made to events outside this period.

Hegemony: Double Meaning and Its Descriptive-Analytical Value

According to Heywood (2002: 201),

> Hegemony (from the Greek *hegemonia*, meaning "leader") is, in its simplest sense, the ascendancy or domination of one element of a system over others (an example being the predominance of a state within a league or confederation). In Marxist theory, the term is used in a more technical and specific sense. In the writings of Antonio Gramsci hegemony refers to the ability of a dominant class to exercise power by winning the consent of those it subjugates, as an alternative to the use of coercion. As a non-coercive form of class rule, hegemony is typically understood as a cultural or ideological process that operates through the dissemination of bourgeois values and beliefs throughout society. However, it also has a political and economic dimension: consent can be manipulated for instance by pay increases or by political or social reform.

In Heywood's first meaning hegemony is observable and measurable, an ontological phenomenon. Gramsci's meaning shifts to domination, bringing episodic power—power as simple capacity and as legitimate capacity (Hindess 1996)—into the debate. Simple capacity implies material and subjective aspects. Power as a legitimate capacity, however, is relational, ideational, intersubjective, and social (Reus-Smit 2004: 42-44). These two aspects of episodic power inform an understanding of hegemony. Simple capacity is illustrated in the Athenian claim that "the strong do what they will and the weak accept what they must" (Reus-Smit 2004: 44). Legitimate capacity informs hegemony as norm-defined and socially sanctioned, and it provides a bridge to the Gramscian concept.

Hegemony in the Gramscian tradition is a form of political culture. In political science the Marxist view is opposite to the behavioral approach (Almond and Verba 1980, 1963). Gramsci argues that the class structure is sustained not only by economic and political inequality but also by "bourgeois hegemony," the spread of bourgeois values and beliefs via civil society: the media, the churches, youth movements, trade unions, and so forth. This "spiritual and cultural supremacy" disposes the subordinated people to accept and legitimize the power of the elite. This reflects legitimate capacity. According to Cox (1981:153), cited by Keohane (1984: 44), "Antonio Gramsci used the concept of hegemony to express a unity between objective material forces and ethico-political ideas—in Marxian terms, a unity of structure and superstructure—in which power based on dominance over production is rationalized through an ideology incorporating compromise or consensus between dominant and subordinate groups" (see also Lentner 2005: 741). Cox (1981: 153, fn 27) continues, "A hegemonial structure of world order is one in which power takes a primarily consensual form, as distinguished from a non-hegemonic order in which there are manifestly rival powers and no power has been able to establish the legitimacy of its dominance." According to Keohane (1984: 45) the advantage of this concept of hegemony is

> that it helps us understand the willingness of the partners of a hegemon to defer to hegemonial leadership. Hegemons require deference to enable them to construct a structure of world capitalist order. It is too expensive, and perhaps self-defeating, to achieve this by force; after all, the key distinction between hegemony and imperialism is that the hegemon, unlike an empire, does not dominate societies through a cumbersome political superstructure, but rather supervises the relationships between politically independent societies through a combination of hierarchies of control and the operation of markets (Wallerstein 1974: 15-17). Hegemony rests on the awareness by elites in secondary states that they are benefiting, as well as on the willingness of the hegemon itself to sacrifice tangible short-term benefits for intangible long-term gains.

Although this Gramscian concept of ideological hegemony is valuable, Keohane (1984: 45) adds that it should be used with caution. Indeed, it is not a good idea to conclude that secondary states are per se the victims of false consciousness (Lukes 2005, 1974) as soon as they accept the ideological hegemony or to perceive the behavior of the elite as betraying the nation's interests for its own sake. Gilpin (1981, 1975) has indicated that, under conditions of the *Pax Britanica* as well as the *Pax Americana*, there were peripheral states that had a higher economic growth rate than the hegemon. That is why deference to the hegemon can be—"under some conditions"—considered as an act of political rationality not only for the elite but also for the economy of the peripheral state. Furthermore, it may be useful to distinguish between the functioning of ideological hegemony in an international context in comparison with domestic conditions. "Opponents of the hegemon can often make nationalism the weapon of the weak and may also seek to invent cosmopolitan ideologies to delegitimize hegemony . . ." As an example Keohane (1984: 46) mentions here the "New International Economic Order." More recently different states have appealed to the *international community* as an ideological potential to challenge the hegemon.

I wish to underscore the double meaning of the concept of hegemony. On the one hand, hegemony is a discursive cultural class concept. On the other hand, hegemony is an observable element of dominance in a particular social order. Both meanings can help to provide a descriptive analysis of hegemony and power in the context of the Atlantic Community. However, to explain these phenomena more fully, it is important to examine the agents that produce the dominance. Thus, I will use the "(autonomous) actor-based" (agency) theory of "groupthink" (Janis 1982/1972) to explain the US unilateral decision to initiate the Iraq war in 2003. Furthermore, I will use the theory of the world-system (Wallerstein 1974) to treat new economic development practices in order to explain whether European states defer the USA hegemon.

In my analytical framework, the Atlantic community embodies a hegemonic system of values and beliefs disseminated by a political, administrative, diplomatic, and economic elite. The stability of the social order is the result of "intellectual and moral leadership" ("*direzione intellectuale e morale,*" Femia 1987: 24 quoting Gramsci 1971: 39; see Lentner 2005: 740). The dominant discourse is the dissemination of an open economy in which private firms produce goods and services that can be exchanged in a trading system without state borders. Individual and property rights are guaranteed by a state of law maintained by governments legitimated in liberal parliamentary regimes. Mainly perceived as a necessary evil, these governments have no objective to plan and steer society in a specific direction. In the dominant neoliberal perspective, societies will develop positively but unplanned under conditions of competitiveness.

Notwithstanding their common ideological features, the two parts of the Atlantic community do have an asymmetrical relation of power. Its military dominance allows the US to pursue its interests by either cooperation or coercion. Although probably not free from hegemonic aspirations, Europe accepts American leadership. In this context, my *central hypothesis* states that the US is divided into a dominant group of neoconservatives (*Mars*) that prefers a unilateral approach based on "hard power" in episodic action and another group comprising the political elite, especially diplomats, that gives priority to multilateral actions with the use above all of "soft power." While some Europeans side with the neoconservatives, the majority of Europeans promote a multilateral approach. This majority promotes dispositional power as a result of the legitimacy of international actions offered by the United Nations and anticipation of being monitored under international norms and a human rights regime. In contrast, a unilateral hard power approach does not enhance dispositional power and as a consequence will not contribute to the establishment of structural power in the long term. That is why a large number of Europeans feel themselves to be in conflict with the dominant neoconservative faction in the Bush administration. Thus, interactions within the Atlantic community are rather complex; both partners are divided, the US within its administrative apparatus and Europe between different states. To explain both parts, I argue that Bush's foreign policy behavior is mainly the result of "groupthink" and that European foreign policy is the result of its own structural experiences and its view on the world system.

Clearly, the relation between power and hegemony is dynamic. In the Atlantic community hegemonic ideology supports a common value system which provides political stability. On the other hand, the asymmetry of power within the community enhances uncertainty among the members. While the US can choose between multilateral cooperation and unilateral coercion, the secondary states must defer to the hegemon or play an unpredictable game and challenge the hegemon. Both driving forces, for stability (continuity) and for challenge (change), imply that power relations are never stable but at best remain in a permanently unstable equilibrium.

US-Europe Relationship: Hegemonic and Internationalist Projects?

This section focuses on some parallel processes in US-EU relations and the internal New European Divide. Although the US seems to be involved in a hegemonic project of dominance and different European states have been engaged in a pragmatic internationalist project, both parts of the Atlantic community are still mutually dependent. Whatever the differences, both projects underscore the ongoing relevance of states as units of sovereign power, at least concerning security and institution building.

A number of commentators (Daalder and Lindsay 2003; Garton Ash 2003a-d; Havel 2002; Kagan 2002, 2003, 2004; Moisi 2001; van Wolferen 2003) have contributed to a public debate about the US-Europe divide. However, they overlook a wider division demonstrated by the participation of countries like Australia and Japan in the western coalition in the war in Iraq.

Historically there was always some opposite framing in the Western partnership. For example, Europeans have often perceived the US as the *promised land*, if not *paradise*. On the other hand, Americans have perceived Europe traditionally as the *old world*, "the ultimate source of American culture and civilization:" human rights, systemic values, and religion (Rietbergen 1998, 1994). Besides this cultural dimension, transatlantic relations have a power dimension, expressed through NATO as military power and through the EU as civic power, as well as a political-economic dimension manifested in Europe-US competition in WTO and the UN.

To explore relations between the US and Europe today I turn towards two specific lines of argumentation which have both analytical and normative features. The first is the "widening divide" hypothesis of Kagan (2003, 2002). In 2004 Kagan added a concern about "America's Crisis of Legitimacy." The second line of argument is found in Vaclav Havel's address to the NATO conference in Prague in 2002. Havel emphasized the normative terms in which the Atlantic community is still relevant, but he questioned how friends should behave. These arguments lead to an explication of the US and the European projects.

Mars and Venus: power and weakness

Kagan (2002: 3-4) writes:

> On the all-important question of [military] power—the efficacy of power, the morality of power, the desirability of power—American and European perspectives are diverging. Europe is turning away from power, or to put it a little differently, it is moving beyond power into a self-contained world of laws and rules and transnational negotiation and cooperation. It is entering a post-historic paradise of peace and prosperity, the realization of Kant's Perpetual Peace. Meanwhile, the US remains mired in history, exercising power in the anarchic Hobbesian world where international laws and rules are unreliable and where true security and the defense and promotion of a liberal order still depend on the possession and use of military might. Americans are from Mars and Europeans are from Venus: They agree on little and understand one another less and less. And this state of affairs is not transitory—in light of the product of one American election or one catastrophic event. The reasons for the transatlantic divide are deep, long in their making, and likely to endure. When it comes to setting national priorities, determining threats, defining challenges, and fashioning and implementing foreign and defense policies, the United States and Europe have parted ways.

Thus, for Kagan, the transatlantic divide cannot be explained by election results and the behavior of the Bush administration or by the September 11 catastrophe. Instead, the divide results from differences in power and from ideological differences. Although the EU was founded for geopolitical reasons, it has evolved through cooperation based on multilateral agreements and has developed an ethos of "civil power." Kagan discovered that Europe prefers a world that is comparable with the EU in which rules and laws have priority over military power. According to Kagan, in this postmodern world concepts such as *raison d'état* and the *amorality* in Machiavelli's theses have been replaced by *moral confidence.*

It is evident that Kagan has used a very limited concept of power in contrast with a three-layered power analysis noted above. Had he employed a more comprehensive concept of power (Haugaard 2002; Scott 2001; Poggi 2001, Goverde et al. 2000), Kagan would not have so easily concluded that Europe lacks power. Although Kagan has lived for many years in Europe, he sketches only a highly generalized picture of the interests and policies of the European states. Remarkably, Kagan suggests that Europe can act in isolation, but in reality it is subjugated in a power relation that will not allow it that choice. On the contrary, the mutual dependency between the US and Europe is so strong that even the hegemon has no free choice to stop playing the role of "reluctant sheriff." The US enrolled in this position, particularly after the fall of the Berlin wall in 1989 and the collapse of the Soviet Union in 1991. Additionally, in a unipolar world it is not in the interest of the US as a leading hegemonic state to permit Europe to go "non-Atlantic" (van Staden 2005). Should the US choose to sever its relationship with Europe, the Europeans would have no other option than to create an independent military capability. Kagan also neglects the relation between foreign policy and domestic affairs both in the US and in Europe. Kagan still regards the US-Europe relationship as the key variable in world politics today. However, the world system is much more complex now. The US has to cope with driving forces produced by at least four rivals: Japan, China, Russian Federation, EU/France/Germany; meanwhile, a fifth potential rival, India, starts to enter the international arena. Finally, if *Mars* and *Venus* are supposed to be relevant metaphors concerning military or "hard" power and civic or "soft" power (Nye 2005: 61), then the cultural variable of "Americanization" relates many people to the US. Kagan underexposes that the American way of life is influencing everyday life of almost every citizen in Europe: globalization is in practice Americanization (Berndtson 2000: 157-169). This cultural resemblance implies that there is a relevant structural power that enhances the Western or at least the Atlantic community. Thus, one should not exaggerate the growth of the US-European divide. Although European isolation would be a tragedy, it is not now a serious threat. Finally, the unilateral role of the US is not unavoidable, even though it could develop into a "self-fulfilling prophecy" (de Wilde 2002: 532).

At this point the normative dimension comes in. If Kagan's thesis does not hold water, then what other issues are important than the suggested divide between the US and Europe? In view of US dominance throughout the world since 1989, how should Europe respond? Is the US dominance the best guarantee for sustaining the Western community? Vaclav Havel's address to NATO offers values and norms as a step toward finding answers to these questions.

"How to behave among friends?" Vaclav Havel's address to NATO

In his Prague speech, Havel discussed the common values of America and Europe, the enlargement of the Atlantic community towards the East to include all the new democracies of Europe, and the dilemma between fighting evil and the value of sovereignty (Garton Ash 2003a). Havel told his NATO audience that we have to weigh very carefully whether the war will be a liberation of a nation from its criminal regime and a protection of mankind against its weapons or whether it will serve as an example of "brotherhood" in the style Brezhnev delivered to Czechoslovakia in 1968. Havel referred to the experiences of his country in 1938 and 1968, and he warned the members of NATO never to make hasty decisions. From his speech I deduce several principles for use by decisionmakers facing difficult dilemmas: 1) as an almost altruistic power, the US was a decisive force in solving two great wars on the European continent; 2) Europe could not have resisted communism without the support of the US; and 3) the US was a driving in solving several European conflicts after 1989. On the other hand, Havel warned, the US should imagine that powers such as China and India on other continents will be challenging its power within a decade or two. Then, it is not only good for the US to remember that its roots lay in the European civilization but also important to keep the power balance in sustainable order because it can rely on an active alliance consisting of 500 million Europeans. Havel developed some principles in regard to "how to behave among friends" that can be summarized as follows:

- The lives of people as well as public values such as freedom and human dignity are more important than sovereignty
- Friendship will never grow on lies
- Before taking decisions and when enhancing friendship, create a public dialogue in mutual openness
- Listen well to the arguments you are not familiar with
- Mutual understanding of other peoples, cultures and traditions does not imply derogation of your norms and criteria nor does it imply a denial of your convictions in order to keep a good diplomatic atmosphere
- Decisions well made in the past are no guarantee for decisions well made in the future
- Falsehood will never free us from accountability for our decisions, neither the good ones nor the poor ones
- All decisions produce responsibility inherent to all citizens as well as to history
- Nip the evil in the bud; that is why a general threat to human lives, freedom, and dignity can justify a preventive intervention against a sovereign state
- Be aware of undesirable "brotherhood."

Of course, these principles could be misinterpreted as a criticism of the recent strategy and policy of the US.[1] However, Havel also revealed that a widening divide between the US and Europe, as suggested by Kagan, is not an irreversible project. The antagonistic behavior within the Atlantic community during the George W. Bush administration appears not to be in the interest of either Western partner. As Garton Ash (2003d) has expressed, "It is time to dance for Europe and the USA."

Three Dichotomies to Compare the US and European Projects

Assuming Kagan's analysis does not stand up, what are the probable consequences of Havel's line of argument? According to Anderson (2003: 36), the American and European projects possess parallels between three dichotomies: unilateral/multilateral; military power/civic power; neoconservative/neoliberal ideologies. These dichotomies have, respectively, three distinct bases: strategies with respect to allies, forms of power, and ideologies of globalization.

Unilateralism can be understood as the use of capabilities by a hegemon to pursue its own interests while avoiding actions that are corrosive to its domestic politics or to rely on the consent of other states (Reus-Smit 2004: 67). The role of the *indispensable nation* requires strong and consistent internationalism (Reus-Smit 2004: 29) in which the hegemon should respect the institutional rules and practices of the world order. According to Cronin (2001: 103), this means "recognizing the equality of all states, observing the rules like others, permitting their responsibilities to delimit their freedom and accommodating secondary powers." From this perspective it can be understood why the US sought legitimacy in the UN Security Council before starting the Iraq war. On the other hand, it is surprising that American authorities treat with disdain the rules of the Geneva Convention. Furthermore, the hegemon must "recognize that new procedural rules and substantive norms must be negotiated, not dictated" (Reus-Smit 2004: 67). When a state has the capacity to act unilaterally, it still has responsibility for its soft power; if a hegemon is concerned with its global political influence in the future it should not neglect the social dimension of power.

> A state can be said to have soft power when its social identity resonates with the principal norms of international society, which then gives its interests and actions a certain legitimacy. Other actors accept such a state's leadership because they see it as the embodiment of prevailing international social norms . . . . But a liberal state that acts illiberally with respect to liberal cosmopolitan norms and the core procedural rules of international society is in serious risk of undermining its soft power (Reus-Smit 2004: 136).

Multilateralism is founded on the following beliefs and features:

- Peace and prosperity can be produced by a system of laws and rules as a result of transnational negotiation and cooperation, but Kant's "Perpetual Peace" cannot be guaranteed
- Economic ("soft") power precedes military ("hard") power
- There are no ambitions to have a monopoly of the means of violence, but military power is necessary in specific episodes in which states or nonstate actors challenge the basic rules of the game, internationally or intranationally
- States with their monopoly of violence in a certain territory (Weber) are still the key players in the internationalist project. However, these actors are willing to share and to pool sovereignty for the *res publica* and the common interest
- The result is "civic power" whose main instruments are deliberations and negotiations, cultural dialogue, fair trade, investments in development, economic pressure (sanctions) when necessary, common foreign policy,

humanitarian aid, and active protection against terrorism based on cooperation between police and intelligence services.
- The multilateral/internationalist project needs an adequate structure for its decision making, which includes the principles of a liberal democratic parliamentary polity. Because of *pooled sovereignty* (Keohane 2002), one state cannot stop common action
- Because multilateralism is also congruent with different national identities in specific territorial spaces (e.g., sports championships in Europe and the Eurovision Song contest) concepts such as *raison d'état* still have meaning.

The third dichotomy between neoconservative and neoliberal ideologies is a recent phenomenon. Since the early 1980s neoliberalism has influenced politics and public administration throughout the world, not only within states but also within international organizations. Although formulated during the Second World War (Hayek 1944), it was only after the economic crisis of the 1970s that the neoliberal approach started to resonate with prevailing economic and social conditions. Neoliberal ideology held that economic crises were not the result of inherent weaknesses in capitalism but rather stemmed from Keynesian economic management and intervention in the market. Faulks (1999: 74) argues that some key features of the neoliberal ideology are based on the belief that the dominance of the West in modern world history can be attributed to an emphasis upon individual freedom to choose (Hayek 1944: 11). Faulks continues:

> For neo-liberals, individuals are perceived as autonomous, self-governing and rational actors who enter into voluntary political, economic and social contracts within civil society. Neo-liberals argue that inequality is both inevitable and desirable. Attempts to offset inequality through state intervention will inevitably lead to the erosion of human freedom, preventing individuals making choices about how to spend their income. The inevitability of human diversity within civil society will ensure that the state acts on only a partial, and therefore distorted, understanding of individuals' needs. This will, argues Hayek, lead at worst to totalitarianism, and at best to an increased conflict between ever-more expectant citizens and a state unable to fulfill its promises. Voluntary exchange within the free market is a far more reliable way of ensuring the fulfillment of individuals' talents because it does not discriminate between people on the grounds of prejudice or ideology, but merely reflects the ability of individuals to manipulate the market to their advantage.

The neoliberal reform program aims first to demonstrate the superiority of markets over politics in providing for human need, generating prosperity, and enhancing personal freedom, and second to defend individuals' market rights, including property rights, the right to assert one's inequality, and the right to choose from a diversity of goods and services in the marketplace (Faulks 1999: 75).

Neoconservative ideology accepts neoliberalism as a set of key values in economic affairs but regards the state as evil but sometimes necessary to guarantee the rights of the individuals. Neoconservatives regard the neoliberal value system not only as a guiding dictum for organizing society but as a product of American culture that should be exploited to support the national interest. Neoconservatives perceive neoliberalism as a power resource, and they have a very specific theory of power as well. Following Reus-Smit (2004: 45-50) this theory can be summarized as follows. The neoconservative theory of power is based on three statements: 1) power is a possession, a commodity that the United States *owns* as a unitary, atomistic actor; 2) the "soft" power of American culture (freedom, democracy, and free enterprise), is a significant power resource that can be used to win hearts and minds of other peoples, particularly because it includes universal values that can be applied across all cultures and all time and is comprehensible and desirable to all peoples; and 3) because these values can only be reproduced, interpreted, and given meaning by American agency, this theory of power points to its inherent subjectivity and as such it is *distinctly nonsocial*; thus, "American power is thought to exist independently of any constitutive international social forces, processes or institutions." Rice (2000: 47) argues that it is the unity of America's national interests and objective universal values, not the endorsement of an imagined community of states, particularly not institutions like the United Nations, that guarantees legitimacy to the US' exercise of power.

Understanding the US project

In order to understand the US and European projects it should be recognized that there are no ideal types in reality. These can be analyzed on a continuum only in practice. In each project there are factions and examples that are closer to one end of a continuum than to the other. For example, Anderson has emphasized that the Bush administration contains both a unilateral approach in the Pentagon and a more multilateral one in the State Department. It should be emphasized that many of those who have articulated the Bush grand strategy were involved for more than a decade in the neoconservative discourse on American power in a New World Order. Many of these politicians, among them Vice-President Dick Cheney, had also participated in the "Project for the New American Century," which sought "to retain global leadership and to preclude the rise of a global rival or a return to multipolarity for the indefinite future" (Khalilzad 1995: 94). In practice, unilateral strategy may be enhanced when solutions for problems are found in military reactions rather than civic ones. For instance, although the terrorist attacks on the WTC twin towers and the Pentagon were directed at the main symbols of global economic and military power, they were converted into a national event (Smith 2002) which produced an "open policy window" (Kingdon 1984) to decide for unilateral military reactions. On the other hand, the unilateral strategy is a high-risk strategy, for it can produce easy involvement in a war. For instance, the US entered the war in Iraq convinced that the international community should legitimize its action. Moreover, a unilateral strategy often destabilizes alliances, and a war is difficult to stop. Even worse, a shift in a power balance can force the hegemonic state into unexpected and undesirable wars (e.g., Machiavelli, *Discorsi*, II, 9).

Of course, for the hegemon a multilateral strategy has potential disadvantages as well as advantages. Multilateralism can mobilize allies (Anderson 2003: 37-38),[2] but these allies are often rival powers with their own interests in foreign interventions, and these interests can constrain the hegemon. Therefore, under multilateralism keeping such rivals subordinate while at the same time dealing with enemies would be an unavoidable but major objective of US foreign policy. Unilateralism has the advantage of excluding allies from key decisions and enabling the hegemon to set a global agenda that suits itself. Particularly when US military power is much more dominant and unrivalled than its civic power, it can be expected that unilateralists are leery of the effectiveness of multilateral institutions like the UN and WTO, in creating world peace or the enhancement of US national interests. However, the logic of action requires that the hegemon will attempt to avoid such risks. It will undertake even multilateral activities to further its dominance.[3] My provisional conclusion is that US foreign policy in the first decade of the 21st century has features of "multilateral unilateralism" rooted in military power with neoconservative aspects in a mostly neoliberal political and economic polity. From this point of view, multilateral behavior in a hegemonic project appears to be mainly window-dressing; it is used to borrow time or to gain legitimacy for decisions that have already been made.

Understanding the European project

The negative impacts or risks of Europe's civic-power-based multilateralism also need to be examined. European integration is based on multilateral behavior of states pursuing their interests in part through supranational institutions in which a power balance among the member states is founded on a system of checks and balances. Above all, the EU is based on a neoliberal ideology with an emphasis on civil power in the market (van Schendelen 2003) and on playing down the role of the state, international borders, security, and military power. Despite the introduction of a common currency, liberal democracy in the EU endures with a low level of legitimacy (Nugent 1991: 165). One disadvantage of Europe's multilateral approach stems from the difficulty of giving the *internationalist* project with its emphasis on international law, transnational institutions, and the multilateral exercise of civil power enough democratic legitimacy in each of its constitutive parts.

Another disadvantage of the European international oriented project is that it is congruent neither with its economic settings nor its political values (Held and McGrew 2002; Held 2000), for there are not yet European political parties. Neither has a European president been elected. Although an internal market exists in the EU-15, none yet has been established in the EU-25. Similarly, EU borders prohibit competition in world markets for many goods, particularly agricultural ones, but this illustrates that the EU is incomplete, subject to criticism from both globalists and anti-globalists. Neither has multilateral civil power yet been supported by a common army.[4] Lacking coercive power, European multilateralism relies on the military capabilities and security policies of the member states. Consequently, as a result of unilateral decisions by the US to go headlong into the war on terror, these European states are back at the center of the political arena.

The European multilateral approach also relies for legitimacy on a largely rhetorical "international community." Often selective in choosing between unsavory regimes, say, Iraq and Haiti but not Zimbabwe and North Korea, Europe pursues multilateralism based not on universal values but rather on national interests.

The greatest risk of the multilateral European project is its dependency on US hegemony in moments of security challenge. As soon as the US takes unilateral military decisions, the weakness of the multilateral internationalist project is revealed. The European powers, particularly Germany and France, were not persuasive in convincing the US that a clear UN mandate was necessary before initiating the Iraq war. As a result, the Western coalition against Iraq was joined by only a few member states of the EU and the CEEC (United Kingdom, Spain, Italy, Denmark, Netherlands, Poland, Bulgaria), while a few others (Finland, Sweden) gave their somewhat concealed support. The US responded with the classic mechanism of "divide and rule" by awarding business contracts to Poland and awarding the post of Secretary-General of NATO to a Dutch minister. The lack of consensus among the European states has been reflected in the pace of the European integration process by delaying approval of the New European Constitution and posing a political obstacle to EU enlargement.

On the other hand, the power of the EU internationalist project implies that there is a potential capacity to offer help (diplomacy, UN-support, peace keeping actions) if the US hegemon has to disentangle itself from unintended and undesirable wars (van Wolferen 2003, Havel 2002). From this perspective, it can be concluded that the European integration process can be positioned now in a twofold way:

• *Short term retardation*: There is a New European Divide. Instead of the division by the Iron Curtain, there is now a divide between those who participate actively in the coalition initiated under American hegemony and those countries that keep out of it. As a result, in all European countries public debates concerning security affairs are dominated by national government agencies. Furthermore, each state decides in a relatively autonomous way its participation, either militarily or politically, in the "war on terror" and "the pre-emptive wars against rogue states." This autonomy is reflected as well in the debate of the EU-25 concerning a new EU constitution. Particularly the states that had reviewed their independence just a decade ago, for instance Poland and Rumania, are ready to mobilize their peripheral power in the double arena of the *European order* as well as the *world order*. It is obvious that the pace of integration will not return quickly since the "no's" to the EU constitution in the French and Dutch referenda in May and June 2005.

• *Enhancement of integration in the long run*: It is also obvious that the unilateral and multilateral strategies cannot be played out in a pure form during a long period and that the New European Divide is neither in the interest of the EU nor of the Atlantic community. In fact, it weakens the common defense system organized in NATO. Furthermore, it will force the US to remain involved in war and peace affairs on the European continent, whereas its resources are more urgently needed in other areas. On the other hand, it probably promotes EU integration, particularly in the second pillar (military and security) as well as in the third pillar (home office and court system) of the EU polity. The EU secretary for European Political Cooperation has declared already that it is not a matter of if, but when there will be an EU military force.

US and European projects: Different but interdependent

In summary, the US and the European projects are different, but they are still mutually dependent. The analysis in this section has emphasized that Kagan's original thesis needs more nuance. The suggested American-European divide is not quite as deep as formulated and it is also not unavoidable. However, the "how to behave among friends" question under circumstances of unexpected and undesirable wars has not yet been answered. Kagan recently (2004: 81-87) accepted the idea that the US is in a crisis of legitimacy:

> Today's debate about multilateralism and legitimacy is thus not only about principles of law, or even about the supreme authority of the UN; it is also about a transatlantic struggle for influence. It is Europe's response to the unipolar predicament. . . . There can be no question . . . that the Bush administration has suffered, abroad and home, from its failure to win Europe's full backing . . . There are indeed sound reasons for the United States to seek European approval. But they are unrelated to international law, the authority of the Security Council, and the as yet nonexistent fabric of the international order. Europe matters because it, and the United States, form the heart of the liberal, democratic world. . . . The challenge for the USA will be to cede some power to Europe without putting US security, as well as the security of Europe and the entire liberal democratic world at risk. . . . Nor will Europeans accord legitimacy to the United States when it seeks to address those challenges by itself, especially if it uses force, which it sometimes finds necessary.

So, Kagan seems now to accept the criticism that military power is a relative resource. Still, he resists the idea that multilateral behavior is not simply another term for approval by Berlin and Paris. Of course, from a hegemonic perspective it is probably difficult to imagine that the Westphalia model, which includes state sovereignty and which is primarily characterized by the different layers of territorial governance, could be challenged by other forms of political organization. In an interdependent global world, however, many transnational problems require solutions beyond sovereignty or pooled sovereignty. That is why different multilateral facilities—such as a juridical corpus, effective multilateral agencies, procedures of assessment and control of universal human rights, as well as technological and administrative advanced control mechanisms, in order to prevent pandemic events and to build a new international world order (De Villepin 2004—are sought. Nevertheless, the remaining issue is still about power. Whatever the character of a region's project, hegemonic or internationalist, the definition of the problem differs. Not only does the episodic use of military power have relevance, but the driving forces behind dispositional and structural power also need to be taken into account.

Power dynamics in the Atlantic community

The European members of the Atlantic community do not possess the capacity to persuade the US to behave according to the juridical principles of the UN; Europe has too little episodic power. However, in the long term the US will probably recognize Europe as its most preferable ally because Europe is the closest to the US, both mentally and culturally as well as in political-economic and political-military terms. In other words, there is still a lot of dispositional power as well as structural power in the relationship between the US and the European states. This is why it can be expected that these countries will continue to respect one another as mutually dependent allies in the long run. However, it is also obvious that in the short term there is no consensus within the Atlantic community in regard to an approach to the Islamic world, the configuration of states in the Middle East and the networks of terrorists in particular. The source of this conflict resides in the divergence in domestic as well as foreign affairs in the states concerned. This development includes the serious risk that the dispositional and structural power available now will erode in the future. That is why the US can lose its credibility and legitimacy in the Atlantic community. Consequently, the European states will probably be either further divided between those who follow the hegemon and those who want to challenge it or will be forced to have aspirations not only in political and economic but also in military affairs.

Hegemonic World Rule and the Logic of the World System

In the previous section Andersons' three dichotomies helped to describe the different projects of the main participants in the Atlantic community. Returning to the concept of hegemony, the description has given us a clear view that the dominating element in the Atlantic Community is a military-industrial-political complex. Although the US and the European states have different projects, the practices associated with these projects do not accord with the pure ideal types of unilateralism and multilateralism. Cohesion remains in the Atlantic Community because of available dispositional and structural power. On the other hand, the episodic use of "hard" power by the US, particularly in the Iraq war since 2003, has called into question certain features of its hegemony (Harvey 2003). The US has lost much credibility and legitimacy in both the Atlantic community and the global setting, a situation mirrored in the long history of empires (Münkler 2005). In this perspective two questions remain. First, what is the explanation for the unilateral decisions at this specific moment and under these particular circumstances? Second, what is the explanation for some following and others challenging the hegemon? The answer to the first question can be found in the theory of groupthink (Janis 1982/72). The second answer lies in the theory of the world-system.

The worldview of Bush's inner circle and the inaccessibility of the "discursive exterior"

In the inner circle of the Bush administration, the most prominent names are Vice-President Dick Cheney, Secretary of Defense Donald Rumsfeld, Assistant Secretary of Defense Paul Wolfowitz, National Security Adviser and later Secretary of State Condoleeza Rice, and Secretary of State Colin Powell. Within this inner circle there was considerable disagreement concerning to what extent the US should use its power to promote America's ideals. In this perspective Daalder and Lindsay (2003: 46-47) have distinguished two factions during the Republican 2000 presidential campaign, in particular the "democratic imperialists" (Wolfowitz and Defense Department adviser Richard Perle) and the "assertive nationalists" (Rice, Cheney, and Rumsfeld). The first "group argued that the United States should actively deploy its overwhelming military, economic, and political might to remake the world in its image." The assertive nationalists "saw the purpose of flexing America's military might as more limited—to deter and defeat potential threat to the nation's security." As Rice (2000: 47) once wrote, "There is nothing wrong with doing something that benefits all humanity, but that is, in a sense, a second-order effect." According to Daalder and Lindsay (2003: 40-41) and in line with the neoconservative theory of power, "the logic that underlay Bush's foreign policy has its roots in the . . . the hegemonist argument that America's immense power and the willingness to wield it, even over the objections of others, is the key to securing America's interests in the world." Besides summarizing the neoconservative discourse (Reus-Smit 2004), Daalder and Lindsay have added the neoconservative arguments concerning globalization, the meaning of leadership, and the disadvantage of multilateral treaties. Bush and his advisors believe that self-interested states are the key actors in world politics, and they refuse the idea of a fundamental reordering of the structure of world politics by trends of globalization which undercut the authority of individual states, with power flowing to nonstate actors. Furthermore, power, in particular military power, is still the coin of the realm even in a globalizing world. But power is more than capability. It is also about will. Leadership is in line with this; as Wolfowitz (1997: A22) once wrote: "leadership consists of demonstrating that your friends will be protected and taken care of, that your enemies will be punished, and that those who refuse to support you will live to regret having done so." Next, multilateral agreements and institutions are neither essential nor necessarily conducive to American interests. "With treaties unable to deliver real security to the United States, Washington would be better able to advance its interests by jettisoning constraints on its freedom of action. This policy of the free hand rested on an important assumption: the benefits of flexibility far outweigh the diplomatic costs of declining to participate in international agreements that are popular with friends and allies." (Daalder and Lindsay 2003: 45)

Groupthink

Particularly during the years 2003-2004 the dominant behavior in the Bush administration's inner circle has functioned as unilateral imperialists. Within this belief system the hegemon has fallen into to a Guantánamo regime, rejection of Geneva Convention, and the scandals of the Abu-Ghraib prison.[5] In consequence, US military power has lost much credibility and legitimacy in public opinion. This cataclysm can be explained by "groupthink," which developed during the 2000 presidential campaign and the team-building period between election and inauguration. Janis' theory of groupthink (1982/72) implies that there are two sides to the coin:

- *Arrogance of power*: the idea among the elite the idea develops that *we* are the task force, therefore *we* are supposed to know what is good and thus *we* do not need to accept counter-signs from the outside world;
- *Pressure to group confirmation*: all members of the task force are permanently pressing each other to remain on board and to confirm to the discourse of the majority of the team.

Groupthink theory is a strong tool for explaining the decisions made by the Bush administration's inner circle. It can also used to explain why, for example, Secretary of State Powell, who was characterized as "a pragmatic internationalist who understood the importance of [military] power but also worried about the costs of alienating other countries" (Daalder and Lindsay 2003: 45-6), was kept on board by group pressure. The arrogance of power can explain particularly why all warnings concerning the threat of Al Qaeda (9/11 Commission Report 2004, Urquhart 2004, Clarke 2004, Daalder and Lindsay 2003) were rejected. Furthermore, a team with a strong coherent belief system in which a state is still the key actor, is probably not responsive to advisors who claim that Al Qaeda, a nonstate actor, should receive more priority than the Iraqi dictatorship. Next, all recommendations issuing that an attack on Iraq should be followed by a clear vision concerning "nation building" were probably refused for the same reasons

(Fukuyama 2004). On the other hand, the theory of groupthink is not able to explain why the President himself can often take an autonomous but determining decision. For this argument an in-depth research concerning power and individual psychology appears to be necessary (Frank 2004). However, as Daalder and Lindsay have argued rather convincingly, Bush himself is not the voice of the groupthink endeavor only. On the contrary, he is the main believer, and as a consequence he takes the key decisions by himself as his doctrine of preemption unveiled (Daalder and Lindsay 2003: 81).

Discursive exterior.

My interpretation of the Bush's decision-making machinery as a process of groupthink implies that any "discursive exterior" (Laclau and Mouffe 1985), represented in the multilateral approach, is inaccessible to Bush's inner circle. Thus, groupthink is the mechanism that produces sufficiently internal dispositional power as well as external episodic power to implement decisions which are coherent with the principles of the belief system of this specific small group. In short, Mars pays no heed to Venus.

According to Laclau and Mouffe, a society can never be "closed"; therefore it is not a unit of analysis. Each society is "overflowed" by a surplus of meanings that makes up the "social." As Howarth (2000: 103) concludes, "no matter how successful a particular political project's discourse might be in dominating a discursive field, it can never in principle completely articulate all elements, as there will always be forces against which it is defined." In fact, a discourse always requires a discursive "outside" to constitute itself. In Kagan's essay, the Mars and Venus metaphor shows that they constitute each other. Without unilateralism there would be no multilateralism. The unilateral belief system has the multilateral belief system as a discursive exterior, whereas for the multilateral discourse, it is the reverse.

Setting world rule or adaptation to structural power of the world-system?

While agents and agency can explain specific behavior of actors in the international arena, this behavior is embedded within the context of the structural power within the world order, a contextual power perspective that helps to explain power within the Atlantic community. The hegemonic and the internationalist discourses, based respectively on the military and civic power as well as the neoconservative and neoliberal belief systems, are in a duality to the world-system. These agents are constitutive to dispose states, civil society, and market to accept conditions of globalization. On the other hand, these agencies are themselves embedded in the existing structural power of the mechanisms of capitalism that, according to Harvey (2003), unavoidably promote the new imperialism. In world-system theory there is a typology of core, semi-periphery, and periphery. These terms refer to processes, not to areas, regions or states. Core processes refer to economic activities adding great value to a product, paying high wages, and thus allowing high levels of consumption. Peripheral processes refer to the opposite situation—low wages, low consumption, and low value added to the product (Taylor and Flint 2000: 20). Semi-peripheral processes exploit the periphery and is exploited by the core. Semi-peripheral processes are often more political than economic. Therefore, the semi-periphery displays processes with relatively more dynamism. Theoretically, core, semi-peripheral, and peripheral processes can be imagined in all spaces and scales. However, core processes are mostly urban while semi- and peripheral processes are mostly rural. Nevertheless, peripheral processes occur also in what Castells (1996-1998) has called the "Fourth World," among the marginalized people in all mega-cities of the world.

Since World War II, the US has been the core power in the world, both militarily and economically. However, its relative position has been changed in regard to Europe and Japan during the last three decades of the twentieth century. Semi-peripheral processes are significant in the rise of Central Europe as a region and, as a consequence of the arms race in the Cold War, the decline of the USSR in the late 1980s (Kennedy 1987). Semi-peripheral processes were demonstrated also in the tremendous growth of the debt of Latin America to the core. For several decades, there has been a renaissance of many *Japans* in Asia as part of the semi-periphery (*new economic tigers*). Nowadays, it seems that large metropolitan areas and specific economic sectors in China and India are starting to participate in the semi-peripheral processes.

From the political and economic perspective of the second half of the twentieth century, US unilateralism and European multilateralism can be regarded as complementary in the core of the world system. However, it is imaginable that due to a change in the configuration of the core, semi-periphery, and periphery this American-European connection within the world system will be challenged in the next decades. Then, from the position of the hegemon, different scenarios can be perceived as plausible. For instance, the global economic transformation and its estimated impact on the configuration of structural power, in other words on hegemonic conditions, is probably a driving force for the US hegemon to continue its activities in the Middle East, particularly to safeguard its influence on oil production in the long run. Then, the US unbound actions will be legitimized with reference to "systemic power," i.e., to save the world from attacks on freedom, democracy, and open economy by either rogue states or networks of terrorists (Harvey 2003, Daalder and Lindsay 2003). Furthermore, it can be expected that for the US the Atlantic community will no longer have top priority. This hegemon will probably attempt to make an alliance not particularly with the EU and not only with Japan and Australia but also with Russia, Pakistan, and India to anticipate the growing episodic regional power of China in the near future. The rapid transfer of western technology in primary and secondary production sectors to China and the outsourcing of many administrative tasks to companies in India nowadays give evidence to this hypothesis. Of course, China, as a potential rival to US hegemony, will appreciate that the US is exhausting itself militarily and politically, while it receives economic knowledge and technology from the hegemon and its allies at the same time.

Because the US and Europe are still engaged in the core processes of the world-system both partners, but Europe as an institutionalized civic power (EU) in particular, has no interest in mutual rivalry other than economic competition. However, if American episodic power performance in the long run controls the main oil resources in the Middle East, the European powers will probably perceive themselves as semi-peripheral, even marginalized by their partner in the Atlantic community (Vidal 2002). Then, the suggested divide within this community could become a reality. As a consequence, the Europeans might be forced to enroll Russia in its polity.[6] On the other hand, should the US act out a bad unilateral hegemonic performance, it seems that only a multilateral European endeavor would be able to tackle the loss of credibility and authority of the Americans both in the western alliance and in the global context. Then the partners in the alliance would face each other on a more equal basis. However, in order to build an adequate authoritative governance capacity on an equal base the Europeans should be able to solve their own violent wars and ethnic conflicts. Then, the creation of an effective EU military power resource (an army of circa 100,000 soldiers with up-to-date logistics and to be mobilized within a short time if necessary) might be a top priority. Although this would imply a shift in the balance of dispositional power, it is expected that both partners from the perspective of mutual dependence in the Atlantic community would better recognize a common interest in cooperative control of the world-system. Because the next phase of capitalism will require core investments in knowledge-based economies (Jessop 2002, Flint 2001), i.e., education, scientific research, and infrastructural logistics, both regions will hopefully conclude that it is not a wise policy to continue to waste resources on wars that cannot achieve such goals as political stability in the Middle East.

Conclusion

Under hegemonic conditions power functions in three layers. The US dominates both the Atlantic community and the world order. In the Gramscian tradition hegemony reflects a spiritual and cultural supremacy of the ruling class, i.e., a world order in which power takes primarily a consensual form. This means "awareness by elites in secondary states that they are benefiting, as well as on the willingness of the hegemon itself to sacrifice short-term benefits for intangible long-term gains" (Keohane 1984: 45). This supremacy is manifested in unilateral and multilateral discourses. These discourses represent the US *hegemonic* and the European *internationalist* belief-systems of policy-makers and politicians in both political systems. As a hegemon, the US presumes the urgency in world politics to demonstrate its leadership by using its resources of episodic hard power. However, apart from some attempts to create multilateral legitimacy for its actions, it neglected the social dimension of power, largely as a result of the dominance of neoconservative theory. Thus the US' exercise of epi-sodic power had a negative influence on the dispositional power of the Atlantic community in the short term and on the foundations of Western structural power in the world order in the long run. In addition, the US was ready to take unilat-eral steps in world politics as a result of the operation of groupthink among the key actors in the Bush administration's inner circle; they excluded all exterior discourse. As a consequence, the Bush inner circle can be characterized by its arrogance of power with respect not only to its partners in the Atlantic commu-nity but also to the world in general. Furthermore, US hegemony can be con-tested by developments in structural power in the world system, i.e., a new phase of capitalism promoting the probable renaissance of new regional powers with rival capacity to exercise power episodically. Finally, this development could strengthen the Atlantic community as well as weaken this hegemonic structure. Either the hegemon will enlarge its bilateral alliances in order to anticipate the episodic power of China as a potential new rival or the USA will enhance the Atlantic community and its consensual dispositional power (hegemonic rules of the game) in order to stabilize its structural hegemonic supremacy in the world system.

In conclusion, whether either Mars or Venus will be a more effective power in the long run is not the essential question. What finally counts is: do the part-ners in the Atlantic community behave as friends in order to be in accordance with a sustainable hegemonic structure in a new configuration of territorial and nongovernmental powers.

Notes

1. However, after President Bush's proclamation of victory on May 1, 2003, aboard the *U.S.S. Abraham Lincoln*, the facts about mass destruction weapons as well as the actual resistance to the occupation in Iraq seem to emphasize the relevance of the principles of "friendship and lies" and "undesirable brotherhood."

2. Keohane (1984: 147) for instance refers to Hirsch and Doyle (1977: 31-32) who have pointed out: "The United States—by providing massive additional financing and accepting trade and payments liberalization by stages—saved rather than abandoned its earlier objective of ultimate multilateralism in 1947-48. Such a policy was then possible because of the fundamental characteristics of the international political economy of the time: United States leadership on the basis of only qualified hegemony. The strategy . . . was a major success . . . and paved the way for a painless adoption of multilateralism at the end of the 1950s." This example demonstrates not only that multilateralism was in the midst of the 20th century a strategy of the US—later often repeated in its influence on the structure of many international organizations—but also that the European partners had much to learn in this domain.

3. Anderson (2003: 48-51) illustrates this position as follows. While Powell con-structed an alliance with the EU, Russia, and the UN for Israel's withdrawal from the West Bank in 2002, a typical multilateral approach, this policy was pure "multilateral unilateralism" as it bought time for Sharon to finish his military target around Arafat's main office in Ramallah.

4. However, in March 2003 the EU declared that it would create an EU defense policy that would be able to mobilize and deploy 60,000 soldiers for peacekeeping operations within two months. This quick intervention force lacks until now a good system for transport, communication, and intelligence. Nevertheless, EU troops are involved some countries such as Macedonia and Congo. Of course, its relation to NATO is a key political issue in the Atlantic Community. Being cautious of the competition, NATO itself has created an operational NATO Response Force (according to NATO's Chief-commander US General J. Jones, October 16, 2003).

5. For social psychologists the excesses in these prisons remind them of experiments concerning commanded obedience and moral behavior (experiments designed, for example, by Zimbardo, Milgram, and Raaijmakers and Meeus: only very well-educated people with strict religious attitudes and principled pacifists could resist group dynamics as well as demonizing enemies).

6. The map of new oil and gas pipelines, now under construction from Russia to Europe, seems to demonstrate that Russia is anticipating a new phase in the Atlantic community. In order to build a strong episodic power position Russia brings these natural resources in separate pipelines to the different European states, using the international bottom of the Baltic Sea as the most adequate logistic corridor: "divide et impera?"

Postmodern and Feminist Approaches

to Hegemony and Power

Chapter 7

Providing Security: White Western Feminists'

Protecting "Other" Women

Elina Penttinen

I remember when I heard it on the radio and could not believe it was true. I was driving in the morning traffic, the sun was piercing through the windshield, and I had trouble adjusting to the changing speed. The news came on and the reporter told how the criminalization of buying sexual services is postponed for a year. I remember lifting my hands up, off the wheel and shouting "Yes!" I could not believe that the criminalization of buying did not go through immediately. The support for it seemed so strong that it had become a dominating discourse among members of parliament, the government, and among feminists. To this discourse there were no real alternatives, except the discourse supporting a sex worker's rights in which sex work is defined the same as any other form of labor and which should be also legally recognized. Between these debates there was no middle ground, at least for a feminist who did not see prostitution as a positive means of earning an income and who did not believe criminalization of buyers was the solution. However, parliament had agreed on including stricter measures against procuring such as enabling the tapping of phone lines of suspected criminals and also harder sentences. They had included the term human trafficking in the legislation and clearly it seemed that the incentive was to combat organized crime and other middlemen and in this way make Finland less attractive as a destination country.

I was surprised that the initiative on criminalizing demand had been postponed and that the emphasis had been shifted to the procurers and organized crime. The debate concerning criminalization of buying sexual services had been going on for about three years, and it was strongly supported by members of parliament, feminist organizations in Finland and also in academia. I had been certain that Finland would criminalize buyers as soon as possible and follow the lead of Sweden on the issue.[1] The criminalization of buying had been included in the government's introduction to the legislation criminalizing human trafficking, legislation, which did not yet exist in Finland and was obviously long overdue. Yet, this move of combining both the criminalization and measures against human trafficking toward combating trafficking in women (from Russia and the Baltic states to Finland) together in the same legal initiative meant that it was very difficult to criticize the buying issue. The opposing views had been ridiculed and also stigmatized as supporting prostitution and violence against women. The male members of the parliament who had opposed the criminalization were easily labeled as clients. According to this dominating discourse the logic followed that if a man was not willing to criminalize buying it must mean that he uses prostitute's services himself. There were rumors that some male members of parliament were planning to be absent the day of the vote, since they did not want to be stigmatized as clients if they voted against criminalization. It seemed that there was no position from which one could oppose organized prostitution and trafficking but not agree that criminalizing buying was the only solution.

A number of ministers, members of parliament, and the government promoted the criminalization of buying sexual services. Finland should not look more tolerant toward prostitution than fellow Nordic countries. This discourse concerning foreign prostitution in the Nordic countries was based on strong arguments that prostitution was violence toward all women. Prostitution as an institution would always be oppressive to all women and as long as prostitution existed there could not be true equality between the sexes (Unioni 2003). In the name of equality between men and women all prostitution should be abolished (Coalition Against Trafficking 2005; Kvinnoforum 2005). The feminist discourses for criminalization of buying argued that all prostitution could be equated to "trafficking in women," that there was no difference between forced and voluntary prostitution, and that all women in prostitution were victims (Central Women's Union 2005). Criminalizing the demand for sexual services would send a clear message that women are not for sale, that women cannot be reduced to sexual objects, and that if some women were subjected to such fate it would imply that all women are always necessarily objectified and subordinate to men. Prostitution was seen as a human rights violation, the women in it as victims. Therefore, a legal measure, which would send a clear moral statement that buying sex from another person was wrong, was needed. The Central Criminal Police objected to this discourse by arguing that such legislation would make their work even harder, since prostitution would be driven underground and that fining individual men would have been an ineffective means to combat prostitution and a waste of police resources. It did not matter to the supporters of criminalization of buying that this legislation might be ineffective in practice, since it was the moral statement that counted (Unioni 2005). The intention was also to prevent prostitution and to help the victims of prostitution, although there were no clear initiatives as to how exactly these women would actually be helped. Issues such as witness protection and women's shelters were raised but not seriously discussed.

My argument is that this dominating discourse on criminalizing the demand became a hegemonic discourse, since it was based on strong alliance and consent (see Fontana, Ch. 2) by many actors involved with the issue, such as legislators, ministers, and feminist political projects. The opposing views were ridiculed or stigmatized as supporting prostitution and thus also inequality of the sexes. The discourse on criminalization was therefore confirmed-structured (see Haugaard, Ch. 3) by the public at large, since there was consent that organized prostitution was a social problem. I am going to show in this paper that what enabled criminalization to become a dominating discourse was that it operated according to the logic of the hegemonic security concept, which is grounded in the protector-protected divide. The only destructuring (see Haugaard, Ch. 3) debate was presented by the organization of Finnish sex workers (Salli 2005) and their views were presented in the Finnish media, but this seemed quite ineffective and they did not have any members of parliament to back them up. Also, the problem for this organization was that they were mainly speaking on behalf of Finnish sex workers, whereas the "problem" of prostitution was mainly associated with the Russian women who come to Finland to prostitute. The Finnish sex workers were able to become visible and their voices heard in the media, but it was not really they that this new legislation was concerned about, but rather the form of organized prostitution that was directed by Russian and Estonian organized crime. The buying issue became constantly confirmed-structured since this measure was combined with the human trafficking issue, which was easily accepted as criminal activity by the public. In addition, the ineffectiveness of the "sex worker's rights" destructuring debate resulted in stronger support for the criminalization of buying as there were no other really considerable alternatives. Normalizing sex work was too radical as an alternative for the legislators, and those who had argued for some other possibilities were labeled as wanting to normalize prostitution.

After the April 1, 2004, when this new initiative was published (Finland, Ministry of Justice 2004) the debate calmed down, and the legislation was passed on July 9, 2004 (Finland, Legislation 2004). After all, the criminalization issue had only been postponed for a year. Another reason is that criminalizing of buying had already been included earlier that year in the new City Ordinance Code of Helsinki, in which public selling and buying of sexual services had been prohibited and the police had already fined some clients on these grounds. In the rest of the country most prostitution took place in private apartments, the clients recruited by the advertisements of phone numbers of prostitutes on the Internet or in specialized magazines. Only in Helsinki had there been such open and consistent street prostitution in Finland. In the rest of the country even the most public forms took place in distant motels and camping grounds where the "business" was not in the streets as in Helsinki. However, small northern communities in Finland have been strongly affected by the open conduct of organized prostitution in the region. Although prostitution was carried on in distant places the northern communities are so closely knit that the local people know what their neighbors and relatives are doing, even moreso than in a city such as Helsinki where people can choose to ignore prostitution and the sex industry in general (Penttinen 2004).

Why this narrative on debate over legislation concerning prostitution in Finland, when my title refers to security? As I already briefly mentioned above, I am going to show in this paper that the debate concerning criminalization was able to gain such large support and become the dominating discourse because it operated through the logic of protection, in which the protected are the women in prostitution. I am going to discuss how the hegemonic security concept as it has been developed in International Relations may contribute to an understanding of white-western feminist projects that aim at "saving other women" with the kind of legal measures described above. This explains why the position of supporting criminalization of buying sexual services is so appealing for them.

I want to open up the discussion on power and hegemony involved in white western feminist projects. With white western feminist[2] projects I am intentionally simplifying the many feminisms there are in order to make the contrast between the ethnicity of the women who are active in "saving" and the ethnicity of the "other" women they want to save. I do acknowledge that there are many forms of feminism and many different stances within feminist theory and epistemology (Harding 1991). However, I want to emphasize here that feminist projects, although they are valuable and have contributed greatly to the amelioration of women's position in western countries, may have a peculiar logic when it comes to saving others. The Finnish case of criminalization of buying sexual services exemplifies this logic and illustrates how the position of the protector is problematic for the feminist, fighting for equality between the sexes. I want to question why logic of protection, which is argued to be masculinist and subordinating to women (Young 2003) is used and is useful to feminist projects. As such my act is one of destructuring the dominant discourse on prostitution in Finland without the intention to normalize prostitution. Therefore I intend to present a counterhegemonic discourse on the issue of prostitution and trafficking in women, which focuses on the issue of prostitution from the perspective of complex global flows. I am going to show how such local solutions as criminalization of buying sexual services are not only ineffective, but may result in terrible consequences for the women in prostitution.

Gendering Security: what Feminists have to say about the Concept of Security in IR

But before going any further, let us step back in time to the time almost forgotten, the time of early IR and the formulation of the constitutive concepts of the discipline such as the concept of security. Let us hear what the feminist IR scholars have to say about this constitutive concept and implications it has on securing women.

To simplify the issue of security, the subject of security means the subject that is to be secured. In mainstream IR and state-centric understanding of security, the subject that is to be secured is the state from outside threats. In turn the state provides security to its citizens, whom the state protects from these outside threats. In this way security is also understood as a negation of outside threats and the state of being secure is the absence of war or conflict. The problematic here is that by focusing on state security as absence of outside threats, the insecurities within the state go unseen (Steans 1998, Peterson 1992). These insecurities within the state that can easily be dismissed in the study of IR as belonging to the sphere of domestic and private have been shown by feminist scholars to be inextricably linked to the international (Höglund 2002, Enloe 1988, Cohn and Enloe 2003). The understanding where international relations takes place shifts away from the cartoon-figure-like relations of superpowers (Sylvester 2002), toward everyday lives of individuals and groups and nations that are not so super (Enloe 2004, Cohn and Enloe 2003). The feminist critique centers on how international relations as power politics create women's insecurities and vulnerabilities (Youngs 2004, Peterson and Runyan 1993). It is important in this criticism to reveal how discourses on security and international relations operate through binary oppositions, which prioritize the masculine over feminine.

Feminist IR theorists have pointed out how the state-centric view on security, which is grounded in the public-private binary, indeed, causes gendered insecurities. Primary emphasis has been placed on how the nation state is grounded in the idea of masculinist protection. The state was criticized for operating as a form of structural violence organized as the patriarchal state. Women have been assigned a place in the private and the inside of the state, and formed as the category to be protected from outside threats (Tickner 1992). Women and children are formed as representative of the nation, its purity and coherence. In turn, as women are constructed as the protected, belonging to the private and the home, their insecurities or their agency in times of war and conflict do not come into view. Therefore, for example, Enloe calls for the collection of women's war stories and how war and militarism (Enloe 2004, Cohn and Enloe 2003) have affected their lives. Höglund (2002) writes how women's daily activitities such as fetching water or buying bread can be seen as acts of heroism in the current conflicts in which war does not follow the rules of international law, and civilians are more and more affected. Although traditionally heroism is reserved as the privilege of the male warrior hero in the context of the wars between nation states, in the current deterritorialized world typical women's work can be seen as courageous acts in a war in which there is no front, such as that in Yugoslavia during the 1990s (Höglund 2002: 14). Still the warrior hero is a place that is definitely masculine and constructed as a form of hegemonic masculinity as Höglund (2002: 13) demonstrates by quoting George W. Bush saying, "Be ready. You will make us proud." This strengthened the image of a male warrior, which resulted in a stream of men who enlisted as volunteers for the war (Young 2003).

The hegemonic security concept, which dismisses women's agency during times of war and conflict, is grounded in the construction of the nation state as the dominating paradigm of IR as it has been formulated since early IR. The gendered public-private divide is the foundation of the construction of sovereign states and their relations. Feminist writers have pointed out how the sovereign state and a state of nature/anarchy, as described by Hobbes, is structurally sexist, and they demonstrate what kind of consequences this sexism has for the understanding of international politics (Sylvester 1994; Steans 1998; Peterson 1992; Burke 2002). Feminist reading shows how Hobbes was not exactly gender blind, but instead in the state of nature women were designated to be in the specific and inescapable space of motherhood. This natural function was considered something that could not be overcome or avoided. The place of women was in the private sphere, excluded from the public/international where sovereign men/states competed for survival and a position of domination over each other. In the state of nature, slaves and prisoners, who were also excluded and dominated by the sovereign men, could indeed free themselves and gain a position of subjectivity, but for women there was no such escape. Sovereign men, on the other hand, had also been detached from all social relations, and from their mothers who had cared for them. It was as if these men had grown up even before they were born. This detachment of social relations enabled the privileged position of the sovereign man as a subject in a state of nature and allowed his domination over the private sphere. In Hobbes's state of nature there is continuing insecurity and vulnerability and therefore also the continuous need for protection that can be provided by the sovereign (Young 2003).

Young (2003: 5-6) explains that Hobbes' state of nature can be read as describing aggressive masculinity and depicts men as selfish aggressors and sexual predators. Because of this constant possibility of threat, the one that belongs to the private sphere should be content that there is someone ready to take over and ensure protection from the sexual predators and aggressive males that exist in the public sphere (or in the international). Again I want to emphasize that this private sphere is characteristically feminine, whereas the public is masculine. The aggressors are masculine. There are no feminine sexual predators. Instead the private is passive and objectified, whereas the public is the sphere of agency and subjectivity.

Feminists have shown that this exclusion of women, by placing them in the private sphere and under the domination of the male subject, is also an important aspect of the representation of states as unified actors. Peterson (1992), for example, explains how the early state formation in ancient Athens involved especially this division of the public sphere of citizens and private sphere of women. The concept of a citizen of the state was based on the notion of the "warrior hero." Women could not be warriors, so indeed they were excluded and limited to the private home, a sphere governed and owned by the [male] citizens. In ancient Athens women lost their right to own property, and in addition each woman became the property of a man. The women's role was nevertheless important, for they represented the nation, which the warrior hero protects and sacrifices himself for. The domestic/international divide hence required women to make the nation that the citizen/warrior heroes would protect and defend. It is in this context that I want to question masculinities and femininities involved in the relation of protectors and the protected when white western feminists *go out* to protect and save "other" women, such as foreign prostitutes in Finland.

Even if today women can become warriors and gain subjectivity in terms of protecting the nation, or become active in the public sphere as in the case of white western feminists, it still does not change the binary logic of protection. As the western feminist takes on the position of the protector toward women of other ethnicities, she reiterates the binary opposition of the protector and protected, in which she takes on the position of subjectivity while reserving the position of the protected to the ethnic other women. This reveals also how the masculinist logic of protection operates in nation building. The hegemonic security concept which has the warrior hero/protector constructed as subject is a useful tool also for the western feminist. It enables the position of subjectivity against the ethnic other woman. As the western feminist appropriates the position of the protector, she or he enforces another line of exclusion. This time it is not the women within the nation (of western feminism) but "other" women. Following the masculinist logic of protection and subjectivity it provides, this logic may also explain why the western feminist projects have been so successful, since it does not present a fundamental challenge to the grounds of western nation building. Instead it can be seen as a project which confirm-structures the binary logic, which objectifies and silences the other.

The warrior hero/western feminist does not represent aggressive masculinity, but instead it can be seen representing self-sacrificing, chivalrous masculinity. The chivalrous masculinity is different from the masculinity of the aggressor/sexual predator. Even if it does not represent the aggressive masculinity, which the feminists see as a problem, it does not change the logic of the protected being subordinate to the protector. The protected is nevertheless denied agency and is silenced, for it is only natural that she or he will submit to the protector's wishes in return for the protection that the chivalrous protector provides (Young 2003). Before continuing this discussion on chivalrous masculinity and its implication on the objectification of the protected, I want to show that the collective of the protected (women and children) is not in practice without agency and is not a coherent unit. The argument is not that women as a coherent unity are denied agency, objectified and oppressed, but that the inherent masculinism/feminism divide of protection determines which forms of agency are valued and, in turn, are visible in international relations.

Feminist writers in IR have shown that women's role in conflicts and wars is not simply the passive role of resources to be protected. Women actually take on a number of roles. Feminists have pointed out how women have been involved as soldiers and freedom fighters in a number of wars (Enloe 1993, 2004). Not only do women engage in battle and fight for their nation but they take part in conflicts also as camp followers: as cooks, caretakers, and nurses for the men in battle; also as prostitutes serving the soldiers in military bases. Feminists have also shown the importance of women's role after the conflict has ended and the peace treaty signed. For women the conflict is not over when the fighting ceases. Indeed, this is the time when the role of women becomes even more crucial. Women are urged to return home, have children, and give up their jobs for the men returning home. Women's position involves reviving the nation again, taking care of the wounded as well as repairing and rebuilding (Enloe 1993, 2004; Steans 1998). Therefore, even if women are constructed as the category of the protected, in practice the gendered forms of agency are more complex.

Similarly, when the object of protection is the foreign prostitute presented as the victim of prostitution, it does not mean that she is simply a passive victim and has no capacity or agency of her own. However, as long as women are constructed as the category to be protected and belonging to the private sphere and indeed constituting the nation this has direct and often terrible consequences to actual women in conflict zones.

Since women have been assigned the role of representing the nation and its purity, women are also the object of battle. Thus, "war rape" is an effective form of war. By raping the women, the enemy is violating the nation, spoiling the men's property and also the purity of the nation. However, rape is problematic, for it is usually seen as a crime that takes place in private (Höglund 2003). War rape is not a novel strategy, but recently it has gained more attention as a war crime than before. Höglund (2003) explains that this is because war rape in former Yugoslavia affected women in such large numbers that this raised attention. The other interpretation is that it is because the raping of the women was so closely connected to ethnic cleansing that it stirred up attention and reactions.

The commonality of war rape in recent conflicts as a part of normal warfare can be seen as a clear example of the gender-specific violence and threats that are connected to the construction of security along public-private and protector-protected divides. Therefore, the specific vulnerability of women in conflict situations cannot be overlooked. Yet, it is just as important to also acknowledge women as "actors" in conflict situations, and not only as the violated, oppressed victims.

I want to emphasize here that these masculine and feminine positions are not essentially positions that are always taken respectively by men and women. In the above discussion I have shown the concern of feminists in IR in revealing women's role in the masculine sphere in combat and war. In the same way it has to be stressed that there are men who also welcome chivalrous protection, and who, even though they embody the male sex, are objectified as the protected within the private sphere of the nation. In other words the feminine and subordinate position can be embodied by both genders, but that does not overcome the masculinist logic of protection.

But there is also something else happening. The chivalrous and masculine protector derives its agency on the grounds that there are threats to the security of those in need of protection. The protector is ready to sacrifice himself in order to ensure the protection, but in order to establish this position the category of the threat must be first created and then maintained. Young (2003) explains that the binary opposite that enables the existence of the chivalrous masculine protector is the category of the aggressive masculinity. It is these unpredictable masculine subjects from whom the home or the nation must be protected. Evil aggressors threaten the safety of women, men, and children and the loving self-sacrificing protector is ready to face them. The existence of the chivalrous masculine protector is grounded on the maintenance of its binary opposite masculinity, the unpredictable, aggressive, and evil masculinity.

Young (2003) explains how this chivalrous masculinity has been very seductive for feminists in the US. After all, the objective is to protect and also save women and children who are threatened by unpredictable aggressive male predators, the terrorists, the oppressive and violent men. For example, the rhetoric of protecting women has been used to ensure support and legitimize the use of force in the war against terrorism (MIT 2005). Attention to the violence against women and violations against women's human rights under the Taliban regime were used as a way to legitimize the war against terrorism and the use of preemptive strikes. Human rights violations and the position of women in Iraq have also been used as a way to legitimize the war in Iraq. Feminists in most cases have not had any trouble with this. Still, the protection operates according to the logic of masculinism and the binary opposition between the protector and the protected. The position of the protected is always one that is passive, one that is silenced. The position of the protected is one of gratitude for the protection she is granted. The women in Afghanistan should have been grateful that they were about to be saved. However, no one was concerned whether these women wanted to be saved by bombing their homes.

I want to emphasize along the lines of Young that it is indeed also the western feminists who take on the position of masculinist, self-sacrificing protector and therefore also objectify the "other" women that they want to save and protect. In this way feminist projects can also operate as a means of silencing and objectifying the other. Western feminists have been criticized for representing third world women as a unified category (Mohanty 1994). Third World women are often depicted as passive and oppressed victims. They may even become the icons of suffering in times of conflict and war, the designated weepers (Sylvester 1994), or the veiled and oppressed, silenced women of Afghanistan (Höglund 2003). Indeed, the same women whose aim was to raise awareness of their suffering render these women mute. What I want stress is that the representation of these women as victims is a means by which the white western feminist ensures her or his own subjectivity. It is what finally enables these women to take on the privileged position of protector. Therefore, the category of the victims needs also to be maintained.

But I want to argue that there is also more at stake. It is not only that there is the unfortunate outcome that the feminists (or George W. Bush and his wife Laura) who mean well end up objectifying the very people they wanted to save (and maybe even empower?). My argument is that by maintaining the category of the suffering victims, the protector, whether male or female, establishes herself or himself as a subject. Therefore the others, whether they are Afghan women, women in the Third World in general, or trafficked prostitutes from Russia to Finland, cannot be saved and empowered according to this logic. They must be kept vulnerable and represented as victims. For if there were no victims, then whom could the western feminist go out to save, or who could the masculine chivalrous protector protect? The category of the vulnerable must be maintained in order for the subject as savior to exist. Hence, I want to raise the question whether, in the project of saving and protecting others the western feminist is only trying to protect herself and ensure her own existence as a subject. In this context I want to ask once more, who is the subject that is to be secured?

Becoming a Subject of Security: Establishing the Position of a White Western Feminist

When prostitution is looked at in the context of globalization and bio-power, the focus changes beyond the debate over whether prostitution is violence against all women, a factor that prevents equality between the sexes, or someone's individual right. This is the argument that I have brought into the Finnish debate concerning prostitution and trafficking. In my PhD thesis (Penttinen 2004) I argued that prostitution is a corporeal consequence of globalization. Therefore, also in measures toward prostitution the aspect of globalization needs to be taken into consideration as to how it conditions the forms the sex industry takes in Finland. This approach has been directed as an alternative to the simplified positions of either being for criminalizing the demand or seeing sex work as an expression of an individual's right. Therefore, I have also wanted to present a counterhegemonic debate to the dominating discourse on the criminalization of buying sexual services.

I have argued that globalization can be seen to operate as a system of Foucauldian bio-power that produces embodied subjectivity. Following Foucault one can see how globalization is inscribed on bodies and how individuals adjust to the bio-power of globalization by incorporating the logic of globalization of the world economy. However, the produced subjectivities are not gender neutral, instead they are very much sex-specific and also ethnicized. In other words globalization produces different forms of agency depending on one's gender and ethnicity. These embodied positions of subjectivity of clients and prostitutes manifest especially in shadow globalization, which is not the opposite of globalization but its underside. This approach to prostitution presents an alternative to the sides presented in the Finnish political debate on whether buying of sexual services should be criminalized. However, holding such a "third" position has been very difficult, if not impossible. The sides in the debate have been clear-cut and constricted; there has been no middle ground. If one opposes criminalization, then she supports prostitution. Or, if one claims to be a feminist, she is included in the abolitionist camp.

As an alternative to the representation of prostitute-client interaction, these positions can be seen as expressions of new kinds of agency and subjectivity that emerge at global conjunctures (Penttinen 2004). They are the result of complex global flows that form what Appadurai (1996) names as landscapes of globalization. In this context abolitionist discourse in Finland is troubling, and I want to raise the question whether the positions of the male client and Finnish feminists are that far from each other. The closeness of the two derives from the western client or feminist being fundamentally different from the "subjectivity" of the ethnic other prostitute. The women in prostitution in the contemporary world are most often of other ethnicities than the clients they serve. The global sex industry not only benefits from this difference but also constructs it by representing the women in prostitution as exotic and erotic others to the western male clients. The new forms of subjectivity that globalization produces manifest themselves in the prostitute-client relationship in Finland. The client represents this new form of agency in the form of new possibilities for consumption and leisure. The Finnish or western feminist is similarly formed as a response to the client-prostitute relationship. But, whereas the client, or the western feminist, exists in the domain of subjects of globalization the prostitute or the trafficked woman exists in and is constrained to be within shadow globalization. For her, globalization manifests as corporeal constraints and necessity to travel or be trafficked to other countries to engage in sex work. Whereas the client/western feminist moves through landscapes of globalization taking advantage of new opportunities of travel, and global flows of information and money and enacts her or his subjectivity in the public sphere, the post-Soviet prostitute moves and is moved in shadow sexscapes of globalization. She has to remain out of sight, in fear of being deported. Yet, this constrained position of the woman in prostitution constructed as the erotic exotic other in the global sex industry needs also to be maintained as exactly that "ethnic other," for it enables the establishment of the truly masculine and western subject, the client. However, presentation of the Russian woman as an ethnic other and as a victim of traffickers is also what enables the western feminist subjectivity as someone who can speak on behalf of the victimized women. Presenting the Russian woman as a victim enables the western feminist to embody the position of a protector.

Instead of being simply the victim of traffickers, the position of the erotic exotic Russian woman, named in Finland as an "Eastern girl," has become a site which someone who is both a woman and from the East can appropriate (Penttinen 2004). It is a product of western imagination. The enactment of the position of the "Eastern girl" is a means to adjust and adapt to the rugged landscape and fitness tests posed by globalization of the world economy. The erotic other is formed as a body that listens, a body that is silent that cannot reveal anything of herself (Irigaray 1985). She is the truly feminine woman, and the male client is also formed as a coherent subject as he can gaze at himself in her. But she forms also the western feminist as a coherent subject, for she represents ethnic and also sexualized otherness to her. The position of the "Eastern girl" is necessarily silenced, objectified, and constrained. It is someone like her that the western feminist needs to create and maintain as a victim in order to establish her own subjectivity as a savior.

Following Foucault's theories of power and subject (Foucault 1983) Butler (1997) discusses how individuals turn themselves into subjects. Butler explains that subjectivization takes place through the eclipse of subjection. The individual subjects to power, and in turn is recognized as a subject and given agency. Therefore, the power that acts on the subjects seems as the subject's own enactment. The acting of power is a form of enacting, it enacts the subject into being. However, this operation of power is never complete; the enactment of the incorporated subject position can be done well or poorly, but it has to be done over and continuously repeated and reiterated. In this reiteration of subjectivization lies also the possibility to break from the power that has produced the subject to new forms and different variations of that subjectivity. What is important in the subjectivization process is that it requires the other, the socially dead, or the abject bodies that are not recognized as subjects. In seeing the socially dead, an individual desires to become a subject, although it first involves subordination and subjecting the abject to power (Butler 1997). In this way an individual is turned into a subject.

This position of the abject is a disorderly and improper body, against which the subject is formed. These abject bodies—such as prostitutes, homosexuals, and AIDS patients—represent the risk of death for the subject (Butler 1993: 3, 1997). The abject is also a category that enables the existence of the subject and thus it is continuously maintained and reconstructed in the process of subjectivization. The established subjects must maintain the category of the abject in order to ensure their own recognition. Although the concept of the abject is derived and refers to dirt that falls off the body, following Butler I want to emphasize the concept of the abject as an analogy referring to social others. But, what is important here is that the abject, as it is derived from the dirt that has fallen off the subject, means that the abject has once belonged to the subject. The abject is the necessary other against which subjectivity and agency are enacted. In the abject the subject sees who she is not, but who she could become if she would not reiterate the position of subjectivity and in turn maintain the category of the abject or socially dead.

In this context the abject really cannot be saved or empowered, for then she could no longer be categorized as the socially dead against which the subjectivity of the client or the feminist protector is formed. The feminist could no longer enact her or his own subjectivity in relation to Russian woman; otherwise, she would have to imagine new ethnic others to be saved from sexual predators and other male aggressors. Even if there would be certain categories of the abjects such as the homosexuals, which Butler explains, were empowered and would gain the status of subjectivity and social recognition, new categories of abjection would have to be formed in order for the subjectivization to take place.

The feminists who form the anti-trafficking movement in Finland want to struggle, obviously, against trafficking in women, organized prostitution, and sexual slavery of women and girls. As the sexualized violence that trafficked women are subjected to is well known, who could object to such a project? However, it is not emphasized enough that the dominating anti-trafficking projects in Finland and globally are based on a specific abolitionist discourse. Instead, this discourse has become normalized as it has formed the hegemonic discourse among feminists, government officials, and legislators. The fact that prostitutes are categorically illustrated as innocent victims who are exploited and who suffer at the hands of traffickers has not been objected to strongly. Instead, they are represented as women and girls who are deceived and lured into prostitution and forced into sexual slavery, thus strengthening the argument that they must be saved. After all, who could object to rescuing innocent victims from whom else but sexual predators! This binary reveals that the discourse on criminalizing the demand operates according to the logic of masculinist protection and thus follows the hegemonic security concept in which the protected are placed in the category of silenced objects. They should be grateful for the protection they receive, although their agency and possibility for subjectivity is denied in return.

My argument is that the actual means by which the feminist projects in Finland aim to save women from prostitution are questionable when the situation of the women in prostitution is taken into consideration. To me, it is clear that the objective of these anti-trafficking feminists is not to empower the trafficked women. They are instead represented continuously as victims of not only traffickers but of gender inequality. They are silenced and objectified even further, and the forms of agency that these women take, within their obviously difficult situation, cannot be seen.

The emphasis has been placed on the prevention of prostitution. Criminalizing the buying of sexual services would send a strong message that women cannot be bought, but it is also believed that it would reduce the demand for commercial sex. Many make the claim that this is exactly what happened in Sweden, as it seems that there are currently fewer (foreign) prostitutes "working" than before the criminalization of buying. It seems that there are fewer Russian women coming to Sweden; it is no longer an attractive country for the traffickers. However, this outcome is highly misleading. Obviously, the preventive legislation does not in any way erase the reasons that lead the women into prostitution, neither can it undo the established connections with the Russian women and their traffickers. The women are just brought to a different place to work, and they still have to pay the debts to the traffickers, whether they can work in the destination country or not. Also, the clients are also on the move. After the criminalization of buying had been passed in Sweden, the Swedish clients came over to Finland to find prostitutes. In fact, organized prostitution in Keminmaa, which is next to the Swedish border in northern Finland, was directed to Swedish clients (Penttinen 2004). But the legislation is directed at the future, not so much to the current situation. The idea is to send a strong message so that future generations will not become buyers or sellers of sexual services. This, of course, is an important goal in many respects, and it strives for gender equality in the future. However, it leads me to question again whom these white western feminists are trying to protect.

It is surprising that the anti-trafficking feminists do not listen to the Central Criminal Police who believe that such legislation as discussed above would also increase the control of the organized criminals over the women who are currently in prostitution. It would be more difficult for the women to solicit the clients in public, and they would need more "help" in getting the clients and in ensuring the safety of the clients. This entails that prostitution would most likely go underground even further, and it might be a risk for the women to take advantage of support services that are directed toward them. The police have criticized this type of legislation also by saying that it would most likely be ineffective, for they do not have the resources to go out and seek the clients just to fine them on the grounds of buying sexual services. The police in Finland do take the issue of organized prostitution and trafficking seriously. Instead of going after the clients, they want to use their resources to go after the real "bad guys" that is the crime syndicates behind most of the Finnish prostitution scene.

One can ask, then, what is the intention of the western feminist when she cooks up such wonderful projects by which she aims to save the other women? Her intention may be genuine, that she honestly believes that she wants to save the other women. However, with saving them in this manner she does not empower the women she wants to save but indeed objectifies and silences them even further. She pushes them into being even more strongly under the control of the traffickers, makes it even more difficult for the women to pay debts to traffickers, and also gives clients relatively more power over them. I am not saying that these women should not be helped. I want simply to raise the question of whether the act of criminalizing the demand at this particular moment in time is the appropriate way to provide help. My argument is that criminalizing buyers is a peculiar way to protect the women in prostitution and save them from violence. Finnish feminists cannot truly claim that the prostitutes will feel safer and more empowered after such legislation would be passed. Then is it really that Finnish anti-trafficking feminists want to save the other women, or do they aim to establish themselves as subjects by appropriating the position of a self-sacrificing savior? The western feminist in her quest to abolish and prevent prostitution by criminalizing the demand takes on the position of the chivalrous masculinist protector and reiterates the binary opposition of protector and protected. Therefore, the outcome is not to save the women currently in prostitution after all, but indeed keep the women down and as vulnerable as possible. For if the ethnic other women were not vulnerable, passive victims, who else would there be to save?

In the end it seems that the only one the Finnish feminist wants to secure is herself.

Conclusion: the Russian Woman Insecured by Feminist Projects of Security

The discourse on the criminalization of buying of sexual services in Finland was able to become a hegemonic discourse, since this initiative was tied with the initiative to include human trafficking in the legislation. Criminalizing human trafficking and including harder sentences for the procuring of prostitution was based on public consent (Fontana, Ch. 2). As there was consent in this issue, the tying of criminalization of demand was difficult to oppose. The legislators, government, and feminists were able to form an alliance, in which opposing views become stigmatized as in favor of prostitution and male members of parliament as possible users. Therefore, the criminalization of buying was confirmed-structured (Haugaard, Ch. 3). At the last minute the criminalization of buyers was withdrawn, since the minister of Justice Johannes Koskinen wanted more information on the effects of such legislation (Heikka 2005). However, the legislation on criminalization of demand will be brought up in November 2005 and will most likely then be passed. So far it has not even been opened to public debate, but it will be passed quietly and without strong objection. This shows how the criminalization of demand discourse has become a hegemonic discourse. A postponement of the initiative does not hurt or weaken it; on the contrary, it becomes only stronger, since the issue becomes in a sense "old news," and it does not receive as much attention in the media.

What was at stake that enabled the abolitionist discourse to become hegemonic was that it followed the binary logic of the hegemonic security concept. As there was an alliance and consent in Finland about trafficking legislation, the abolitionists or western feminists were able to embody the position of the protector. However, what they were trying to protect with the type of measures they were presenting was slightly unclear. The objective was of course to prevent prostitution, send a clear moral message, and enable equality of the sexes to take place. It just seems that the Russian women in prostitution were not included in this "equality between the sexes plan"; instead, it was quite the opposite.

When we talk about security what is at stake most of all is subjectivity and agency. In talking about security, also, the subject of security is constructed, that is the subject that is to be secured. Subjectivity and agency are especially the positions of the one who secures, and the secured is the object of securing and hence also passive. This protector and protected divide correlates with the masculine-feminine binary, in which the previous term is always privileged above the other. The feminist scholars in IR have been raising awareness of gender security, and how women's security is often overlooked (Young 2004, Enloe 2004). As women are seen belonging to the private and to the realm of the protected, they are not only objectified as a passive category but their forms of agency go unseen. Similarly, in the abolitionist discourse as it presents women in prostitution as categorically the victims of prostitution, the forms of agency of the Russian women cannot be seen (Central Women's Union in Finland 2005). The way in which they cope with difficult conditions, adjust to the rugged landscapes and fitness tests of globalization by being involved in the dangerous, and risky business of prostitution goes without acknowledgment. The needs of these women are not addressed or cared for. They are not empowered, and their voices are not heard.

I do acknowledge that, for example, the Coalition Against Trafficking in Women operates in many countries, offers shelter, and tries to bring women into witness protection programs. In Finland as well there is discussion on the possibilities of helping the victims of traffickers, and this involves considering trafficking as grounds for a residence permit (Coalition Against Trafficking in Women 2005; Kvinnoforum 2005). However, this initiative is also highly problematic, since suspicion of selling sexual services, or having false papers, is grounds for deportation at the border. It is then up to the Border Guard authorities in Finland to decide who needs protection from traffickers in the form of a residence permit and who should be deported.[3] Again I am not convinced that this will work for the benefit of the women in prostitution.

The white western feminist projects of saving other women are grounded in the masculinist logic of protection, whether the objects of saving were the women in Afghanistan oppressed under the Taliban regime, women in Iraq suffering from human rights violations, or the Russian prostitutes being trafficked to Finland, Sweden or Norway. I do not want to imply that the feminist political projects are all wrong and ineffective. Indeed, feminist projects are necessary. Gender equality

is definitely a worthwhile goal to struggle for. In terms of combat against trafficking in women, the introduction of victim protection programs, shelters and residence permits for women involved do make sense and are necessary if the target of
struggle is organized crime. It is also necessary that white western feminists' projects are given media attention and also gain consent in the public, since the objective is gender equality and universalization of human rights. However, these projects should also be subjected to close examination in terms of power and hegemony involved. These issues have been raised by feminist IR scholars who have
been ready to discuss feminist political projects critically and to address the dichotomies between gender and ethnicity. In addition, Burke (2002) has promoted a
discussion on the concept of security and a feminist proposal for comprehensive
security. However, the projects I have examined seem to reinforce rather than
overcome the problems addressed.

As Young (2003) explains, the masculinist logic of protection is always subordinating and silencing. It depends on the construction of two forms of
masculinisms that are used to balance each other. The chivalrous, self-sacrificing
masculinity is constructed as the other of the aggressive, predatory masculinity that
threatens women and children. Both these forms of masculinity are derived from
Hobbes's framework of the state of nature. The chivalrous masculinity seems
better than aggressive masculinity, since it is established as a sacrifice to protect
the other. However, it is still in the same way a form of domination. In order to
gain protection the "woman" that is protected must give up something. It is always
a form of bargaining. And what needs to be given up is agency and subjectivity.
This seems almost natural, that in order to gain the security that the protector is
willing to provide, the protected submits to the will of the protector in gratitude.
She will then ensure her own bit in the relationship and obey the protectors' wishes
in order for the protector to carry out his task. Therefore, the Russian prostitute
should also be happy to be categorized as a victim, for this puts her in the position
of the protected.

As I have already stated many times that what is at stake in providing security
is subjectivity and agency. In order to have subjectivity and agency the protector
not only needs the threat from which she tries to protect the objects of protection.
The protector in this case also needs the category of the protected that is necessarily silenced and subjected by the protection. The subjectivity and following agency
of the protector is derived from creating and maintaining this category. If there
were no one to save, there is no point in enacting a position of a savior. Why would
the chivalrous masculine protector sacrifice herself if there were no one to sacrifice
oneself for?

According to this argument, it does not make sense to save or empower the
abjects and thus grant them agency, for this would threaten the coherence of the
subjectivity of the self-sacrificing feminist. Quite the opposite, it makes sense
rather to keep the other women that the feminists want to save as vulnerable as
possible. This is done by labeling a woman in prostitution categorically as a victim
and by introducing legislation that seriously makes her position as a prostitute even
more vulnerable to traffickers and procurers. Maintaining the ethnic other women

in an objectified and silenced position, therefore, secures the position of the white western feminist protector. The only thing that these feminists have forgotten has been to question critically whether the trafficked women and women from Afghanistan or Iraq want to be saved on these terms. According to the logic of masculinist protection it does not make sense to ask or see what the protected women think about the strategies of protection they are subjected to. The protected could not speak or even be heard as the protector-protected binary constructs them as silenced and passive victims. Asking, listening, and seeing what the protected need or want would disrupt the subjectivity of the protector and her or his position of domination, as it would imply that the protector does not know what is best for the protected. This does not go well with western projects.

Then, whom are they really trying to save, these women and men who mean so well? And whose discourse of chivalrous protecting is so appealing that it gains popular consent and thus becomes hegemonic? In the end it seems that these feminists in the protector position are more concerned with their own safety, security of their own nation, the nation of western-feminism and the nation of western subjectivity, and maintaining these boundaries that are threatened by terrorists, organized criminals, or immoral women who prostitute. Using a discourse of saving, or securing the other is a means to disguise the project of maintaining and enacting western subjectivity. Objectifying and silencing the other seems then an act of benevolence, although when it comes right down to it, it has nothing to do with helping the vulnerable groups of women (or men) in their struggles in the current deterritorialized world but only about ensuring the continuity of western subjectivity.

Notes

1. A critical comment on the underlying logic behind the legislation on the criminalization of buying sexual services is presented in Arthur Gould (2002).

2. The white-western feminist is also strongly problematized by Arab and Arab-American feminists in the special issue on Gender Nation and Belonging of the MIT Electronic journal of Middle East studies Vol 5 Spring 2005. In the various articles of this issue the white-western feminists are criticized to be silencing the Arab women who are presented simply as victims of oppression in patriarchal societies and portrayed in these simplified terms and therefore the forms of agency and difference among Arab women are not acknowledged.

3. Discussion during a Roundtable "Toward an agenda for action against human trafficking. Preventive means and victim protection." 23. 9. 2005. Dr. Janice Raymond discussed the work of CATW. The roundtable was organized within the framework of the Estonian-Finnish project between NGO's Living for Tomorrow and Unioni Naisasialiitto Suomessa Ry:N (Women's Union in Finland).

Chapter 8

A Critical Naturalist Approach to Power and Hegemony: Analyzing Giving Practices*

Tomohisa Hattori

At the core of debates over power and hegemony are philosophical questions regarding what exists, what we know and how we know it, and what constitutes evidence for scientific knowledge. By applying the critical naturalist version of the realist philosophy of science to these debates, this chapter prioritizes ontology over epistemology and methodology in conceptualizing power. A critical naturalist approach shares with other forms of naturalism the principle of the fundamental unity of natural and social sciences and, thus, the common objective of discovering the underlying causal mechanisms behind natural and social phenomena. Accordingly, this chapter endeavors to anchor the concept of power to a structurally based notion of causation. Following the insight of Bhaskar, the philosopher most associated with this approach, this chapter recognizes a key distinction between intransitive and transitive dimensions of knowledge: that is, between the object of scientific knowledge as it exists independently of scientists and the actually existing scientific knowledge as constructed by scientists at a particular time and place. By way of contrast, the constructivist approach relies heavily on the transitive dimension of knowledge (e.g., Bourdieu discussed below in this chapter and Haugaard's chapter in this volume). A Marxist approach, on the other hand, relies heavily on the intransitive dimension of knowledge (e.g., Gramsci discussed below in this chapter and Fontana's chapter in this volume). Critical naturalism provides a counterbalance to these two approaches, presenting an alternative post-positivist approach that is premised on both the contested nature of knowledge and the independence of the reality (including power as part of it) from human knowledge.

To elaborate briefly on this philosophy of social science, critical naturalism rejects the atomist ontology of positivism and shares with poststructuralism, constructivism, and Marxism the premise that social reality is inherently relational. It also affirms the Marxist insight that social reality is not encompassed in knowledge broadly conceived but rather exists independently of it. Beyond these ontological premises, a critical naturalist approach regards reality as layered. That is to say that the same phenomenon can be analyzed by different scientists as relations among a neutron, a proton, and an electron, among molecules, or among cells. Physicists, chemists, and biologists each examine a distinct layer of reality, which, in turn, is explained by underlying causal mechanisms connected to the other layers. The reality of a particular phenomenon in this sense is deeper than physicists or chemists alone can explain. Because reality is ontologically deep and open to many causal mechanisms, the constant conjunctions between events emphasized by positivists, while often providing a clue for further research, explain nothing in themselves; skepticism is the wisest methodological stance. Discovering the truth about reality, while difficult, is nonetheless achievable. This puts a critical naturalist approach at odds with Foucault's poststructuralist view of truth as a relative concept. It also diverges from Bourdieu's constructivism, which distinguishes social science from natural science due to the limits to naturalism in social science (Bourdieu et al 1991).[1] Critical naturalism, in short, argues for both the existence of the real apart from science and the possibility of the fundamental unity of natural and social sciences (Bhaskar 1989). Finally, whereas most Marxists agree with this approach, they tend to reduce all social relations to relations of production, a claim that critical naturalists are not ready to make. The disagreement here is not philosophical but empirical.

Critical naturalists entered the power debates relatively recently (Isaac 1987). Past debates on power in political science have been grounded in the philosophical commitment to positivism, that is, logical deductivism and a Humean notion of causation based on the constant conjunction of events as constitutive of the practices of both natural and social sciences. Beginning with the debate between Mills' (1956) notion of a "power elite" and Dahl's (1957) concept of A's "power over" B to do what B would not otherwise do, debates over power often focused less on what power is than on the empirical and methodological problems of demonstrating and measuring the effect of power (Dahl 1958).[2] Responding to Dahl's criticism, defenders of Mills' approach produced empirical studies of interlocking memberships in corporate boards of directors to substantiate the existence of a "power elite" (Domhoff 1968, 1978; Mintz and Schwartz 1985; Useem 1983). Likewise, in a debate with Bachrach and Baratz (1962, 1963, 1970), who developed the second face of power that highlighted the significance of nondecision and agenda-setting, the methodological concerns of Polsby, Dahl's student, set the critical tone: "How to study this second face of power? To what manifestations of social reality might the mobilization of bias refer? Are phenomena of this sort in principle amenable to empirical investigation?" (Polsby 1980: 190).[3] Lukes' further elaboration, "a third face of power" based on the objective interests of an agent (1974), was defended by an extensive empirical documentation of its use and operation to counter such methodological criticisms (Gaventa 1980).

The poststructuralist notion of power developed by Foucault radically shifted the terms of the power debates by destabilizing the authority of positivist knowledge and relativizing the positivist claim to truth. Power, for Foucault, takes the form of discursive knowledge institutionalized as the authority of expertise. Rather than the empirical effects of power, Foucault (1975; 1988; 1979) focused on how experts produce and use this knowledge across a wide range of medical, psychiatric, and penitentiary institutions, identifying the production and use of knowledge as a deployment of power through authorized and authenticated interpretations of reality. The truth so produced, he argued, is at once knowledge *and* power (Foucault 1970: xxi-xxiii).[4] Applications of Foucault's conception of "power/knowledge" have focused on the discursive analysis of expert knowledge as a political instrument, such as Ferguson's (1990) study of how the World Bank economists constructed knowledge about Lesotho's economy depoliticized a very political process involved in their advice on economic development plans.[5]

Bourdieu's critical contribution to the power debates builds on Foucault's skepticism about knowledge construction and use with the concept of symbolic power. This concept allows Bourdieu to detect and construct objective power relations that are not immediately apparent. Symbolic power is a gentle, sometimes invisible, form of power that is "disguised" and "euphemized" (Bourdieu 1977: 191). He reminds us that it is "an aspect of most forms of power" that "presupposes a kind of active complicity" (Thompson 1991: 23), as, for example, when an employee laughs at her boss's joke even when the joke is not funny. This laugh becomes a symbolic indicator of the existence of an objective social relation. While distinct from a spontaneous laugh, it is not generally recognized as the operation of power because it is premised on habitus, or a set of acquired traits or dispositions (in this case, subservient and deferential traits as an employee) that internalize the objective relation and thus produce this type of response (Bourdieu 1977: 72).[6] Bourdieu uses this type of analysis to approach objective social relations. In the above case, for example, he would start with an analysis of the subjective experience of the existing social order (e.g., the subordinate's laugh) which misrecognizes real power relations as self-evident, taken for granted, and undisputed. The subjective experience of the social world which, in this view, emerges as what it has always been and what it should be—a doxic experience—is characterized by a correspondence between a social division between the boss (actively giving an order) and the employee (passively taking his order) and a symbolic division between the active joke-giver (the witty one) and the passive joke-recipient (the less witty) (Bourdieu 1977: 222, note 27). The subjective experience of laughing at a boss's joke helps misrecognize the real distinction between ortho-doxy (my boss is funny) and hetero-doxy (my boss is not really funny) (Bourdieu 1977: 168). In the process, the objective fact that she laughed at her boss' joke because he is her boss is masked. The task of Bourdieu's sociology is to detect and postulate the real objective relation that is masked behind this experience: "the real does not exist before or outside science" (Bourdieu et al 1991: 84). It is science that constructs the real.

In contrast, Gramsci's analysis of power, based on Marx's anti-positivist philosophy of social science, is firmly grounded in the real, or the internal social relation which constitutes the identities, interests, and capabilities of individuals (Bhaskar 1989: 42-3; Ollman 1993).[7] The key internal relation for Gramsci, following Marx, is the social-property relations between the owners and nonowners of the means of production, which can be found in wage relations between workers and employers, as well as in commodity relations between producers and expropriators of the product of cooperative production. Together, as a geohistorically specific set of relations of production, they constitute the capitalist mode of production, a social structure. For Gramsci as well as other Marxists, relations of production constitute various power relations in capitalist society. Gramsci's contribution to the power debates is to characterize how power is used politically in capitalist society as the dialectic of coercion and consent: "hegemony" (Fontana 1993: 2-3). Distinguishing capitalist power relations from power relations in precapitalist societies, Gramsci recognized the significance of "hegemonic projects" in which a capitalist class or its subgroup establishes their moral or intellectual leadership over other capitalist subgroups or other classes, thus inducing society-wide consent (Gill 1990). Gramsci's concept of hegemony, in other words, was not designed for a causal analysis of the conditions for a social phenomenon but for the role of specific activities in maintaining relations of production (i.e., hegemony) or inspiring efforts to overthrow such relations (i.e., counterhegemony).[8] It is a concept, in short, that already knows how causal power operates through internal relations (i.e., relations of production).

This chapter applies a critical naturalist approach to questions of power and hegemony in a particular practice whose analyses have been vexed: bilateral, multilateral, and nongovernmental foreign aid, which I reconceptualize for this purpose as a form of giving. Most scholarship on foreign aid has been carried out by foreign policy scholars and practitioners whose primary concern has not been the causes of foreign aid but its effectiveness in achieving the donors' objectives. As a result, past studies have correlated foreign aid with its impact, such as strengthening alliance between donor and recipient (Zunes 1996), encouraging exports, economic growth, and peace (Arvin 1997; Nyoni 1998; Boyce and Pastor 1998), and promoting democracy or a strong state (Knack 2004; Frisch and Hofnung 1997). These studies often characterize foreign aid as beneficial when the donors' objectives were achieved.[9] I start with Baldwin's classic synthesis of Dahl's positivist notion of coercive power with the positivist analytical framework of social exchange where foreign aid can also be understood as mutually beneficial. This positivist approach, however, fails to explain a striking correspondence between donor-recipient relations and creditor-debtor relations and allows for the introduction of two anti-positivist approaches. Bourdieu's notion of symbolic power is used to approach the specific case of bilateral grant aid as a means of euphemizing material power relations. This approach demonstrates the utility of symbolic power as a means of detecting the operation of power in giving practices that goes beyond the appearance of mutual gains and cooperation. The case of multilateral and nongovernmental grant aid is approached as what Gramsci called a hegemonic project. Both the Bourdieuian and the Gramscian analyses demonstrate the symbolic dimension of social reality, or how the social construction of a symbolic experience can naturalize and legitimize objective social relations. Through these analyses, this chapter highlights the significance of an ontologically based conception of power. The conclusion discusses the ethical implications of the critical naturalist approach to power, including the ethical significance of the distance between science and policy advice, the causal responsibility beyond human and corporate agency, the ethical role of scientific truth, and the possibility of ethical naturalism.

The Exchange Approach: Influence and Mutual Gains

Baldwin is an early pioneer in the study of foreign aid as an instrument of foreign policy (1966a; 1966b; 1985: 290-335). He is most widely known for having integrated the conceptual issue of power into the existing exchange approach of Homans (1961) and Blau (1964), resulting in a conception that is both coercive and consensual, conflictual and cooperative (Baldwin 1989). This intellectual synthesis should be understood in the context of the predominance of neoclassical economics and the behaviorist approach to social science in the United States in the 1950s and 1960s. According to Homans, a key pioneer of the social exchange approach, although social behavior is different from genetically prefigured behavior, it can be analytically reduced to an actual exchange of activity between persons (1961: 13). Key variables in social exchange, as in market exchange, are value and quantity exchanged (1961: 36-49). This allowed Homans to quantify influence as a function of the indebtedness of one party to the other for goods or services they cannot obtain by themselves (1961: 83-111, 283-315). The key achievement of Baldwin was to integrate Dahl's coercive concept of power into an analytical framework that emphasizes mutual gains and cooperation. By extending the exchange analysis of influence to interstate relations that had been characterized primarily by the coercive notion of power, Baldwin was able to analyze both the coercive and consensual dimensions of policy instruments, such as (dis)information, diplomatic deals, or weapons that recipient states may not be able to obtain (Baldwin 1985: 13-4).

What allowed Baldwin to combine the exchange approach with Dahl's concept of power is the philosophical compatibility in the conception of the relation in both theories. Distinct from the notion of internal relations that Marx and Gramsci used, exchanges are relations between autonomous agents, who are considered ontologically prior to the institutions in which they assume positions and roles (Baldwin 1989: 16-8; Homans 1961: 56). Exchanges, therefore, can be understood as external relations, wherein the powers, interests, and identities of agents are exogenously given (Barnett and Duvall 2005: 45-7). As such, this approach was particularly suited to the question of how countries use foreign policy instruments such as foreign aid to get recipient countries to do what they would not otherwise do.[10] In the process, Baldwin overcame a key weakness of attempts to apply neoclassical economics to politics: the tendency to depoliticize the power dimension of exchange

(1978; 1989: 10-44).

Baldwin's synthesis resulted in a conception of power that is, on the surface, compatible with Bourdieu or Gramsci: both coercive and consensual, conflictual and cooperative (Baldwin 1978: 1235, footnote 10 in 1235, 1239-41; Leng 1998). However, this appearance is misleading because the very different philosophical premises lead to different characterizations of the use of power. For Baldwin, as for Homans, only individual agents are real. This conception of the real, in which individuals are given abstractly, that is, independently of their relations to others in society, is ontologically individualist (Collier 1994: 70-6; Lukes 1973: 73-8).[11] Indeed, Baldwin (1978: 1239) regards both the Hobbesian and the Lockean social contract between an abstract individual and another abstract agent, the state, as forms of social exchange, despite the fundamentally unequal power relation and the reality of state coercion just beneath the surface.

This ontological premise is supported by epistemological individualism, which locates the source and nature of knowledge within the individual or corporate agent. The form of epistemological individualism that Homans and Baldwin use is empiricism: the experience of agents is the basis of knowledge about social behavior. In this view, each person's experience can be understood without reference to another's (Collier 1994: 70-6; Lukes 1973: 107-9). In a somewhat extreme manner, Homans believed that stripping factors like institutions from the conception of "elementary" social behavior would lead to a core understanding of social behavior that was shared by all human beings. The observation of "face-to-face" exchange between individuals outside social contexts is the basis of his knowledge (Homans 1961: 7-8). Power relations in such desocialized contexts mean very little. However, one does not have to go to this extreme to be an epistemological individualist. Baldwin, in particular, has been interested in the context-specificity—the domain (over what actors?) and the scope (with respect to what?)—of influence in social exchange in the complex institutional settings of international relations, where states are often the most important unit of analysis. By specifying such institutional contexts, Baldwin was able to recalibrate the terms of exchange or, in the language of power, the cost of influence.

This epistemological individualism is also supported by methodological individualism, which holds that "facts about societies, and social phenomena generally, are to be explained solely in terms of facts about individuals" (Bhaskar 1989: 27). Social elements are rephrased in individualist terms. For example, that "leadership does not depend on the personality of the leader but on the nature of the relationship between the leader and his followers" was rephrased by Homans (1961: 287, 391) as the leader's "ability to provide rare and valued rewards for his followers." Institutional factors were routinely undermined). So, for example, if gift exchange takes place as a result of inheritance or a prior distribution of resources, it should not be considered elementary social behavior and is, therefore, outside the scope of Homans' (1961: 317-20) study. He thus excludes the most significant type of gift exchange: the kind that results from a prior distribution of resources. In the process, his analysis of gift exchange loses its complexity and becomes little more than common sense. Once again, unlike Homans, Baldwin attempts to take institutional settings into account, treating them as exogenous factors that need to be specified for policy relevance (Leng 1998; Patchen 1998; Baldwin 1998: 145). In the final analysis, however, it is facts about the individual agent, not institutional factors, that determine an agent's behavior (Baldwin 1985: 291-4), and institutionally based power relations are underemphasized.

Finally, the social exchange approach has clear normative implications.[12] Its use of models illustrates this point. The exchange approach elevates the norms of reciprocity, equivalence, fairness, and mutual gains in their models, any deviation from which can be analyzed and criticized. Like neoclassical economics, there is a danger in this approach of normalizing the model (e.g., validating the norm of reciprocity), regarding empirical observations (e.g., neglecting the lack of reciprocity) as deviations from the norm. When the data do not fit their model, they tend to prescribe policy remedies before—or often lieu of—going back to the drawing board and tyring to figure out what really happened (Lawson 1997: 44-5).[13] The interest in balancing coercion and consent, conflict and cooperation, to offer another case, can blind researchers to the inherently conflictual social relations that underlie such otherwise benign appearances. Even master-slave relations can be analyzed as mutually gainful exchanges according to Baldwin (1998: 142).

These ontological, epistemological, methodological, and normative underpinnings mediate Baldwin's analysis of coercive and consensual power relations in otherwise coercive international relations. Baldwin captured the appearance of both the donor's influence and the recipient's gains in foreign aid by integrating the conception of power into the exchange approach—at the cost, however, of failing to recognize the obviously conflictual relation underlying the surface exchange between rich and poor states in international relations (Baldwin 1966a, 1966b, 1985). The most obvious condition he overlooked was the fact that the bilateral donor-recipient relation almost exactly coincides with the bilateral creditor-debtor relation (DAC various years; World Bank Annual Report various years; IMF Annual Report various years). The simple fact that foreign aid recipients have only rarely become donors in the last half century identifies the exchange of grant foreign aid as unreciprocated in a material sense (DAC various years). The striking correspondence—the rich are donor and creditor states, and the poor are recipient and debtor states—suggests an inference that the greater wealth of the donors is the material condition for being both a donor and a creditor. There is no basis in the exchange approach, however, from which to pursue this obvious line of inquiry. The search for some internal relation that plausibly constitutes both the donor-recipient and the debtor-creditor relation is outside its analytical reach: it can only approach them as two autonomous inquiries. An exceptional case presented by Al-Madhagi (1994) that a poor indebted state can be somehow free to choose its donors and creditors would appear plausible to the exchange approach. The call by President Muammar Al-Qaddafi to refuse grant aid from the West during the recent meeting of the African Union would also appear reasonable from an exchange perspective even though it was roundly ignored by all other African heads of state

(Abubakr 2005). In another version of the exchange approach, network theory, the basic material need of poor states that compels them to accept whatever aid they are offered is recast in methodological individualist terms: a patron-client relation can be established as a result of exchanges of grant aid (Catrina 1988).

The next two sections apply two anti-positivist approaches to coercive and consensual power to the question of foreign aid to illustrate the contribution of philosophical inquiry to the power debates. The following section applies Bourdieu's notion of symbolic power to bilateral grants. This is followed by an analysis of multilateral and nongovernmental grant aid practice applying Gramsci's concept of hegemony. Both of these approaches focus on the subjective dimension of knowledge: Bourdieu's for the scientists' construction of the subjective experience that corresponds with the objective social relation and Gramsci's for the mass' collective and subjective transformation of the existing social relation.

Unreciprocated Giving as a Mechanism of Acquiescence: Naturalization

Bilateral grant foreign aid appears as a voluntary transfer of resources from one state to another. The lack of immediate reciprocation results in the common social etiquette of a recipient thanking a giver. However, bilateral grant aid is rarely reciprocated in a material sense: givers remain givers; and recipients remain recipients (Hattori 2001). Bourdieu (1977: 4-9) argues that even if giver and recipient are otherwise equal in their normal social interaction, a temporary "symbolic" power imbalance emerges as the recipient recognizes her obligation to reciprocate and expresses gratitude until this obligation is discharged. The balancing of this imbalance, on the other hand, does not actually occur when the original recipient reciprocates by giving a gift because he misrecognizes his prior gift, thus expressing only gratitude for the gift just received. Bourdieu's contribution to the analysis of giving is to regard these exchanges as an irreversible process in which intervals and timing play important roles. This approach effectively rejects the prior focus of exchange studies on the observation of reciprocity (Mauss 1967; Gouldner 1961). Although Bourdieu did not study unreciprocated giving practices, Homans (1961: 319) observed that failure to reciprocate could indeed signal the material inferiority of the recipient. The correspondence between the symbolic and the material imbalance of power in bilateral grant aid noted above can be understood as what Bourdieu (1977: 164-68) calls a doxic experience, or an experience in which the objective material order corresponds more or less with the subjective experience of it, contributing, in short, to the appearance of the existing social order as self-evident, taken for granted, and undisputed.

Unreciprocated giving practices like bilateral grant aid are quite distinct, not only from reciprocal gift exchange but also from generalized reciprocity where a strict sense of reciprocation does not apply due to the long delay between giving and reciprocating and the involvement of different agents. According to Sahlins (1972), in a highly cohesive society the norm of reciprocity may be temporarily suspended or diffused, as between generations (e.g., between parents and children, who later become parents and give) or between relatives of different means. The failure to reciprocate in the short term does not prevent a rich uncle from giving something to his poor nephew, who will try to repay. If the uncle has passed away by the time he is able to repay, however, he will be generous toward other members of the extended family. This kind of generalized reciprocity "refers to transactions that are putatively altruistic, transactions on the line of assistance given and, if possible and necessary, returned" (Sahlins 1972: 193-4). The temporary nature of inequality (e.g., between the uncle and the nephew over a relatively long time) is still a precondition. Relative proximity in kinship is also another precondition. It is difficult to find the equivalent of such close relations in international relations; that is, the type of relations for which the "reckoning of debts outstanding cannot be overt and is typically left out of account" (Sahlins 1972: 194). The kind of turnover described above—children or a poor nephew becoming able to give in the long term —seems lacking. A small program called the South-South Cooperation (SSC) or Technical Cooperation among Developing Countries (TCDC) administered by the United Nations Development Programme attempts to replicate this kind of turn-over in the relation between states. It has been negligible in volume, however, and has grown very little over the past twenty-five years. More typical cases in international relations involve the kind of giving that does not involve either specific or generalized reciprocity.

According to ethnographer Parry (1986), though instances of unreciprocated giving are rare in African ethnography, they are more common in India. He suggests that the kind of social formation that supports this type of giving practice is qualitatively different from those analyzed by Mauss and his followers, who established the core theories of reciprocal giving. Elaborating on this observation, Parry (1986: 467) concludes that unreciprocated giving practices are most likely to be found in societies with a well-established state, an advanced division of labor, a commercial sector, and a universalistic religion and that the material conditions include social relations that are structured, both politically and economically, to produce large surpluses which can be stored well beyond self-sustenance. Unreciprocated giving, in short, is found in geohistorically specific societies quite distinct from hunting-gathering societies or subsistence agrarian societies from which the original anthropological insights into giving practices were drawn. The social divide between donor and recipient is wider and more enduring than the social divide of "primordial" societies. And beneath donor-recipient relations lie some internal social relations that structure this material divide, materializing an underlying social hierarchy. Exactly how such internal relations emerge in unreciprocated giving is geohistorically variable. The internal relations that enabled *euergetai* in ancient Greco-Roman world, for example, were quite different from those that enabled charity in medieval Europe or *sadaqa* in medieval West Asia (Veyne 1990; Hands 1968; Rubin 1987; Flynn 1989; Rosenthal 1972; Sabra 2000; Singer 2002; Barnes

1987; McChesney 1991).

Integrating Parry's insight and historical studies of the material conditions of unreciprocated giving with Bourdieu's insight into symbolic power relations gives us a window on the correspondence between the material and the symbolic in these societies. Extending this insight to bilateral foreign aid, it is easy to see how this practice euphemized the profound material divide between rich and poor states in the recent past. In the bilateral creditor-debtor relations of Debt Crisis, debtor states are obliged to repay what they owe; when they can not, creditor states can appeal to the Paris Club (at the French Finance Ministry), which develops and imposes conditions for rescheduling the debts (Kearney 1993). Under the Debt Crisis, in short, all notions of voluntary exchange were lost: the creditor-debtor relation turned into a power relation in Dahl's sense (creditor states make a debtor state carry out structural adjustment policies it would not otherwise do) as well as Bachrach and Baratz's sense (they set the harsh agenda for economic recovery of the indebted). Bilateral grants in this circumstance—a form of unreciprocated giving—is a strange sideshow: far smaller in volume and plagued by all sorts of ambiguities and practical flaws. Viewed as a form of symbolic power, however, the gesture becomes significant: all across the debtor world, gratitude is being expressed even as harsh conditions are imposed. In accepting this unreciprocated gift of foreign aid from a creditor state, recpient states become complicit in the material order that weighs them down; a critical source of their poverty is misrecognized in these gestures of generosity and gratitude. In short, they dare not refuse the gift. In the symbolic scheme of things, this would be taken as a show of no resistance (Scott 1990: 26).

In order to see how the interplay of material and symbolic power creates the doxic experience, social scientists must go beyond their "sense of limits, commonly called the sense of reality, i.e., the correspondence between the objective classes and the internalized classes, social structures and mental structures, which is the basis of the most ineradicable adherence to the established order" (Bourdieu 1977: 164). When the known world and the known sense of reality are socially constructed, specifying how causal power creates this world requires a theory of knowledge that questions existing knowledge and common sense and searches for scientific truth that is neither immediately observed nor self-evident. Bourdieu's sociology emphasizes the break with the self-evident or observable empiricist analysis in this sense (Bourdieu et al 1991). It is not sufficient, however, to clarify the correspondence between the material power of the creditor states and their symbolic demonstration of it through foreign aid. It is ultimately necessary to understand where this material power comes from. There is a real basis, in other words, for the specific limits to the naturalization of arbitrariness in any given social formation: although many things may be naturalized in the sense of Bourdieu's doxic experience, other things may not be legitimized in the sense of Gramsci's notion of hegemony, an inquiry to which I now turn.

Philanthropy as a Mechanism of Consent: Legitimation

I have refrained from identifying bilateral grant aid as a mechanism of consent. It has emerged, instead, as a naturalizer of relations of domination in the current international order. Even though the doxic experience described above is a world that is taken for granted, it is not a *legitimized* world, discursively speaking. Gramsci understood that the effort to legitimize the existing order through moral and intellectual leadership is a feature that distinguishes capitalism from precapitalist social formations. Because societies with no legitimizing discourse for their ortho-doxy are either archaic, in the sense that hetero-doxy becomes institutionalized and cornered into sorcery, or authoritarian, in the sense norms are coercively guarded, the interplay between material and symbolic power is quite different from the Gramscian notion of hegemony, which seeks active consent in the context of conflicting classes, class subgroups, and other groups under capitalism.[14] In a famous story described by former Czech President Vaclav Havel (1985: 27-39), a Czech grocer had a poster hailing the Communist Party on the front door. But the day after the fall of the Communist regime, the poster was gone. The doxa in such a circumstance was just a thin veil over the actual coercion beneath. Discursive legitimation of the moral and intellectual leadership in this case was imposed. The Communist Party doxa was, in short, not a case of hegemony but a case of supremacy, that is, more of coercion than consent.[15]

Here, I briefly clarify the concept of hegemony as a specific form of the interplay of material and symbolic power that legitimizes the correspondence between material and symbolic relations under capitalism. Going beyond the mechanism of acquiescence, hegemonic projects give rise to (1) an ethical discourse that justifies these projects and (2) institutions of moral accounting through which the honor of moral and intellectual leadership is conferred, in this case, upon a group or coalition of leading states, corporations, nonprofit and multilateral organizations, and individuals. Power in hegemonic projects operates in the specific geohistorical context of capitalism, creating the appearance of not just a self-evident or taken-for-granted order but a legitimate and ethically justified one.[16] Although the notion of hegemony contains a dialectic of coercion and consent, neo-Gramscians in international relations have deemphasized this dialectic and highlighted the concept of hegemony, emphasizing instead the mechanism of consent in an otherwise coercive international order. According to Gill (1990: 42), hegemony "generally refers to a relation between social classes, in which one class fraction or class grouping takes a leading role by the active consent of other classes and groups. Hegemony, therefore, is not a relation of coercive force as such (as it is viewed in political realist theory), but rather one of consent gained through 'intellectual and moral leadership.'" In the case of grant foreign aid, this mechanism of consent often appears alongside the mechanism of acquiescence. The reason for emphasizing this fact is that, while these mechanisms sometimes appear in the concrete world of even the same project (e.g., co-funding), a critical naturalist approach helps differentiate what is unique about the capitalist form of hegemony from other forms of interplay of material and symbolic power.

I have argued elsewhere that the practice of multilateral and nongovernmental grant aid as an international form of modern philanthropy is a hegemonic project operating as a mechanism of consent under the capitalist order (Hattori 2003). Modern philanthropy is a type of unreciprocated giving that is mediated by organizations that receive donations and distribute gifts. By distancing donors from recipients, these international aid organizations create a sense of the anonymity and altruism of donors contributing to good causes and social ideals. These organizations develop an ethical discourse that justifies donations on the basis of the good they do and the social ideals they serve. They also scrutinize the donors, praising the manner (and, of course, the munificence) of their donations. The annual reports of these organizations are filled with praise for major donors and the good their donations enable them to do. In short, international aid organizations institutionalize not only the ideals to which wealthy donors contribute through ethical discourses which praise them; they also create a form of moral accounting through which public scrutiny and praise occurs. Two things follow. On the one hand, by providing an opportunity for the wealthy to contribute to social ideals, these organizations help materialize virtue, identifying the wealthy as the virtuous. Donations demonstrate a virtuous use of wealth, thus contributing to the legitimacy of the donor's wealth. On the other hand, by praising donors and their virtue publicly, aid organizations encourage wider social acceptance of the "grand" donations of social leaders, identifying donor states, corporations, and grand individuals as fit for rulership. The honor bestowed in such cases is a difference-creating practice, distinguishing generous donors from the rest of society, including the stingier rich.

International aid organizations engage in a similar interplay of material and symbolic power.[17] Accepting donations from such organizations, whether Catholic Relief Service or UNICEF, is an active deed that can be distinguished from the more passive acceptance associated with earlier giving practices like Greco-Roman *euergetai*, medieval Christian charity, and Semitic *sadaqa*. In particular, gifts from such organizations reveal a key aspect of the underlying internal relation of capitalism: the notion of the *deservedness* of recipients. With modern capitalist philanthropy, recipients are also scrutinized for virtue. Indeed, it is the vested interest of such organizations to reassure donors that recipients possess dispositions of self-help and hard work—and, if not, that their donations are helping to foster them. Beneath the virtues of self-reliance (be resourceful even when the pay is low) and integrity (do not steal or cheat) is the core internal relation of capitalism—and, by extension, the historical process of reconstituting individuals as abstract citizens and free laborers. To the extent that the recipients of foreign aid are also the laborers or potential laborers of the capitalist world, the donors and donor states of foreign aid have an indirect material interest in shaping the dispositions of laborers toward self-help, hard work, and integrity. Because, broadly speaking, the surplus accumulated from such labor-power is what enables the donors and donor states to give in the first place, self-help, hard work, and integrity are precisely the virtues that contribute to the higher productivity of laborers. Even though this connection is abstract, that is, difficult to pin on any concrete transfers to capitalists or specific reconstitution of individual workers, the process of giving and receiving in this case *defines* what is deserving. Praise for the work ethic and the admonishment of laziness in the ethical discourse of philanthropic organizations—domestic or international— articulate the ontologically deep operation of material power that generates and transfers surplus from recipients to donors.

It is, therefore, no surprise that the assumption of good causes and social ideals articulated by aid organizations is hard to break, even when negative effects are exposed (Kennedy 2004). The sheer range of causes and ideals is baffling as compared with the specificity of the internal social relations that make philanthropy possible. And public acceptance of these causes and ideals, even when they do not exactly match the intentions of donors, is part of the mechanism of consent that generates the appearance of anonymity and altruism. Any effort to identify such a mechanism of consent in the face of such ethical hegemony faces methodological hurdles in an academic world dominated by positivism, which doubts sources of knowledge beyond human experience or actual incidence not detected by human senses.

Because Gramscians share a realist philosophy of science with critical naturalism, the debates on power and hegemony between them are largely over the degree of the explanatory power that can be attributed to relations of production under capitalism. Because Gramscians and other Marxists believe generally that all social relations in a capitalist social formation are internally related to capitalist relations of production, their only real philosophical concern is the *intransitive* dimension of knowledge, i.e., the reality that exists independently of social scientists or science (Gramsci 1971; Ollman 1976). There is little need in this view for the transitive dimension of knowledge. This is where critical naturalists part company. For critical naturalists, whether social relations are internally connected to the relations of production is an empirical question, not a precommitment. To put this another way, some social relations might yet remain as external relations, that is, not yet scientifically explained by the social relations of production (Sayer 1995: 26-33). This is not the case for multilateral and nongovernmental aid, however: the internal relation behind the donor-recipient relation is clearly a set of relations of production. As a hegemonic project, multilateral and nongovernmental grant aid plays a significant role in neutralizing the case for domestic and international redistribution, something that is clearly outside the material interest of capitalist donors and donor states.[18]

Conclusion

In this chapter, I have applied a critical naturalist approach to Baldwin's, Bourdieu's and Gramsci's notions of power, all of which identified power as both consensual and coercive. The questions of what exists, what we know and how we know it, and what constitutes evidence for scientific knowledge framed my analysis, and the context of giving practices, especially in international relations, provided me with further elaborations. To summarize briefly, I have argued that the positivist notion of agency-oriented power in the exchange approach makes the structural analysis of giving in general and grant foreign aid in particular difficult. Baldwin, who attempted to bridge the behaviorist literatures of social exchange and power, identified foreign aid as a policy instrument influencing recipients and set the agenda of a generation of policy-oriented and donor-oriented work on foreign aid. Bourdieu's constructivist scholarship on giving practices, by contrast, allows us to break away from the positivist verification of self-evident explanation and to approach the objective social relations that underlie the appearance of things. Mauss' classic study of the process of giving, receiving, and reciprocating was reframed from this perspective as an anti-positivist cycle of an irreversible practice that naturalizes the otherwise arbitrary division of social power by constructing a correspondence between symbolic and material power. In applying the latter approach to grant foreign aid, I also distinguished Bourdieu's transhistorical mechanism of acquiescence from Gramsci's mechanism of consent. Although they have much in common—both, for example, materialize a social hierarchy—Bourdieu's mechanism of acquiescence applies to a far wider range of phenomena across time and space than Gramsi's mechanism of consent, which applies to alliance building in the specific context of conflicting classes, class subgroups, and other groups under capitalism. The grants of international aid organizations, like other forms of capitalist philanthropy, institutionalize ethical discourses that justify the virtues of their donors and donor states, while scrutinizing both donors and recipients for virtues and dispositions of hard work, self-help, and integrity that are integral to the enhancement of the productivity of labor. By specifying the relations of production as the material basis of such ethical discourses, this chapter goes beyond Bourdieu's constructivist analysis of the doxic experience as a mere correspondence between material and symbolic relations, thus also moving away from his anti-naturalist tendencies. For critical naturalists, as for Gramscians, the real—in this case, relations of production—exists independently of the scientists who construct the model (the transitive dimension of knowledge).

This chapter has also argued that uncovering hegemony requires a critical naturalist philosophy of social science which insists on ontological depth of social reality. By continuously questioning the conditions of possibility—of, for example, giving without reciprocation—it is possible to bring those deeper layers of social reality to light, layers that are explicitly rejected by the exchange approach and implicitly neglected by Bourdieu. Because philanthropy in both its domestic and international forms is fortified in ethical terms which blur the correspondence between material and symbolic relations, the effort to see through the ethical discourses to the underlying material reality requires an ontology that supports a coherent epistemology and methodology aimed at discovering truth in a complex, open social system. Because a positivist exchange approach locates causal power only in agents, it has no way of grasping the Gramscian notion of hegemonic projects, in which causal power is rooted in a causal mechanism that involves not just agents, but institutions and social structure. Hegemony, in other words, is considerably more than "power-over": it is grounded in institutionally and structurally conditioned power capabilities.

By way of conclusion, let me elaborate briefly on the ethical implications of my argument. First, in contrast to the concept of influence emphasized by Baldwin and others, my emphasis on causal power distances grant foreign aid from the agency of donors and policy makers, allowing aid scholars to examine critically the institutions and practices of foreign aid as a whole.

Second, my approach shifts the ethical responsibility for causal action away from individual and corporate agents to social relations. The implication is significant. By failing to clarify the causal mechanism of giving, the best an individualist ethics can do is to motivate individual or corporate agents to do what is deemed, usually self-evidently, right (Pogge 2003; Singer 2002). Untangling the causal role of structures and institutions is the first step in the huge but necessary task of socializing ethics, that is, holding institutions and structures to account (Collier 1999).

Third, by emphasizing the discovery of truth as the supreme ethical as well as scientific virtue, a critical naturalist approach avoids a major pitfall of constructivism, whose relativistic view of truth can be politically exploited: emphasizing the notion of knowledge as a contested truth claim—the transitive dimension of knowledge—leaves no room for ethical guidance (Haugaard 1997). By focusing on the ethical properties of a society, a critical naturalist approach can indeed reveal false or limited ethical claims of an existing society, as in the virtue attributed to capitalist donors described above. Such an ethical naturalism, in short, holds out the possibility of ethical truth, which, though still a transitive dimension of knowledge, is neither mystified nor derailed by socially constructed ethical claims (Collier 1999).

Finally, the critical naturalist approach emphasized here acknowledges a primacy of scientific knowledge; any practical action should postulate its implications. Balancing the emphasis on discovering truth with a healthy skepticism about the ability to find it leaves ample room for the revolutionary ethic elaborated by Gramsci. His emphasis on the subjective understanding of the objective social relations of capitalism as a guide to practical resistance is based on a scientific knowledge of those social relations (Fontana 1993: 150-62; Gill 1993). When his foresight is proven right as in the hegemonic project of aid giving organizations described above, it is only practical to follow his ethical lead.

Notes

* This chapter was written during a sabbatical leave. I acknowledge the financial support of Lehman College, the City University of New York.

1. Ontological, epistemological, and relational limits to naturalism may be summarized as follows: (1) social structures do not exist independently of the activities they govern; (2) the objects of scientific inquiry manifest themselves in open systems; and (3) social scientific knowledge and the objects of social scientific inquiry are causally interdependent. See Giddens' (1984) point about double hermeneutics in social science. For a defense of critical naturalism, see Bhaskar (1989: 38, 45-7, 174-8).

2. The empiricist version of positivism was dominant in social science in the 1950s and 1960s and formed the intellectual background of Dahl's (1961) emphasis on concrete decisions and the measurement of constant and regular effects of power.

3. Bachrach and Baratz and their supporters provided an ample empirical literature on the role of nondecisions, the exclusion of issues and participants from decision-making, and agenda-setting in the politics surrounding air pollution (Crenson 1971; Bachrach and Baratz 1970).

4. Thus, for Foucault, "by truth I do not mean 'ensemble of truths which are to be discovered and accepted', but rather 'the ensemble of rules according to which the true and the false are separated and specific effects of power attached to the true'" (Foucault 1980: 132).

5. For an interesting poststructuralist study on security clearance in a nuclear laboratory, see Gusterson (1998).

6. Habitus is a concept that Bourdieu developed for both the relational criticism of the atomist notion of agency and the anti-positivist criticism of deductivism and a Humean notion of causation. On the one hand, habitus is a concept that allows Bourdieu to develop a relational constitution of agents who internalize aspects of social structure in the process of their socialization. Habitus is constructed as an dialectical locus of social structures and agents. On the other hand, habitus is a methodological intervention into constructing a concept that checks social scientists "against the immediate, against sensations," against the self-evident (Bourdieu et al 1991: 83).

7. A relation between A and B is internal if A's essential properties, such as identities and interests, are not what they are unless B is related to A in the way it is (Bhaskar 1989: 42-3). For example, a relation between a slave and a master is an internal relation because slave's identities, interests, and powers are constituted in relation to his master; that is, who he is, what he needs and knows, and what he can do are all constituted therein. It is this internal relation, not slave's master, that constitutes them. See also Ollman (1993).

8. Thus, distinct from hegemony, neo-Gramscians characterized the relations between states under capitalism as struggles over "supremacy" (Augelli and Murphy 1988). Because Gramsci's notions of hegemony and supremacy are the characterizations of how power under capitalism is used rather than what power is, they are not agnostic with regard to practical action. The difference between Gramsci and critical naturalists is that whereas Gramsci's strategic focus on the possibility for transformation presumes how causal mechanisms under capitalism work, critical naturalists do not yet fully know that. Gramsci also had a key insight into the possibility for revolution: although people must become aware of objective reality in order to change it, people's subjective understanding of social reality can inform the strategies of practical action (Gill 1993: 21-48; Fontana 1993: 150-62).

9. Aid program evaluations that focus on positive outcomes for recipients include Cassen and Associates (1994) and World Bank (1998), both commissioned by the World Bank.

10. In applying Dahl's conception of power to policy analysis, Baldwin (1989: 7; 1985: 9, fn. 6) focused on agency-specificity, the means-ends question, the target (who or what is influenced?), the domain (over what actors?) and the scope (with respect to what?).

11. In this ontologically individualist world, a structure refers to a pattern of exchanges. Similarly, Waltz's notion of structure as the distribution of capabilities is an ontologically individualist notion of structure (1979), according to Wendt (1987).

12. Normative orientations of the knowledge geared toward pragmatic concerns—or what Baldwin calls "statecraft" (1985: 8-28)— are also important. Because it is designed to benefit a particular state and facilitate its policy makers, it has a clear normative orientation. A discovery of social scientific truth about the nature of power relations is at best a byproduct of the policy-relevant knowledge production. The limited access to this form of often "classified" knowledge—practical knowledge for a limited audience—also reduces the possibility for open criticism, a crucial condition for scientific advance.

13. The exchange approach may be used in a large number of questions as a research method like the rational choice approach, presenting a dangerous tendency toward a method-driven research instead of a question-driven research (Cf. Green and Shapiro 1994).

14. This chapter discusses foreign aid as a hegemonic project. Because a hegemonic project is a specific interplay of material and symbolic relations under capitalism, this chapter does not engage with Joseph's (2002) general concept of hegemony.

15. On supremacy, see Augelli and Murphy (1988).

16. See Hattori (2003) for this argument in more detail.

17. Independent moral bookkeepers, such as associations of philanthropic organizations, have been established. InterAction, a peak organization for internationally oriented nongovernmental organizations in the United States, was replicated in Europe and Japan. Development Assistance Committee of the Organization for Economic Cooperation and Development is an equivalent organization for scrutinizing the aid practices of its members and multilateral aid organizations. See Hattori (2003).

18. There is considerable evidence to support the argument that philanthropists resisted rather than advanced the transition to a welfare state (Piven and Cloward 971: 32-36; Owen 1964: 501-97). The discourse of philanthropy, emphasizing the moral differences between the rich and the poor, was precisely what had to be overcome to ensure the moral legitimacy of the welfare state that redistributes the wealth of the rich to the poor.

Chapter 9

Does Power Have a Place? Hegemony, Antagonism, and Radical Politics

Saul Newman

"This relationship of domination is no more a 'relationship' than the place where it occurs is a place"   —Michel Foucault (1984: 85).

Gramsci's notion of hegemony has been of crucial importance not only to Marxist and post-Marxist theories of revolutionary strategy and political identification, but also to subsequent understandings of the way power functions in society. As Bendetto Fontana has shown, hegemony for Gramsci refers not simply to the ability of one group or class to dominate others, but, importantly, the ability to do so without resorting to coercion and violence.[1] Hegemony therefore suggests an operation of power that is far more subtle and pervasive than outright repression. Gramsci argued that the bourgeoisie in capitalist societies maintained its dominant position, not so much through a coercive state apparatus, but through a diffuse series of relationships, institutions, ideas and values that were coextensive with civil society. Not only the state, in other words, but also the Church, schools, universities, private associations, scientific discourses, and cultural and moral values, could all be seen as constructing a bourgeois hegemony—a general ideological domination that permeated society, and relied not on the direct use of force (although this was always available in the last instance) but on the everyday interactions, as well as the participation and consent, of people in civil society. Indeed, it no longer made any sense to separate civil society from the state—both were interlinked in a complex series of power relations that formed an "integral State." Gramsci developed this theory of hegemony to explain the failure of the working class to effectively undermine the position of the bourgeoisie. Unlike in Eastern societies, where the state was centralized and authoritarian, thus overwhelming and dominating civil society, in developed Western societies the state was much more reliant on civil society, and therefore more closely interlinked with it. According to Gramsci, then, the Leninist strategy of seizing control of a centralized state apparatus was conceivable in societies such as Russia; while in the West, a different strategy had to be devised—no longer the "war of movement" but the "war of position." In other words, the working class and other subaltern groups in society had to develop, through the intellectual and moral leadership of the Party, a counterhegemony which would rival that of the bourgeoisie: they had to develop their own institutions, modes of identification, shared ideas and values—their own "collective will."

Implicit in Gramsci's account is the idea that, in Western capitalist societies at least, power could no longer be situated in a single, identifiable location or place. Even though the State apparatus and its coercive machinery were still present, they were not the only, or even the most important, sites of power—rather, as we have seen, there were multiple instances of power (various institutions, cultural values, ideas, etc) all of which added up to a generalized ideological domination. Gramsci's theory of hegemony thus led to the need to substantially revise the concept of power itself—a revision that, I would suggest, finds its ultimate conclusion with Foucault. In Foucault's "micro-analysis," power no longer has an identifiable source and is, rather, dispersed throughout the social field, coextensive with a whole series of relationships, discourses, and practices. In Foucault's understanding of the socio-political field, then, there is no longer what might be termed a "place of power"—a central symbolic location which gives meaning and coherence to power relation-ships. Power relationships therefore become wholly diffuse, multiple and localized, and—although they can give rise to forms of domination—they remain in their "everyday" form simply as a mode of "action upon the actions of others" (Foucault 1982: 211).

In this chapter I want to explore the effects that this dispersal of power—this shift from the sovereign *place* of power to multiple "power relationships"—has had on radical political theory. The "decapitation" of the sovereign figure of power has meant that the political field can no longer be seen in Manichean terms, as a struggle between power and the subject that seeks to emancipate himself from it. I argue that this reconfiguration of the concept of power involves a remapping of the political field itself, where there is no longer a central revolutionary struggle—defined through the category of class—but rather a series of localized struggles and fragmented identities. I suggest that while it is impossible to return to the central Marxist idea of class struggle, the Foucauldian "model" of localized politics constituted through antagonistic power relations brings with it its own set of problems and limitations. Here I will propose an alternative theoretical model of antagonism to the one developed by Foucault—one instead constructed around the notion of an "empty" place, that is derived from Lacanian psychoanalytic theory. The implications of this for radical post-Marxist political theory will be explored through the work of Lefort and Laclau. Both these thinkers presuppose a socio-political field in which identities are contingent rather than fixed, and emerge around a central tension between two poles or principles: between "the people" and power in Lefort; and between the particular and universal in Laclau. This constitutive tension or antagonism, I suggest, offers new ways of thinking about not only power and hegemony, but also democracy and ethics.

The Place of Power

By "place of power" I am referring to an abstract symbolic position through which both power relations and political identities are organized and constituted. Thus, in classical political theory power was embodied in the figure of the sovereign. In monarchical society, for instance, power was invested symbolically in the body of the king as the incarnation of Divine Right. With Hobbes, we find the desire to make power more transparent: thus power was gathered in the Commonwealth and forged through a "contract." While the form in which this power appeared was immaterial —its purpose was solely to quell disorder—it was still centralized in an absolute place in society. Moreover, in the Hobbesian universe, this power continued to be embodied in an image of a sovereign body — this time an "artificial" one. The image of the Body is, in this way, mapped onto political society, functioning as a way of organizing power relations around sovereign institutions and laws. Modern political theory is also inhabited by this image. The sovereign head and its associated limbs are embodied in the state and its various agencies and bureaucracies. In liberalism, the place of power was legitimized through the social contract. In radical political philosophies—namely Marxism, socialism, and anarchism—the place of power was seen as an oppressive and illegitimate arrangement. Both political traditions were united, however, by this notion of the centrality of power.

There is another side to this logic of the place of power, however. While, on the one hand, the place of power is the symbolic centrality through which power and political identity are invested, this produces a counterdynamic in the logic of the revolution designed to overturn or "displace" this place. The political revolution aimed at seizing or overthrowing power in society is the logical counterpart to the centrality of power in society. However, it has often been the case that revolutions against power have ended up reaffirming it. There would appear to be something in the very nature of revolutions that perpetuates power, often in new and more authoritarian forms. Thus, the form of power changes, but its *place*—its structural imperative—remains the same. Therefore, we might say that there are two aspects to the place of power. The first is the one we have discussed—the symbolic and structural centrality of power in society. However, this centrality is always instantiated in a second aspect—the *perpetuation* of power in revolutionary politics. It is as if the place of power is always haunted by an inverse double—the specter of power that is reaffirmed in its very overthrowing.

A reference to this two-sided operation of the place of power is found in the theoretical debate during the nineteenth century between classical Marxism and anarchism. Although Marxism and anarchism emerged from similar traditions in socialist thought and shared a common critique of capitalism, they were radically split over the question of the state and centralized political authority. While Marx saw domination in capitalist societies as emanating from the economic power of the bourgeoisie, the anarchists believed that this neglected the mechanism of the state itself as a source of domination. The state, they argued, was a largely autonomous institution, beyond the control of class, and which had its own specific logic and imperatives—self-perpetuation. Therefore the Marxist notion of the "transitional state"—the state that would be controlled by the working class, prior to its "withering away" after communism had been established—was a naïve illusion, according to the anarchists. They argued that the transitional state would simply be one of the guises of state power through which it would articulate itself in increasingly authoritarian ways. In other words, it did not matter which class controlled the state—what was important was the structural principle or the place of state power itself. Bakunin argued that Marxism paid too much attention to the *forms* of state power while not taking enough account of the way in which state power operates: "They (Marxists) do not know that despotism resides not so much in the form of the State but in the very principle of the State and political power" (Bakunin 1984: 221). So the state is oppressive no matter what form it takes—whether it be a "bourgeois" state or a "workers'" state. Indeed, Bakunin predicted that the Marxist workers' state would resolve itself, not in the abolition of class, but in the creation of a new set of class divisions—between a new bureaucratic class and the rest of the population (1984: 289). Therefore the state could not be seen as a neutral tool of revolution, as Marx proposed. It was, in essence, a structure of domination that was irreducible to class or economic relations. Therefore, the aim of a socialist revolution, according to the anarchists, should not be the seizure of state power, but rather its destruction.

The major theoretical achievement of anarchism was precisely to unmask both the autonomous dimension of political power, and the dangers of its reaffirmation in a revolution if neglected. Power was to be understood in terms of an abstract position or *place* in the social, and as having its own structural imperative, which instantiated itself in different forms, including that of the Marxist workers' revolution itself. Therefore the place of power was not something that could be easily overcome, and was always in danger of being reaffirmed unless addressed specifically. Anarchism thus exposed the limitations of Marxist theory in dealing with the problem of power and authority. Blinded as it was by its economic determinism, Marxism failed to see power as an autonomous phenomenon that was irreducible to economic factors, and that required its own specific analysis. The anarchist critique of classical Marxism allowed radical political theory to conceptualize an autonomous political domain that was at least as important as the economic domain.

The Manichean Paradigm

The political philosophy of anarchism can only be understood in terms of radical conceptual division between two ontological principles—*natural authority* and *artificial authority*. According to Bakunin, natural authority, which is embodied in "natural laws," is essential to man's existence, determining subjectivity and forming the ground for an essential social commonality, constituted by rational and ethical relations between individuals (1984: 239; see also Kropotkin 1947:45). This order is opposed to "artificial authority"—the centralized power and authority embodied in political institutions such as the state, and in man-made laws. This authority is external to human nature and an oppressive intrusion upon the subject and the natural functioning of society. Political power is seen, then, as fundamentally oppressive, thwarting the full development of the subject's humanity. Central to anarchism, then, is the dialectical struggle of the subject against the external, "artificial" obstacles of power and authority that stand in his way—that deny his freedom and humanity, and distort rational social objectivity.

So there is an essential antithesis in anarchist discourse between the order of power and the order of humanity. Jacques Donzelot sees this Manichean logic as endemic to radical political discourse:

> Political culture is also the systematic pursuit of an antagonism between two essences, the tracing of a line of demarcation between two principles, two levels of reality which are easily placed in opposition. There is no political culture that is not Manichean (1979: 74).

Moreover, it could be argued that anarchism, in subscribing to this oppositional logic and making the state the focus of its analysis instead of the bourgeoisie, has fallen into the same reductionist trap as Marxism (Donzelot 1979: 74). In substituting the state for the economy in this way, anarchism remained within classical conceptual categories that bound Marxism. Both discourses involved a reduction of the political field to a central struggle between a place of power and a place of subjectivity.

Manicheism therefore constructs a clear demarcation in the political imaginary between power and subjectivity. In fact, we might see in this logic something resembling Gramsci's notion of hegemony and counterhegemony, where the hegemony of the dominant class can only be resisted—and eventually overcome—by the development of a rival "historical bloc" of the subaltern classes. Revolutionary struggle thus comes down to a "war of position" in Gramsci's analysis—a relationship of antagonistic dualism that closely mirrors the Manichean imaginary of revolutionary politics. However, I would suggest that there is also an important difference here: in Gramsci, a counterhegemonic bloc does not emerge in a predetermined or essentialist way—through "natural laws" or historical forces—as in the classical anarchist and Marxist accounts of the development of a revolutionary subjectivity. Rather, for Gramsci, the "collective will" of the subaltern classes is something that is constructed in a wholly *synthetic and contingent* way, through the formation of alliances between different classes—the working class and the peasants, for instance. There is no essential relation or coincidence between the political aspirations of these different identities; to forge a "collective will" from these heterogeneous and even conflicting wills is the task of those engaged in a counterhegemonic struggle, and here the role of intellectual and moral leadership is crucial for Gramsci (see 1971: 60-61, 123-202) We shall return to this idea of a contingent rather than essentialist link between different identities engaged in political struggles when discussing Laclau's theory of hegemony, which is derived in large part from Gramsci.

Foucault's "Decapitation" of Sovereign Power

The Manichean paradigm central to revolutionary politics, nevertheless, suggests a extremely paradoxical relationship between power and the subject presumed to oppose it. In this relationship of opposition there is also a hidden and deep-rooted mutual dependence between power and the subject. The identity of the subject is constituted only through its relationship of opposition to the power that denies it. In anarchism, for instance, it is the state, as an external obstacle to the progressive self-realization of the subject, which at the same time allows the identity of the subject to be constituted in opposition to it. The identity of the subject is characterized as essentially "rational" and "moral"—that is, capable of a full realization of humanity —only in so far as the unfolding of these innate faculties and qualities is prevented by the state. Without the existence of political authority, in other words, the subject would be unable to see itself in this way. The existence of political power is therefore a means of constructing this *absent fullness* in the subject.

This hidden dependence of the subject on the power that he ostensibly contests is one of the central political and theoretical problems identified by Foucault. Foucault's "analytics" of power contended that power relations could no longer be confined to a central place, but rather were constitutive of all social identities. One of Foucault's main contributions to the theory of power was his attempt to study power in its own right, rather than reducing it to the central mechanism of class or economic domination. Like the anarchists, he believed that to see power in these terms was to neglect its actual operation (Foucault 1980: 116).

However, Foucault also went beyond the possibilities of the anarchist analysis of power in two fundamental methodological respects. First, for Foucault, power could no longer be seen as being embodied in a central symbolic or structural place in society. To see power in this way, as both Marxism and anarchism did, was a form of reductionism designed to avoid the problem of power—the fact that power permeates all levels of society. Just as power cannot be reduced to the economic dominance of the bourgeoisie, neither can it be reduced to the institution of the state. Indeed, both anarchism and Marxism are two instances of what Foucault considers to be the excessive emphasis placed on the problem of the state: anarchism sees the state as the primary oppressive force in society, while Marxism, although it sees the state through the lens of its economic analysis, still overvalues the importance of the state in maintaining capitalist productive relations (Foucault 1991: 103). Foucault suggests, then, that the only way to avoid the reaffirmation of power is precisely to reject explanations that confine power to a central place. Marxist and anarchist conceptions of power would be two sides of the same coin in this respect. They remain caught within a traditional "juridico-discursive" notion of power: namely that power is centralized within a symbolic place of authority, be this the king, the state, the bourgeoisie, etc. For Foucault, this is an outdated notion that no longer has any relevance to political theory. "What we need," as Foucault said famously, "is a political philosophy that isn't erected around the problem of sovereignty ... We need to cut off the King's head" (1980: 121). Instead, Foucault maintains that the analysis of power must start from its "infinitesimal mechanisms": from the multiplicity of practices, relations, techniques and discursive operations that intersect at all levels of social reality, running through institutions like the prison, the factory, the hospital, or the psychiatric ward.

The second methodological consideration is that, for Foucault, power is fundamentally *productive* rather than repressive. Unlike the classical paradigm, in which the operation of power was seen to deny human subjectivity, prohibit freedom, and distort the objective truth of social relations, Foucault saw power as that which *produces and incites*; subjectivity itself is produced, rather than denied, by power. In other words, the identity of the subject is constructed discursively through relations of power/knowledge and "regimes of truth" which, through their power effects, require the subject to speak the "truth" about himself and his identity. There can be no Manichean separation between the subject and power—the subject is always already fully implicated in power relations, the effects of power constituting the very core of his being.

This reconfiguration of power presents classical radical politics with a number of problems. First, by pointing to the permeation of power throughout society, it denies radical politics an identifiable target of revolution—like the state—and in so doing, undermines the conceptual division between society and power. Second, it denies radical politics a privileged political subject—the subject who is to be emancipated from power. It makes problematical the very notion of the place of power and the place of revolution, upon which traditional radical politics is based. In other words, there is no longer an essential, universal position of emancipation beyond power: "there is no single locus of great Refusal, no soul of revolt, source of all rebellions, or pure law of the revolutionary" (Foucault 1978: 95-96).

A "Strategic" Model of Politics

What Foucault's "micro-political" analysis amounts to, then, is a *displacement* of the concept of power itself. The image that inscribes power and politics, for Foucault, is no longer one of sovereignty but one of *war*. Indeed, in his lectures in 1975-1976 at the College de France, Foucault suggests that war might serve as a model for deciphering power relations. Here conflict and struggle would be seen as the ontological condition for power relations and politics itself. Foucault's methodology of power, then, is based on the idea of conflicting force relations:

> ... if power is indeed the implementation and deployment of a relationship of force, rather than analyzing it in terms of surrender, contract, and alienation, or rather than analyzing it in functional terms as the reproduction of the relations of production, shouldn't we be analyzing it first and foremost in terms of conflict, confrontation, and war? (Foucault 2003: 15).

This antagonism of forces is perpetual, and inscribes itself into the political field —becoming recodified into laws, institutions, and even in language itself. This "strategic" understanding of politics and power unmasks the radical diffusion of forces behind the sovereign image of place. Indeed, in his outline of a Nietzschean genealogy, Foucault describes a fundamental struggle of "forces" that occurs in a "nonplace"—a purely differentiated relation of antagonism, without the stable political identities that would otherwise unify the political field: "only a single drama is ever staged in this 'non-place', the endlessly repeated play of dominations" (Foucault 1984: 85). The struggle of forces that underlies identities and power relations—as well relations of resistance to power—is therefore so absolute and antagonistic that it undermines any sense of a common political ground.

One of the consequences of organizing power, subjectivity and resistance methodologically around relations of antagonism has been a crisis in the radical political imaginary. Radical politics could no longer be organized around a spatial opposition between power and the universal subject. Rather, the political field would have to be seen in terms of an ongoing antagonism of forces—localized forms of resistance being generated by specific relations of power, without the hope of a final emancipation. Foucault's intervention here may be seen as part of the "postmodern political condition" characterized by the breakdown of once central political narratives and ideologies, the dissolution of stable political identities and institutions, and the decline of utopian projects and discourses (Heller and Fehér 1988). In this new "paradigm" politics is seen as thoroughly indeterminate and contingent. For instance, as Laclau and Mouffe (2001: 159) show, the radical political field that had hitherto been united by the universal subjectivity of the proletariat and its struggle against capitalism, has been succeeded by an explosion of new political identities and struggles—women, ethnic and sexual minorities, environmental groups, and so on.

However, the problem with this diffusion of identities and struggles is that it can lead to a complete fragmentation of the political field. If we are to see the political field in terms of relations of force, the problem is that this antagonism can lead to the dissolution of the very political dimension it constitutes. This is because the political field also relies on some universal dimension—the possibility of a common ground or "counter-hegemony," in Gramscian terms—being articulated between different struggles and identities. So if identities and struggles become increasingly particularized—as has been the general trend in contemporary postindustrial societies—the political field will disappear altogether. This is a problem identified by Laclau (2000: 86):

> This, in my view, is the main political question confronting us at this end of the century: what is the destiny of the universal in our societies? Is a proliferation of particularisms—or their correlative side: authoritarian unification—the only alternative in a world in which dreams of global human emancipation are rapidly fading away?

In classical radical politics, this common emancipative horizon was provided by the universal revolutionary subject. However, if, following Foucault, this notion of the universal revolutionary struggle is no longer sustainable, then how can a universal political dimension be sustained? Indeed, Foucault speaks of a struggle of differences and representations that takes place in "a pure distance, which indicates that the adversaries do not belong to a common space" (Foucault 1984: 85). Perhaps this "nonplace" that Foucault refers to is precisely this erosion of the political.

Power, Antagonism and the Real

However, what if we were to conceive of antagonism in a different way—one which, paradoxically, allowed a universal dimension to emerge from these relations themselves? What if we were to conceive of antagonism, not on the basis of Foucault's force relations, but rather on the basis of some kind of constitutive "lack?" To theorize this alternative notion of antagonism, we shall turn to Lacanian psychoanalytic theory. While it might seem strange that what would most people would see as a discourse concerned with the individual psyche should enter into a discussion about the politics, it must be remembered that even for Freud, psychoanalysis—because it is a mode of inquiry that seeks to explain the interactions of the individual with broader society—goes beyond the realm of individual psychology and refers to the intersubjective field of social relations. Indeed, as Freud (1995: 627) says, psychoanalysis is intrinsically concerned with "social phenomena." Lacan (1998: 20), as we shall see, develops this idea, seeing the unconscious itself—because it is structured "as a language"—as a thoroughly social and intersubjective, rather than individual, domain.

Central to Lacanian theory is a model of subjectivity that is based, not on some sort of essential fullness or on any Cartesian notion of rational self-transparency or autonomy, but rather on a fundamental lack or gap in the subject's identity. This idea comes from Freud notion of *Spaltung* (splitting)—which is a process found in fetishism and psychosis, where two contradictory perceptions of reality can coexist in the ego (Freud 1940). Lacan takes this idea of splitting and applies it to the condition of subjectivity in general: the subject, for Lacan, is always divided between that part of him that is knowable (the ego), and that part of him that remains unknown (the unconscious). Therefore the ego's sense of self-identity is ultimately an illusion; it is disrupted by a knowledge that is "not known"—namely, the unconscious.

This division is further reflected by the position of the subject within the external world of language. Here Lacan radicalizes Freudian theory by "reading" it through structuralist linguistics. Lacan sees the subject's identity as being constituted through and within language—through the signifying structures that bestow meaning on the world. Put simply, the subject can only construct a meaning for himself and develop a coherent identity through language, through the signifiers that "name" him as a subject. The "I" only has meaning and a sense of its "self" in relation to the signifier that stands in to represent it (Lacan 1977: 3). However, this entry into the world of language is marked by a fundamental experience of alienation: because signifiers only refer to each other within a chain of signifiers, then the subject cannot wholly identify with, or find a place for himself within, this symbolic order. This means that the subject cannot achieve a coherent or complete identity: there is always a sense in which language fails fully to account for or represent the subject. Therefore there is an irreconcilable lack between meaning and identity; because of this, identity itself is always lacking, incomplete, and only partly constituted. Indeed, the subject in Lacanian psychoanalytic theory is constituted precisely through this gap between identity and meaning. Subjectivity is based on a *failed* identification, and thus identity itself is to some degree incoherent and unstable. That is why Lacan writes the subject as *s( )* - *s* barred: this recognizes the failure of the signifier to represent the subject. If we compare this understanding of the subject to Foucault's, an important difference become evident: while for both thinkers the subject is constituted through external structures—power/knowledge for Foucault, and language for Lacan—for Foucault, the subject is wholly constituted by these structures (there is no aspect of the subject that is not colonized by power/knowledge) whereas for Lacan, they only *partly* constitute the subject.

Why is there this failure in identification? The inability of the subject to be wholly represented in the external world of language points not to some hidden essence of the subject that is too unique or singular to be symbolized. Rather, for Lacan, there is a sort of structural failure in the process of symbolization itself: there is an element that is, paradoxically, internal to the signifying chain yet, at the same time, excluded or "missing" from it. It might be thought of as a structural void within the symbolic order—a void which, at the same time, destabilizes meaning and allows it to be constituted. Language always points to a beyond—to something that is beyond its own limits of representation; in psychoanalytic terms, this would be the impossible enjoyment (*jouissance*)—the imaginary state of fusion between the infant and mother—that is forever lost to the subject. This void is what Lacan terms the "real" (*reel*). The real is a kind of "impossible" domain that is outside language—that which *cannot be symbolized*—thus constituting, at the same time, its internal limit. Thus the subject's identity is disrupted by this real: "This cut in the signifying chain alone verifies the structure of the subject as discontinuity in the real" (Lacan 1977: 299). The real, in Lacan's formulation, has nothing to do with *reality* as such; rather, it is precisely what displaces what is commonly understood by "reality." In other words, our reality—the reality of our identities and our way of seeing the world—is fundamentally conditioned by symbolic and fantasy structures; and it is the real—that which cannot be integrated into these structures—which jeopardizes this reality, making our identities precarious and at times incoherent. The real is therefore the point at which these symbolic structures break down and the contingency of their operation is revealed. It may be seen as an irreducible void around which identity is both partly constituted and dislocated.

According to Laclau, whose thinking is influenced by Lacanian theory, the notion of the real has direct political effects. Because the real is both outside and inside the symbolic—because it functions as the *internal limit* to symbolization—it sets in place an endless series of political identifications in the attempt to fill the void in the symbolic, an operation that is ultimately impossible. In other words, the real has *hegemonic* effects: that is, because it makes the fullness of identity structurally impossible, it generates the imperative—*desire* in Lacanian terms—at the level of the symbolic, to attempt to fill this lack with one's own identity. To give an example, the Marxist notion of class struggle would be an attempt to symbolize or come to terms with what was ultimately *unsymbolizable*—the traumatic dislocation at the heart of social representation itself. It is here that the real provides a different way of approaching the notion of antagonism. Laclau argues that society is an "impossible object"—that is, it can never be fully represented or grasped precisely because of the internal limit of representation itself. This applies to any ideological attempt—whether conservative, liberal, or radical—to represent the social field. Indeed, that is why there are competing political and ideological representations of society—not because of an actual antagonism that rends society apart but because of the discursive limits of society's own objectivity and therefore its fundamental inability to be wholly represented:

> In terms of the theory of hegemony, this presents a strict homology with the notion of "antagonism" as a real kernel preventing the closure of the symbolic order . . . antagonisms are not objective relations but the point where the limit of all objectivity is shown (Laclau 2000: 72).

It is here that *antagonism qua real* is different from the Foucauldian understanding. Foucault's notion of antagonism as a series of conflicting force relations underlying power and identity leads, as we have seen, to the dispersal of identity itself. It implies a Nietzschean idea of "absolute difference" between adversaries, so that there can exist no common ground between them, only a fluidity of positions and relations. By contrast, the notion of antagonism qua real entails a *partial fixity* of the politico-ideological field. Antagonism here performs two methodological operations: (a) it *displaces* identity, opening it to contingency and indeterminacy; and (b) at the same time, it also *constitutes* identity—on the basis of its own limit. In other words, rather than identity and relations being entirely fluid and differential, they are partly fixed. Rather than the field of antagonism being completely diffuse, it would be structured around its own constitutive lack. So, as well as antagonism destabilizing political and social identities, it also provides an internal limit around which they are constructed.

This idea of partial fixity refers to Lacan's notion of the *point de capiton* or "anchoring point." According to Lacan, while signifying systems which constitute meaning are characterized by the *metaphoric* and *metonymic* movements between signifiers, so that meaning is never wholly determined or complete—which is why we are always engaged in searching after an impossible fullness of meaning—nevertheless, there are "master signifiers" in this chain which, at certain privileged "nodal points," anchor the signifier to signified, thus allowing meaning to be partly fixed. An example of this is provided in Lacan's discussion of psychosis. According to Lacan, psychosis—which is the inability of the subject to constitute meaning—is characterized by "foreclosure" (*Verwerfung*), the radical failure of the subject to register the "Name of the Father" (*nom du père*). The "Name of the Father" operates here as a "master signifier" which fixes meaning through a kind of structural interdiction or prohibition (against incest). This does not refer to an actual father's "no" but rather a structural function of the signifier that provides an anchoring point around which meaning can be partially constituted. When this function fails—when the subject fails to register this interdiction—his system of meaning, around which his world is formed, breaks down. Lacan (1997: 102) likens this to the removal of the "woof from the tapestry"—in other words, a particular "thread" that quilts the entire field of meaning vertically, and without which meaning disintegrates.

This idea of anchoring or "quilting" points that fix meaning at certain places, may be applied directly to the politico-ideological field. We see that our understanding of politics—the way we constitute our political identities—is ultimately dependent upon the ideological and discursive systems of meaning through which we make sense of our world. The breaking down of essentialist identities and universal paradigms—for instance, the notion of the dialectic as the motor of history, the status of the proletariat as the embodiment of the universality of society, the idea of an objective social reality whose "natural laws" determine political and social events, and so on—has meant that politics is ultimately an indeterminate and contingent enterprise. This is why political identities are said to be antagonistic—that is, constituted through the undecidability of representations. However, the other side to this operation, as I have shown, is that meanings and identities are also partly fixed. Certain key signifiers operate in the political world to organize meaning. For instance, Žižek talks about the way that "Communism" functions as an ideological quilting point around which different representations are constituted:

> If we "quilt" the floating signifiers through "Communism," for instance, "class struggle" confers a precise and fixed signification to all other elements: to democracy (so called "real-democracy" as opposed to "bourgeois formal democracy" as a legal form of exploitation; to feminism (the exploitation of women as resulting from the class-conditioned division of labour); to ecologism (the destruction of natural resources as a logical consequence of profit-oriented capitalist production; to the peace movement (the principle danger to peace is adventuristic imperialism), and so on (Žižek 1989: 87-88).

This would be an example of the operation of the "nodal point" in the politico-ideological field—that which fixes meaning to different discursive elements when they are refracted through it. We can see in this the two methodological functions performed by the notion of antagonism qua real: both displacement of meaning, through "floating signifiers" as well as the partial constitution and stabilization of meaning achieved *through this very displacement*.

If we accept these two fundamental functions of antagonism qua real we have a somewhat different conception of the political field from the one envisioned by Foucault. While, for Foucault, the political field itself is dissolved through the struggle of heterogeneous forces, for the Lacanian-inspired "discourse analysts"—Laclau, Žižek, Lefort—the political field is open and indeterminate, yet "sutured," or held together through the discursive limits of this openness. What are the consequences of this for the notion of "place" however? As I have argued, the idea of an essentialist place—the Manichean division between the place of power and the place of emancipation — is no longer sustainable. However, as I will show in the following section, we can theorize a notion of a *partly constituted* place—one that allows a contingency of identities and political actions yet at the same time provides certain discursive and, indeed, ethical limits to the political field. I will explore this possibility by discussing two different, yet related approaches to the problem of place in contemporary political theory: Lefort's idea of the "place of power" in democratic theory and Laclau's argument about the role of the universal and particular in the politics of hegemony. Both thinkers, as I will show, engage with the problem of how to theorize an *empty place* in politics.

Lefort and the Democratic "Empty Place" of Power

In the previous section I introduced an alternative methodological conception of antagonism to the one developed by Foucault—antagonism as partial indeterminacy/partial fixity (via the Lacanian real) rather than antagonism as absolute difference and heterogeneity. Let us apply this notion to the question of power directly. As I have shown, for Foucault, the notion of antagonistic force relations underlying power means that power itself is thoroughly dispersed and decentralized, eschewing the idea of a central mechanism or symbolic place. As Žižek points out, however, the problem with Foucault is that it there is always a disavowed specter of Power that haunts his "concrete" analyses of particular, localized power relations and practices. That is to say, Foucault's theory of power only makes sense if one acknowledges that behind the plurality of practices, relations and discourses, there looms a symbolic dimension of Power which these practices and discourses implicitly refer to—and yet it is precisely this dimension that is denied by Foucault. Therefore, there is always an unbridgeable gap in Foucault's "bottom up" analysis between micropractices and power (Žižek 1999: 66).

So, while Foucault's analysis might appear to be more "concrete" in the sense that it claims to be discarding symbolic "sovereign" notions of Power, focusing instead on the direct, local "power effects," there is in fact nothing concrete about this. Paradoxically, power only has "concrete" meaning if it refers to an "abstract" symbolic dimension. One could argue, then, that there is a tension in Foucault's account of power between the methodological and analytical levels of explanation. Methodologically, power is seen through the metaphor of war, as decentralized force relations. Yet, analytically, power is seen as not only being inscribed in dominating institutions and discourses—such as the prison and sexuality—but also as implying clear normative questions, such as that of resistance to various practices which seek to tie the individual to a discursive identity.[2]

As an alternative to this, perhaps we could say that power does indeed have a central mechanism—a "deeper" symbolic and structural identity—albeit one that is flawed and incomplete. As Balibar shows, this return to the notion of a "structure" or "apparatus" of power does not mean that power is to be seen as absolute—rather, *as a structure*, it is deficient and lacking:

I would say against Foucault... that *there is power*, even a power apparatus, which has several centres, however complex and multiple these "centres" may be... But, having said this, I shall parody Lacan and add: power cannot be all; in fact, in essence it is "not-all" [*pas-tout*], that is, deficient (Balibar 2002: 136).

This would be a way of seeing power relations as organized around a symbolic mechanism or place—albeit one that is lacking and constitutively "empty." The point here is that what is important about power—what gives it an identity and what allows us to understand its operation today—is precisely this "abstract" structural and symbolic dimension that is dismissed in Foucault's account. For instance, it would allow us to understand resistance to power as emerging from its very deficiency and dislocation: "every power structure is necessarily split, inconsistent; there is a crack in the very foundation of its edifice—and this crack can be used as a lever for the effective subversion of the power structure..." (Žižek 1996: 3).

Furthermore, the dislocation or emptiness in the identity of power may allow us to perceive the conditions for the legitimate exercise of power—for example, democratic power. For classical radical politics, power was illegitimate and irrational because it sustained a gap between itself and "the people." For instance, Marxism saw the state as illegitimate because it represented the particular interests of the bourgeoisie rather than the universal interests of society. For anarchists, the state was illegitimate because it ruled in its own interests and was not under the control of society as a whole. What both of these conceptions of power pointed to was a crisis in representation: in other words, there was always a gap between power—which was seen in terms of particular interests—and the universal or general interest, which was embodied in, for anarchists, the figure of "the people," and for Marxists, the proletariat.[3] Power was therefore seen, in both these paradigms, as not only illegitimate but also as an irrational distortion of the interests of society—something that had to be abolished before society could be reconciled with itself and become fully transparent and rational. However, as Žižek points out, what if this distance between the people and power is precisely what is characteristic of modern democracy—in other words, of the *legitimate* function of power? (Butler et al 2000: 94) In other words, Žižek is suggesting that democracy itself relies on this gap in representation between "the people" and the institutions and political identities that claim to represent them. The idea that this gap in representation can be overcome rests on the mistaken assumption that social reality is entirely transparent and identical to itself and that there is no need for these representative political structures. However, a discourse analysis approach suggests that social reality cannot be seen as transparent in this way—that a "universal" identity such as "the people" is ultimately incoherent and meaningless unless it is represented or symbolized through a certain particular position, identity or struggle that fixes a meaning on it. In other words, "the people" cannot be entirely universal or commensurate with society because society itself does not have this consistency or intelligibility. Rather, "the people" can only be articulated politically in certain concrete, and ultimately fractured, and incomplete ways. Moreover, given that the social order is not transparent or unified in the way that these revolutionary discourses imagined—given that society is opaque, heterogeneous, and pluralistic—then any notion of a revolution that entirely eliminates the "distortions" of power would imply an attempt to enforce a certain uniform identity upon society at the expense of the differences that constitute it, an enterprise that has certain totalitarian implications. What is being suggested here, then, is that democratic politics depends not on eliminating this gap in representation between "the people" and power, but, rather, in sustaining a certain tension between these poles.

It is here that Lefort's notion of democratic power is important. Lefort employs this notion of the deficiency and structural emptiness of power to argue that democratic societies are constituted on the basis of their own discursive limits. It is precisely this symbolic distance between "the people" and power that is the defining feature of democracy. According to Lefort, modern political systems are no longer characterized by the symbolic consistency of the sovereign image of power. Democracy, he says, is "instituted and sustained by the *dissolution of the markers of certainty*" (Lefort 1988: 19). Power in sovereign systems of rule was embodied in the figure of the king, and it was this that gave society a body. However, the "decapitation" of this sovereign head left political societies with an *empty place of power*. In other words, the symbolic place of power once occupied by the figure of the king still remains, but it is now empty. There is no political identity that embodies this place fully, and it is marked by a radical absence and indeterminacy:

> Modern democratic society seems to me, in fact, like a society in which power, law and knowledge are exposed to a radical indetermination, a society that has become the theatre of an uncontrollable adventure, so that what is instituted never becomes established (Lefort 1986: 305).

Modern democratic systems are therefore organized and constituted around this empty place of power. Democracies are always characterized by a tension between two imperatives—the egalitarian, universal imperative, embodied in the social (the will of "the people") and the sovereign, institutional imperative embodied in the legal apparatus. One provides a check or "counterweight" to the power of the other, ensuring that the place of power remains empty, that no political identity or group becomes "consubstantial" with it. In this way, democratic systems are characterized by a central and constitutive antagonism between these two logics; indeed they are the very "institutionalization of conflict" (Lefort 1988: 17).

Let us explore Lefort's notion of institutionalized conflict. First, this idea of conflict differs from that inscribed in the oppositional logic central to classical radical politics. As we have seen in the Manichean universe, there is a central conflict between two essential points of departure—the place of power and the place of subjectivity. This conflict is, however, dialectically mediated towards its own overcoming. The aim of revolutionary politics is to overthrow the irrational and oppressive political structures that deny universality to society, and to overcome the alienating division between the people and power. According to this logic, social conflict and antagonism will cease, the distortions of power, ideology and religion will fall away, and society will become transparent and reconciled with itself. By contrast, Lefort's notion of conflict is irreducible and nonessentialist. Rather than emanating from fixed political positions, conflict is what allows these positions to be constituted and reconstituted. In other words, it is precisely the indeterminacy in the social that is produced by this tension, which allows new political identities and representations to be articulated. What is sustained by the place of power as empty is the structural imperative for various political actors and identities to seek to "fill it" by claiming to represent the "whole of society" or the "majority will." However, because it is impossible for this place to be filled, because no identity can become "consubstantial" with it, as Lefort argues, this creates a contingency in the process of political identification, transforming existing political identities and allowing new ones to take their place. In other words, because the place of power is symbolically "empty"—that is, failed and incomplete—politics in democratic societies is characterized by a fundamental indeterminacy. So, rather than being overcome in a dialectical fashion, this antagonism is the vital constitutive dimension of society. It is precisely what produces new political identities in a contingent and non-essentialist way.

It is precisely on this point, moreover, that Lefort's notion of conflict differs from Foucault's. Unlike the Foucauldian idea of conflict which leads, as I have said, to the dissolution of society—to elimination of place entirely—Lefort's idea of conflict retains the idea of place, yet sees it as *empty*. In other words, for Lefort, political identities and positions in society are partly fixed. The conflict, that for Foucault leads to a diffusion of the social into a series of force relations, for Lefort is precisely what allows society to be constituted, to achieve an identity. In other words, conflict—or antagonism—provides the discursive limits through which social identity emerges. Again we see the two crucial implications of antagonism qua real—*partial indeterminacy* and *partial fixity*.

Laclau's Politics of Hegemony: Universalism and Particularism

Lefort's notion of the "empty place" thus allows the political field to be seen as partially constituted. Laclau also attempts to articulate a notion of place in politics, one which is discursively constructed through hegemonic relations and which, moreover, provides a universal dimension for a radical emancipative politics. Laclau's thinking may be seen as an engagement with the political implications of the "postmodern condition." Contemporary political struggles are no longer founded, he argues, on the essentialist subjectivity of the proletariat, or the centricity of the struggle against capitalism. Indeed, radical politics today must fully assert the contingency of identity, and the indeterminate and open ended nature of struggle.

At the same time, however, Laclau is skeptical of the so called "politics of difference" that is said to characterize contemporary multicultural societies: in other words, the idea that political identities are purely differential, particularized, and incommensurate with one another. This fragmentation of the political field into a series of competing particular identities—social, national, cultural, and ethnic—is seen as symptomatic of the death of the universal Subject and the emergence in its place of a multitude of "subject positions." Indeed, the dispersal of identities and the "localized" struggles of resistance implicit in Foucault can also be seen in this context of the death of the Subject and the politics of difference.[4] However, Laclau sees the idea of a purely particular or differential "subject position" as problematic because it implies a fixed position or location within a totality—and, as Laclau (1996: 21) argues: "what could this totality be but the object of experience of an absolute subject?" In other words, what is implied, yet disavowed, in the "politics of difference" is precisely a place of enunciation which forms a background upon which these differential "subject positions" and identities are constituted.

Let us try to formulate this in structural terms. According to Saussure, language is a series of signs within a formal system of differences. A linguistic sign (composed of signifier and signified) only has an identity insofar as it is different from another linguistic sign. In other words, what constitutes the identity of the sign is not its relation to the thing or concept to which it is attached (the signified)—this relationship is purely arbitrary—but rather its relation to other signifiers within a structure. Thus A is A because it is not B, or C, or D, etc. The differences between signs, however, can only be established if they refer to a fixed background or system that constitutes them. That is to say, something only has a differential identity if its position within a system of differences can be fixed at a certain point. For instance, what would happen if this fixed system of differences were to break down completely? The linguistic signs within this system would entirely lose their meaning because their differentiation from other signs could no longer be established. This realization of the fundamental instability or indeterminacy of the sign is the basis of a poststructuralist account of linguistics, rather than the structuralist approach of Saussure's.

Let us apply this argument to the political field. If we are to understand political identities as being discursively constructed—that is, that different social identities and struggles are only intelligible through discourse, language, etc.—we see that the politics of "pure difference" paradoxically presupposes a kind of universal limit or common background (structure) which constitutes and fixes these identities in their differences. However, the quandary for political theory is, as Laclau argues, that this universal dimension can no longer be seen as an essentialist, objective foundation outside politics—as in the dialectic or some notion of rational social objectivity—but rather, must be seen as thoroughly *within* the field of politics and constituted through these differences themselves: "Now, the only way of defining a context is, as we have seen, through its limits, and the only way of defining those limits is to point out what is beyond them" (Laclau 1996: 52). As Laclau shows, however, what is beyond these limits can only be other differences, and therefore it is impossible to establish whether these limits are internal or external to the context. What this amounts to, then, is the very *undecidability* of the limit itself, and, if we accept that political identities are only constituted in relation to this limit, this means that these identities themselves are indeterminate and unstable. We can see here again the methodological notion of partial instability/partial fixity that I have outlined. Like Lefort, Laclau sees politics as operating not amongst relations of absolute difference—as in Foucault—but in relation to a universal dimension or place which is empty, and which only partly fixes political identities.

It is here that Laclau's notion of hegemony—which he derives in part from Gramsci—can help us. For Laclau, the political field is constituted by two irreducible poles or principles—the *universal* and the *particular*—and the dynamic that operates between them. We have seen that because there is no longer any universal subject or metaphysical foundation for politics, this dimension of the universal is "empty"—that is, it can no longer be embodied in an objective content. The universal remains as the empty horizon of politics—the "empty signifier"—that cannot be filled and yet, precisely because of this, generates the desire or structural imperative in political identities (the particular) to fill or embody it. "Society" may be seen as an example of an empty universality: as we know from the analysis above, society is ultimately a meaningless and inconsistent identity which means different things to different people. Thus it has no objective content as such, but rather embodies an "absent fullness"—a permanent horizon which different political identities and ideologies interpret and try to embody in different ways. However, it is structurally impossible to completely embody this identity—"society" as the horizon of politics always exceeds these various attempts at symbolization. It is this political operation of attempting to fill the "unfillable" place of politics that Laclau refers to as the logic of "hegemony": "*The universal is an empty place, a void which can be filled only by the particular, but which, through its very emptiness, produces a series of crucial effects in the structuration/destructuration of social relations*" (Butler et al 2000: 58). We can see, then, the way in which Laclau's universal empty place parallels the empty place of power in Lefort: both employ the Lacanian notion of an absent fullness created by the real, which is the void or internal limit to the symbolic order. In other words, for both thinkers, there is a political dimension or place that is symbolically empty and which can only be articulated through a contingent relation of representation, in which a particular political identity comes partly to embody it.[5] Both notions of this empty place have concrete effects—"structuration/ destructuration" or fixity/destabilization—on the political field, as they generate the very contingency in political identity which is constitutive of it.

So, similarly to Lefort, Laclau shows that politics can be reduced neither to essentialist determinacy nor to a complete "postmodern" dispersal of identities; neither, in other words, to absolute universality nor absolute particularity. Both are reductionist paradigms that deny a properly political domain. Rather, politics must be seen as involving a *contamination* of the universal and the particular. Political identities are split between their own particularity and the dimension of the universal that constitutes them in their particularity. Political identities, no matter how particular, cannot exist without a dimension of universality that contaminates them. It is impossible for a group to assert a purely separate and differential identity, because part of the definition of this particular identity is constituted in the context of relations with other groups (Laclau 1996: 48). For instance, the demand of a particular minority for cultural autonomy always bears reference to a universal dimension: the demand for the right to be different is also a demand for equal rights with other groups. It is also the case, however, that the universal is contaminated by the particular. As we have seen, the universal is formally empty, so it can only articulate itself if it is represented by a particular political identity. However, we also know that because the universal is formally empty, no identity can completely represent or embody it. In other words, the universal, for Laclau, is an "impossible object"—like Lacan's object *petit a*—in that its representation is, at the same time, impossible *and* necessary. For instance, the idea of society is an impossible "discursive" object whose universality can only be represented if a particular ideology or political identity—like Communism, for example—can articulate a certain vision of it. While no particularity can fully symbolize this universal, its partial symbolization is crucial if we are to have any notion of politics at all. Therefore, the universal requires that a particular element "stand in" for it, without which the universal itself loses all meaning. Here we see, then, that although the universal and the particular are the opposite poles of the political field, each is dependent on the other as its positive condition.

So in this *hegemonic* relationship of mutual contamination, the universal is split between its universality and its need to be represented through a concrete particularity; while the particular is split between its particularity and its reference to a universality which constitutes its horizon (Laclau 2000: 56). As I have shown, even the most particular of identities, if it is to engage in any form of political activism, has to refer to some universal dimension, such as the notion of equality of rights with other identities. So to articulate a certain demand, a political identity must form what Laclau calls "chains of equivalence" with other identities and groups. To give an example, the demand of students for better conditions and more funding, cannot remain within this specificity for long: these demands will eventually overlap with the demands of other political identities in forming relations of united opposition to the power that denies them. Thus, the government that denies students their rights also denies workers *their* rights, and so on. In this way, the groups in this chain are increasingly unable to maintain their own particularity, as they become united in opposition to a common enemy—thus constructing, in Gramscian terms, a "collective will."

It is important to note here that this hegemonic political relationship, in which one particular identity "stands in" for the others, is not determined in an essentialist way. In other words, there is no *a priori* link—as there was in Marxism with the proletariat—between the universal and the particular identity that comes to incarnate it. According to Laclau, the relation of incarnation is entirely contingent and synthetic. The "stand in" is decided in an open field of discursive articulation and political contestation. Theoretically, any identity, if it manages to articulate adequate chains of equivalence, can come to represent a common political struggle. Furthermore, the particularity that "stands in" for the universal does so only temporarily, and its identity is destabilized by the universality it "represents" (Laclau 1996: 53). In other words, its status as a representative is increasingly made more difficult to sustain as the struggle progresses, as it is caught between the imperatives of its own particularity and the universality it is required to embody. Therefore, because this link is indeterminate and contingent, this opens the political field to other identities to attempt to fulfill this incarnating function.

The "Ethics" of Place

It is here that I can perhaps draw briefly upon the question of ethics and politics. Central to Gramsci's theory of hegemony is the role of intellectual and, particularly, *moral* leadership in the construction of a "collective will." To counter the ideological hegemony of the bourgeoisie, "organic intellectuals" must develop an alternative ensemble of "ideas" and "values" that would be shared among subaltern groups. Gramsci does not define what these ideas and values should be—these are not to be predetermined in any way but depend on an entirely contingent articulation. Nevertheless, counterhegemonic politics implies, it would seem, the need for some sort of common ethical horizon. Moreover, while Lefort and Laclau do not develop a theory of ethics as such, I would suggest that there is an ethical dimension implicit in their politics.[6] The question of ethics is important here because, from a hegemonic perspective, politics takes place in a contingent and indeterminate field. That is to say, there no longer exist absolute rational or moral grounds for deciding which identity is to fulfill the hegemonic function. Laclau raises this question explicitly: "I have been confronted many times with one or other version of the following question: if hegemony involves a decision taken in a radically contingent terrain, what are the grounds for deciding one way or another?" (Butler et al 2000: 79) This was also a question that in some ways dogged Foucault's notion of resistance to domination: what are the criteria by which forms of resistance can be normatively justified? Here, however, I would follow Laclau and draw a distinction between the *normative* and the *ethical*. The category of the normative involves pre-established criteria for justifying certain actions, whereas the ethical involves precisely an impossible gap between the subject and the normative criteria that are supposed to guide his action. The ethical action or decision, in other words, takes place in an abyss or void in which pre-established normative criteria are not clearly perceived. In Derridean terms, ethics involves a *moment of madness*. According to Laclau, hegemony is the name given to this unstable relationship between the ethical and the normative (Butler et al 2000: 81). In other words, in the hegemonic relationship described above, there is always a gap between the universal and particular, between the empty place of the universal and the particular identity which attempts, ultimately unsuccessfully, to embody it. We find the same relationship of impossibility in Lefort, where there too is a gap in democratic societies between the empty place of power and the political identities that try to fill it. The point here is that this gap or lack in representation does not signify the failure or breakdown of ethics, but is, on the contrary, ethical in itself.[7] This is because it opens the field of politics to different identities, to a radical freedom and undecidability of decision. To fill the gap, to overcome the lack in representation, would amount to a totalitarian closure of the political field.

If political ethics involves sustaining a gap between the universal and the particular, then it must also involve, as I have alluded to before, a contamination of these two terms. In fact, we can refer here to a political *ethics of contamination*, in which identities are caught between their own particularity and the universality they inevitably invoke. There are three possible articulations of this ethics of contamination. First, as we have seen, contemporary radical politics cannot be reduced to a minoritarian politics of difference; identity politics, in this sense, is ultimately self-defeating if it attempts to maintain a purely separatist political position. Nor can it be reduced to a foundationalism based on a universal subjectivity or a Manichean division of the world, as was the case with anarchism and Marxism. Rather, radical politics is the effect of a contamination between particular concerns, interests and identities, and the universal emancipative horizon which they inevitably bear reference to. Second, if we are to see the particular as pertaining to the standpoint of the individual, and the universal as referring to the standpoint of the community, we can say that radical politics today, if it is to be emancipative, has to involve a contamination of both concerns, or indeed, a deconstruction of the classical division between them.[8] Third, we can also see the universal as pointing to the principle of *equality*, and the particular to the principle of *liberty*. Classical liberal theory has generally drawn a distinction between these two principles, seeing them as mutually limiting. By contrast, the radical left tradition has seen liberty and equality as interconnected and dependent upon one another, contending that freedom was only possible in society when all were equally free (Bakunin 1984: 267). Perhaps contemporary radical politics can take from this a notion of *liberty/equality*—or "equaliberty" in Balibar's terms (1995: 72)—as an *unconditional and necessarily excessive* ethical demand. In other words, what would perhaps be constitutive of radical political ethics would be a refusal to separate liberty and equality, a refusal to see one as imposing limits on the other, and a conviction that it is simply unjust to do so. This would form a kind of ethical horizon—or even an ethical demand—which would inform radical political struggles of today. While hegemonic politics insists on a gap between the ethical and the normative—entailing therefore a constant negotiation between these two poles—what I am suggesting here is that this demand for full equality with full liberty exists as an unfulfilled and *unfulfillable* demand, something that forms an open horizon which can never be grounded in any concrete normative order. In a similar manner to Derrida's notion of the "democracy to come"—which, rather than existing as defined teleological goal, is an open project that is "infinitely perfectible" (Derrida 1997: 306)—we might say that this link between equality and liberty is also an infinitely perfectible project that may be articulated in different ways through different political struggles. Because hegemonic politics can only allow synthetic and contingent links between political identities and ethical positions, an open-ended ethical project is the only one possible; however, precisely because there is this contingency in the formation of political alliances, hegemonic politics at the same time demands certain ethical parameters—a certain ethical "quilting point" that defines the contours of political struggle. Liberty/equality, in this sense, might

Saul Newman

provide these ethical contours, characterizing hegemonic politics as radically egalitarian, libertarian and democratic.

What this implies is an ethics of the "empty place"—an ever expanding horizon for radical politics that can never be entirely grasped, and which thus generates ongoing struggles of emancipation. I have suggested here that place is an irreducible and necessary symbolic category in radical political theory, allowing us to conceptualize power relations, resistance and subjectivity. I have also discussed three articulations of the problem of place, as well as three concomitant modes of antagonism that are constitutive of it: first, the Manichean paradigm of classical radical politics, in which the place of power is ontologically separated from the place of subjectivity and resistance, and where the antagonism between the two is dialectically mediated towards the overcoming of power itself; second, the Foucauldian "displacement" of the sovereign place of power through the diffuse antagonism of heterogeneous force relations—an antagonism which denies consistency to the political field itself; and third, the notion of the *empty place* of power, articulated through an alternate model of antagonism—one implying both partial displacement and partial fixity of political identities. Through a discussion of its application in the work of Lefort and Laclau, I have suggested that this last understanding of antagonism and place is the most fruitful for radical politics, allowing us to navigate a "middle road" between, on the one hand, essentialist universality, and on the other, the politics of difference and particularity.

Notes

1. See Fontana's "State and Society" in this volume.
2. Foucault (1982: 216): "Maybe the target nowadays is not to discover who we are, but to refuse who we are. . . . The political, ethical, social, philosophical problem of our days is not to liberate the individual from the State and its institutions, but to liberate ourselves from the State and the type of individualization linked to it."
3. The proletariat, for Marx (1978: 538), is "a class which is the dissolution of all classes, a sphere of society which has a universal character because its sufferings are universal..."
4. Hence Foucault's (1973: 387) wager that "Man would be erased, like a face drawn in sand at the edge of the sea."
5. Here Laclau (2001: 12) takes Lefort's argument about the empty place of power even further: "That is why Claude Lefort's argument, according to which in democracy the place of power is empty, should, I think, be supplemented by the following statement: democracy requires the constant and active production of that emptiness."
6. There have, however, been a number of debates on the relationship between ethics and hegemony between Laclau and Critchley (1998).
7. Laclau (2000: 81) refers to the ethical as the "infinite process of investments which draws its dignity from its very failure."
8. Indeed, as Laclau 2000: 80) argues, the "moment of the ethical is the moment of the universality of the community."

Chapter 10

Hegemony and the Power to Act

Kevin Ryan

The significance of hegemony for political analysis has long been associated with the work of Antonio Gramsci and the problem of "domination through consent." More recently, its root in geopolitical discourse has again come to the fore where it frames a renewed interest in matters of empire, or more specifically, with the motives of the United States as it disengages from the established norms of international relations (see chapters by Goverde, Cerny, and Lentner). In particular the doctrine of "preemptive war" has generated debate concerning the motives of the US, interpreted on the one hand as a bid for global hegemony, and on the other as an attempt to establish a more insidious form of rule. Chomsky's *Hegemony or Survival: America's Quest for Global Dominance* is a recent contribution to this debate which comes down on the side of the latter, although it must be noted that Chomsky's use of the term hegemony is somewhat inconsistent. On several occasions it is used to denote the threat or use of military force (2003: 3, 11, 227), and on one occasion describes an ideological project as the US attempts to represent its actions as "the realization of history's purpose" (2003: 43). Another contribution is Mann's *Incoherent Empire*. In contrast to Chomsky, Mann tells us that reliance on force directly undermines US hegemony because hegemony presupposes a form of rule "to which the ruled routinely consent" (2003: 11-12, 252). For Mann hegemony is not produced through the "barrel of a gun" but by the "everyday actions" of people; actions which reflect the taken-for-granted order of things.

The literature is testimony to the fact that the "source" of hegemony can be specified in a number of ways, and yet a common theme emerges in the notion of a concentration of power—a hegemonic state, class, or ruler—so that "hegemony" denotes both a subject and a mode of subjection. The relation between one and the other becomes more intricate given that the subject of hegemony is at once those who benefit from the existing configuration of power *and* those who seem to acquiesce in their subjection to it. Between the subject and mode of subjection we find the concept of hegemony tracing out a relation of actual or possible contestation—a horizon of contingency which leads us into the task of mapping its complex composition and its fundamentally political character.

Working from the premise that hegemony is both reproduced and resisted at the level of "everyday actions" (Mann), what I want to do in this chapter is examine hegemony as a power bloc or field of force relations which is both contingent and vulnerable to new articulations at the level of the social, a starting point that requires the relation between subject and subjection be brought into sharper focus. In doing this I will be drawing on the work of Ernesto Laclau and Chantal Mouffe. Laclau and Mouffe have been developing a theory of hegemony for several decades now, using poststructuralist thought to rework Gramsci's theory, and more recently working closely with the Lacanian scholar Slavoj Žižek. While I suspect that Žižek would balk at the prospect of being labeled a poststructuralist, for the purpose of organizing the discussion all three thinkers will be gathered under that heading. This only gets us only part of the way to the source of hegemony however, for as we look through the lens of their theory for the moment when hegemony is contested, we meet with a certain void which conjoins the subject and the structure. There are good reasons for this "empty" rendering of political subjectivity. In part it reflects a critique of the centered and essential subject as implicated in discourses of class, nation, gender, race, and so on. It also reflects the assumption that some form of collective subject is required to effect structural change. While broadly endorsing the poststructuralist position I also think it is possible to pass through the subject-as-void to a socially situated and "centered" subject, and it is here that we can locate the moment and place where hegemony is reproduced or contested. I will be arguing that the social ontology of poststructuralism enables us to think the "power to act" in a number of ways, and doing so delivers sharper analytical tools for studying hegemony, power and the subject in the contemporary world. I should also mention that this will require retracing some of the ground covered by Saul Newman in the preceding chapter, the purpose of which is to offer an alternative reading of the Lacanian register of void/lack. The chapter is divided into six sections, the first three examining the poststructuralist rendering of hegemony, with particular emphasis on the radical (counterhegemonic) act. The remaining sections set about relocating the source of hegemony and the power to act at the level of a certain "self-trangressing" individual.

From Subject Position to Identification: Opening Out the Void

When Gramsci wrote about hegemony he used it both descriptively, to characterize the modern bourgeois state, and prescriptively, to formulate a revolutionary strategy (Martin 1998: 65-6; Fontana, this volume). In their neo-Gramscian theory of hegemony Laclau and Mouffe reproduce both of these uses. On the first count they empty out the remaining trace of (class) essentialism from Gramsci's absolute historicism so that all social formations and social identities are fundamentally contingent. On the second count they continue Gramsci's interest in the role of the organic intellectual by defining and defending a radical project for the political Left. In this way the poststructuralist rendering of hegemony brings the "is" and the "ought" together, specifying how the social as a contingent field of objects and relations is ordered and how it can and should be transformed. As a theory of social formation and transformation, this rendering of hegemony necessarily converges on questions of power and the subject, both of which are implicated in the double movement from the hegemonic "decision" (order/closure) to "undecidability" (dislocation/rupture), and the reverse of this. We can take this double movement as our point of departure, beginning with the role of discourse in the institution of hegemony.

Laclau and Mouffe (2001: 107) use a conception of discourse which goes beyond the "discursive/nondiscursive" distinction drawn by Foucault in his archaeological works (Foucault 1972: 157). In making this move they emphasize the contingency of all social identities and social practices, focusing on the role of meaning in the constitution and institution of what is sometimes called the "non-discursive" or "material" level of the social. Used in this way the category "discourse" becomes coextensive with the social and can be understood as "publicly available and essentially incomplete frameworks of meaning which enable social life to be conducted" (Howarth 2000: 104; Laclau 1990: 90). The crucial term in this quote is "incomplete," which points to an ineradicable surplus of meaning or horizon of contingency which contaminates any and all discursive formations. From the poststructuralist perspective, it is precisely because the social world is discursively structured as a grid of possibilities and limitations—systems of meaning that "direct" thought, speech and action in the Gramscian sense, or what Foucault (from Georges Canguilhem) called "the true" —that it remains permanently vulnerable to that which it excludes. The specific names given to this radical surplus are "dislocation" and "social antagonism," and both concern a type of conflict which has no *a priori* positive form or content and cannot be traced back to some essential structure (the mode of production) or privileged subject (the working class).

The antagonism/dislocation couplet has undergone several incarnations. In Laclau and Mouffe's seminal work, *Hegemony and Socialist Strategy* (2001: 122-7), antagonism was indistinguishable from dislocation). Following Žižek's intervention into that text (1990) Laclau conceded that antagonism was a *response* to the dislocation of social order, thus aligning antagonism specifically to political subjectivity (Torfing 1999: 129). More recently Jacob Torfing argues that antagonism can also be the *source* of dislocation, a point to which we will return (1999: 131). Whether the relation is one of cause/effect or simultaneity, antagonism/dislocation denotes the limit of any hegemony, a limit which takes the form of a lacking subject and an incomplete structure. Because the ordering of social space entails the exclusion of meanings, so a surplus of possibilities is always immanent to a given order. However, in and of itself the surplus has no representational or signifying form. It is only when the surplus is implicated in the negation of identity—when groups identify with the meanings which have been excluded—that social antagonism is possible. An example would be the phenomenon of stagflation during the 1970s, which undermined welfare capitalism and opened out conditions of possibility for new hegemonic practices. The contingency of order became manifest in an event that initially "exceeded" the truth of established discourses such as Keynesianism. As the event was ordered into discourse so it was used to reorder the social, with the political right using a theme of national pride and steadfastness to advance a program of neoliberal reform, winning the support of the working class and negating the identity of the political left. In this type of "undecidable" situation, meaning is made available for rearticulation and a struggle for (counter-) hegemony ensues (Smith 1994; Torfing 1999: 130; cf. Clegg 1989: 224-5). And this brings us to the subject of this problematic, which has itself been the subject of some debate.

In *Hegemony and Socialist Strategy* Laclau and Mouffe worked with the concept of subject position, in this respect at least adhering to the legacy of structuralism (Foucault 1972: 12-14, 122). This theorization of the subject has played a critical role in problematizing the centrality of Reason and Truth in modern social and political thought by dispersing the sovereign bearer of both—whether the autonomous self of liberalism or the class "for itself" of Marxism—across a range of social positions (one can simultaneously be a worker, a woman, an ecologist, a member of an ethnic minority, etc.). The *social*, which is to say *collective* subject is positioned within a historically specific field of relations and practices which both constitutes and circumscribes subjectivity, shifting the emphasis from the autonomy of the subject to its subjection. However while emphasizing the precarious and incomplete nature of all identity/subjectivity, this answer to the problem of subjectivism tends to eclipse agency altogether, as in the case of Louis Althusser's (1994) theory of ideological interpellation, whereby the subject is "hailed" into position by the structure. Slavoj Žižek's interventions into *Hegemony and Socialist Strategy* engendered a theoretical development in the form of the subject *prior* to its subjectivation (Žižek 1989, 174-5). In the categories of dislocation and antagonism Žižek recognizes the Lacanian "split" subject (Žižek 1990). Just as dislocation denotes the incomplete nature of the structure, so antagonism corresponds to the fundamental contingency of the subject, which takes the form of an original and constitutive *lack*. Žižek argues that if we begin from the concept of subject position and "make an abstraction, if we subtract all the richness of the different modes of subjectivation, all the fullness of experience present in the way the individuals are 'living' their subject-positions; this original void, this lack of symbolic structure, *is* the subject, the subject of the signifier" (Žižek 1989: 175, original emphasis). Laclau agrees when he explains that "subject equals the pure form of the structure's dislocation," in which case "the subject exists because of dislocations in the structure" (1990: 60).

In the couplet antagonism/dislocation we find a theory of contingency which conjoins subject and structure, with the eruption of contingency opening out the possibility for new articulations—the moment when hegemony is contested by agents seeking to emancipate themselves. The negative space of void/lack is thus the condition of possibility for emancipation (Laclau 1990). However, as we look for the bearer of this freedom what we find is a *social* subject (the subject of environmentalism, feminism, religious fundamentalism...) which articulates a constitutive lack and a dislocated context. The subject is not what it *is* but what it is *not*, and this lack is given positive form only as antagonism goes to work on the disordered structure. Political subjectivity emerges as the lacking subject identifies with some object cause of desire, something that would fill its lack and make it whole (Torfing 1999: 56; Stavrakakis 1999: 13). What is overlooked or misrecognised by the subject in this act of identification is the impossibility of that which is desired: a fully constituted identity and a social order which is complete. Desiring a state of plenitude, the lacking subject acts as if meaning can be fixed once and for all, and yet the act of identification can never transcend its own contingency. Other than through the act of identification —which is also the moment of foreclosing and hence repression within any hegemony—there is no escaping the contingency of social being: the fact that the relation between social order and subject positioning is articulated by hegemonic practices which fill the void, or at least promise to negate the lack which compels the subject to act (see Stavrakakis 1999: 34). However, because filling the void *necessarily* entails the exclusion of meanings and possibilities, so any hegemony remains vulnerable to its immanent and ineliminable horizon of contingency. Contingency continues to inhabit the "decision" of hegemonic closure, which thus fails to fully suture the essential undecidability of the social. In other words, antagonism and dislocation remain an ever-present possibility.

Hegemony and Power: Filling the Void

While contingency is ineliminable, it is also the case that what defines the social *as such* is the more general context of order. From Saussure we know that language (or discourse) is a system of differences that bounds itself as a relational whole. Hegemony is bounded by limiting contingency so that it constitutes a form of "universality." However poststructuralist thought does not subscribe to the context-transcendent universality defended by Habermas, but neither does it abandon the universal as in the case of Lyotard's paralogics. Both, according to Laclau and Mouffe, signal the death of politics, the first because it assumes the exhaustion of meaning as a "totally reconciled human essence," the latter because a free-floating constellation of language games cannot form a common political ground (Laclau 2000: 208-9). Hegemony is neither one nor the other because it tends towards both. If a body of social agents opposes some repressive force, then this shared identification ("we would be free if only...") becomes a common political horizon or "frontier." But to function as a political force it becomes necessary to represent the alliance in its totality. As Newman shows in some detail (Chap. 8), this representational function is the place of the universal, a symbolic or essentially "empty place" into which steps one of the elements as it becomes constitutively split between its own particularity and its function of representing the whole (Laclau 1996: 26, 43). The representation of order and unity is thus split by being both one thing and everything, and will endure only to the extent that it continues to incorporate or repress its immanent horizon of contingency (Laclau 1996: 22; Laclau and Mouffe, 2001: 111-2).

The representational "filling function" is the ideological dimension of hegemony, which is theorized as "myth" and "social imaginary" (Laclau 1990). A mythical representation such as "Class Struggle" or "the Nation" attempts to displace the essential contingency of the structure, stabilizing the social field by anchoring meaning in nodal points[1] (Laclau 1990: 63, 1996: 44; Laclau and Mouffe 2001: 112-4). Nodal points are in effect empty signifiers which are capable of unifying the social field precisely because they are available for interpretation on the part of a multiplicity of agents. A dislocation defined as "crisis" for example is hegemonized by publicly narrating it, directing its meaning in such a way that the mythical representation secures popular support for specific reform programs (Hay 1996 cited in Martin 1998: 124). In contrast to myth, a social imaginary is a surface of inscription which is meaning-given, or a myth which has become so encompassing that it is no longer merely one object among other objects but is the structure supporting the being of objects as such[2] (Laclau 1990: 93-4). Examples of a social imaginary would be the Enlightenment conception of progress or the Communist ideal of a classless society (Torfing 1999: 115).

The filling function of myths and the fixing function of nodal points correspond to specific structural relations, defined as chains or logics of "equivalence and difference" (Laclau and Mouffe 2001: 127-34; Laclau 1996: 44). Condensing the social field into a tightly ordered ensemble of elements, which in Gramscian terms would be a hegemonic bloc or national-popular collective will, the logic of equivalence orders the disordered social field into a political frontier which is defined against some common threat. Such an enemy may be external, for example "international terrorism," or internal, such as "big government." The logic of difference moves in the opposite direction by retaining the differential character of the elements. In crude terms a differential chain describes a divide and rule type situation so that antagonism is diffused. The predominance of one or the other logic will have a bearing on how social space is actually ordered and divided, whether as a multiplicity of articulations or as a dichotomous division of two opposing blocs or frontiers (Norval 2000: 220-1; Mouffe 2000; Laclau 1990: 17; Laclau and Mouffe 2001: 128-9).

To summarize: dislocation and antagonism mark out a complex event—the eruption of contingency, the emergence of political subjectivity, and the reordering of social space. Taken together, this describes the process of hegemonic formation and re-formation. It is also here that power relations become visible, or rather invisible as a result of reification. Laclau tells us that the being of objects "is nothing but the sedimented form of power" whose traces have been erased, so that power is "merely the trace of contingency" inhabiting any objectivity (Laclau 1990: 60). He also tells us that "any decision presupposes an act of power" through the inclusion and exclusion of possibilities, and yet power itself remains ambiguous. On the one hand a power that represses "entails the *capacity to repress*," while on the other a power that represses discloses "the *need* to repress, which involves limitation of power" (Laclau 1990: 60, original emphasis). Relations of power articulate the hegemonic decision as meaning is partially and provisionally stabilized, which also fixes the being of objects, but again only provisionally, as the decision is contaminated by contingency—or the trace of power. Power is constitutive and transformative, while its effects are never more than provisional, because power is ineradicable. Power is also unevenly distributed given the presuppositions of the mythical filling function, which is a capacity on the part of a particular element to hegemonize the disordered field by representing the whole (Laclau 2000: 207-8; Stavrakakis 1999: 20). Hegemony then is a provisional state of order which remains vulnerable to that which it excludes —its immanent surplus of meaning or "horizon of subversion"—which is also the condition of possibility for emancipation on the part of those who are subjected. But the ineliminable trace of contingency is also the impossibility of a once-and-for-all freedom. Precisely because any instituted totality, any universality, presupposes exclusion, so the meaning of emancipation can never be exhausted and it becomes meaningless to think of emancipation as the total elimination of power (Laclau 2000: 208). Instead emancipation entails the ongoing rearticulation of power relations, which leads into the prescriptive dimension of the poststructuralist project.

Political Subjectivity and the Radical Act

This is succinctly phrased in the preface to the second edition of *Hegemony and Socialist Strategy*:

> If one is to build a chain of equivalence among democratic struggles, one needs to establish a frontier and define an adversary, but this is not enough. One also needs to know for what one is fighting, what kind of society one wants to establish. This requires from the Left an adequate grasp of the nature of power relations, and the dynamics of politics. What is at stake is the building of a new hegemony. So our motto is: "Back to the hegemonic struggle" (Laclau and Mouffe 2001: xix).

The answer to the problem of social orders characterized by domination is another hegemony, one that facilitates emancipations. A confrontation with the prevailing neoliberal hegemony for example requires those who identify with the political Left to come together as an equivalential field of force or frontier which itself aims to hegemonize the social field. There is apparently no way out of the hegemonic circle. Hegemony is the how of politics, for good or ill. For Gramsci hegemony was implicated in directing social forces in the historical context of an organic crisis. Laclau and Mouffe's counter-hegemonic program for the Left is also a directing force, but one that operates in a different context.

Counterhegemony no longer foresees a revolution that will overcome the problem of domination once and for all, but is a strategy to prevent closure over the social field so that domination can be continually contested. But how is this critical engagement with hegemony instantiated? Does the counterhegemonic subject wait passively in the wings for structural dislocation or for its identity to be repressed so that it will experience its lack? Or in more pointed terms, what is it that constitutes the "act"?

Žižek draws on Lacanian theory to define the "authentic" or "radical act" in a way that resembles Foucault's well known refusal of "Enlightenment blackmail": his refusal to be either for or against the present (Foucault 1984: 42-3). The danger of such a choice is that the logic of either/or forecloses on alternatives, with both sides of the choice reproducing the prevailing order by interpellating the dissident gesture back into the standing conditions that make the choice meaningful. In the face of such a nonchoice the act of refusal is not a negative stance of evasion but rather a positive act of subversion. Precisely because the surplus is internal to discourse (in Lacanian terms, the Real is internal to the Symbolic), so it is possible to reach the surplus *through* the instituted systems of meaning. Faced with a decision that obliges us to make a solemn choice between, say, class struggle and postmodernism, Žižek's answer is "Yes Please!" (2000). Rather than participating in petty disputes waged under the terms of the prevailing hegemonic order, an authentic act engages in the radical gesture of subverting the very principles structuring the field: refusing the given horizon of the possible and redefining its parameters by retroactively creating the conditions of its own possibility (Žižek 2000: 121). The authentic act is radical precisely because it refuses the blackmail of a spurious choice, instead positing a new horizon of possibilities as presupposed: the thing that we want is already there because we just put it there (Žižek 1989: 215-31). However it remains unclear what sort of agent is responsible for this subversive gesture: is the lacking subject capable of taking the initiative, and would this presuppose a capacity for conscious reflection and decision?

In her recent work Mouffe approaches this problem when she uses the social logics of equivalence and difference to theorize the role of antagonism in liberal democracy. Her argument is that the seemingly natural relation between the liberal and democratic political traditions is in fact a contingent historical articulation (2000). The relation between liberty and equality, between the logics of difference and equivalence, is one of irreconcilable tension. For Mouffe neither logic/tradition is necessarily in and of itself progressive or regressive; in fact the relation of mutual contamination creates a tension or paradox at the heart of modern political life. In view of this Mouffe stands against the idea that the paradox can or should be resolved, arguing instead that the crucial objective today is to prevent closure over this ineliminable gap, which is the possibility for critical thought and radical action. Depending on the context, then one logic/tradition can be used to challenge the overdetermination of the other. For example in the case of ethnonationalism, the liberal tradition provides a political grammar[3] to challenge the essentialist and exclusionary articulation of democratic discourse.

Alternatively the individualizing hegemony of neoliberalism can be challenged by using democratic discourse to press for greater equality and solidarity. This would suggest that political interventions might be strategically enacted, implying a capacity for initiation, or perhaps even *anticipation* outside of the context of dislocation, a capacity which is not however provided for in the theory. Mouffe continues to assume that the moment of antagonism/dislocation marks the birth of political subjectivity, and again there is no conceptual space for the subject outside of the moment of structural instability.

We have seen that dislocation and antagonism move towards fragmentation as a void is opened out in the social field, a void conjoining the lack in the subject and the incomplete structure. Accepting that order presupposes some kind of closure over the sliding of meaning, then the void is essentially a partial vacuum which is filled as agents rearticulate the social field and institute a new hegemony. However unless there is a possibility of *initiating* this process then we are left with a mode of political subjectivity which is structurally determined by the tension between contingency and necessity, thus reworking the old Marxist metaphysic. While the determinacy of historical materialism is abandoned we are still left with the structural determination of the possible, albeit in the negative form of the void. Granted there are important developments in this approach: the dislocated structure does not determine its own future rearticulation (Torfing 1999: 151), and just as importantly, the "frontier-effect" of antagonism/dislocation is not a privileged and unified subject such as the working class, but a chain of political subjectivities which, though united by what they oppose, retain their singularity (and their essential contingency) (Norval 2000: 219-23). Nevertheless, for hegemony to be contested the social field must be conflicted —at the level of structural relations—to such an extent that it has reached some kind of critical mass. Without these conditions we have only a latent agency which has yet to emerge from the slumber of interpellation. The subject as initiator is foreclosed because this apparently requires a theory of the subject as autonomous and in conscious possession of things such as "interests" and "intentions," which would be an illegal move within the constraints of the theory. We will return to this shortly; first I want to problematize the poststructuralist conception of political subjectivity.

The Power to Act

The way I will organize this is by formulating a question with the help of Hardt and Negri (other studies which move in the same general direction include Lash 2002; Bauman 2002a, 2002b; Dean 1999; Beck 1992). Hardt and Negri's work on *Empire* is very different from the studies of the new imperialism by Mann and Chomsky mentioned above. While the US may articulate the logic of *Empire* it cannot be its centre because there is no centre (Hardt and Negri 2001: 384). Arguing that a "paradigm shift" has taken place which has produced a new global "apparatus of rule," Hardt and Negri propose a decentered and deterritorialized mode of sovereignty that suspends historical coordinates and fully envelops the spatial totality; an enfolding which negates the existence of an outside. The new logic of rule sweeps everything within the order of the whole so that "power is both everywhere and nowhere." It is an apparatus with "no external standpoint" and it operates through the "triple imperative" of incorporating, differentiating, and managing its instabilities—feeding on rather than threatened by its contingency. *Empire* produces order through the inclusion of difference, and is not only "resistant to the old weapons [of critique] but actually thrives on them, and thus joins its would-be antagonists in applying them to the fullest" (2001: 138). Hardt and Negri's assessment of the efficacy of social theory in the face of this new apparatus of rule is particularly troubling in its implications for the so-called radical approaches of postmodernist, poststructuralist, postcolonialist, and other anti-essentialist/ constructivist forms of critique. In the words of Hardt and Negri "[t]he danger is that postmodernist theories focus their attention so resolutely on the old forms of power they are running from, with their heads turned backwards, that they tumble unwittingly into the welcoming arms of the new power" (2001: 191). It is not simply that the new apparatus of rule has become resistant to critique; it goes much further by incorporating and enlisting the arguments and insights drawn from these critical frameworks (cf. Bauman 2002a: 23). For Hardt and Negri the only viable possibility for getting beyond the rule of *Empire* rests in the creative power of what they call the "multitude": a fluid force of wills, desires, bodies, and affects engaging in multiple acts of refusal.

According to poststructuralist theory a context marked by "crisis" (antagonism/dislocation) wakes the sleeping beast of contingency and precipitates social movement as the lacking subject looks for something that it can desire, something that will allow it to rest again in its (impossible) dream of plenitude. There is no impetus to act without structural instability. *Empire* however is a situation of "omni-crisis", and it governs by managing its own essential contingency. To transform the rule of *Empire* requires not a latent political subjectivity in the negative form of lack but a positive transformative force which is relentlessly enacted through a proliferation of creative innovations (i.e., the multitude). The multitude's "power to act" takes the positive form of creative and, if so perceived, subversive gestures; it is a "constituent power" of "ontological construction" (2001: 358). The act is one of radical *innovation*: not only refusing to be dominated but also creating new possibilities (2001: 48, 357, 369). We are clearly within the realm of Žižek's authentic act here, but there is a fundamental difference. In thinking the problem of political subjectivity in the context of *Empire* Hardt and Negri move in the opposite direction from the poststructuralists: resistance comes first (2001: 360, 469n). However, Hardt and Negri do not provide an account of how the power to act is (to be) initiated (nor are they particularly clear on the meaning of the multitude). How do we resist or refuse a mode of ordering which does not fear but thrives on its contingency and enlists the support of critical social theory? The theory of *Empire* would seem to be a communist manifesto for postmodernity, perhaps aiming to reformulate Marx's militant and emotive battle cry: "workers of the world unite," with the power of the multitude an assertion of what might be. While the transformative power of the multitude is in part an aspiration on the part of the authors of *Empire*, and thus exhibits a certain fictitious status, we can nonetheless use it to think about the "power to act" and to consider what political subjectivity might look like in the context of *Empire*. This is not simply about refusing that which is meaning-given but about creating spaces for the positing of new possibilities. What is required is an account of the act as *initiated*, or a plausible answer to Hardt and Negri's question: "how are rupture and innovation possible...?" (2001: 387).

What I want to do is use *Empire* to pose the following question: how subversive is the idea of contingency as articulated by the negative concepts of dislocation/antagonism/void/lack? Hardt and Negri's thesis suggests a seismic shift in the order of things—a new *episteme* in Foucaultian terminology, or *imaginary* in Laclau's. If this is correct and the theoretical insights predicated on antagonism/dislocation and counterhegemonic frontier-formation *have* been domesticated by new apparatuses of rule, then at best they lose their status as radical, and at worst can no longer claim to be the basis of real alternatives. This does not mean that these insights should or can be abandoned, but it does require a reassessment of the proposed measures to resist or overcome a social order characterized by domination.

This question will serve as a hinge in moving the discussion laterally from one theoretical framework to another. If Hardt and Negri are correct, then the poststructuralist project to use and direct contingency against the (current neoliberal) hegemony is unlikely to produce the transformative effects it hopes for. In Žižek's account of the authentic act the subject does not express or actualize her inner nature but "transforms the...undead ghosts that haunt the living subject" (2000: 123). The act is drawn towards the immanent horizon of contingency, and is not merely about doing the impossible by retroactively producing its own conditions of possibility; it must also "traverse the social fantasy" by intervening in the symbolic field at its point of failure, thus transforming its "hidden, disavowed structuring principle" (2000: 125). In a classic deconstructionist move, the act looks for that which is off the spectrum of the sayable as a dirty little secret shared by all but uttered by none. Putting this slightly differently, and against those who equate postmodern critique with moral and epistemic relativism, the authentic act does not exist in a vacuum. Instead it presupposes a historical and cultural context which is structured by concrete possibilities and limitations. Insofar as the knowledge produced by poststructuralist theory may itself be implicated in the new apparatus of rule, then it may *be* a point of failure in the symbolic field, so that the act requires that we reach into the void and touch the surplus that contaminates *its* discourse: that which *it* disavows. What is intended is to insert a moment of individual innovation into the poststructuralist rendering of hegemony—an innovation at the level of the reflective self—and to examine this as the site of transformative power. I want to explore the possibility of a certain subject characterized as "centered but

non-unified" being the locus of the radical act. This is not a structurally determined subject position, nor a subject "split" in the Lacanian sense, but a subject
positioned within—without being entirely caged by—the orders of discourse.

From Identification to Self-Transgression

In his theory of power, knowledge and structure (Chap. 3, this volume),
Haugaard makes conceptual space for goal-directed action, with the power to
realize goals on the part of the individual actor a type of decision which is very
different from the role of the decision (hegemonic closure) in poststructuralist
thought. As a form of decision which operates at the interface between subjectivity and subjection, this traces hegemony all the way down to its source, with the
power to act the moment when hegemony may be reenacted or refused – the latter being its point of failure. Before examining this further I want to sketch the
conceptual terrain where Haugaard's theory shades into Laclau and Mouffe's.
The point of contact is Foucault's work on power/knowledge, which allows us to
move across to Haugaard's theory without meeting the obstacle of
incommensurability.
      When Foucault discussed "the true" he was concerned with the practical
effects produced as people set about directing, governing, and conducting themselves and each other (Foucault 1982: 220-21). The society-effect of truth is the
constitution of relatively well defined possibilities regarding what can be said
and what can be done: specific ways of knowing things and related ways of doing things that come together as regimes of social practices. To think about the
social as a "regime of truth" is to study how the social field of objects and relations is discursively ordered and problematized, which for Foucault is the essence of the political (Foucault 1991: 79, 82, 1980: 131). When Foucault traced
out the historical struggles and conflicts which are gathered into the truth of our
present, and when he wrote of the tactical use that can be made of "subjugated
knowledges" (Foucault 1980: 80-3), it is clear that his method of critique was
concerned with disclosing the contingency and the traces of exclusion—the
ineradicable surplus—which inhabits the appearance of necessity (cf. Haugaard
1997: 205-19). There is clearly a strong family resemblance between the
Foucaultian notion of truth and the Gramscian theory of hegemony.
      Foucault used this conception of (social) truth to open out the study of
power as productive and diffuse rather than repressive and concentrated. Yet
despite Foucault's interest in social power, the commentary on his work more or
less agrees that he tended to focus on the constraining rather than the facilitative
effects of this positive power. Incorporating Foucault's insights into their respective frameworks, both Haugaard and Laclau and Mouffe open out the question of
resistance by emphasizing that which power makes possible. For Laclau and
Mouffe relations of power can be directed—in the Gramscian sense—toward the
production of counterhegemonic frontiers and myths. For his part Haugaard
notes that shared systems of meaning—i.e., social knowledge and social prac-

tices —facilitate "the pursuit of goals *through the agency of others* by making cooperative interaction possible" (1997: 123, emphasis added). Goal-directed action in the strong sense of innovation is possible, and is possible at the level of the individual, but this is facilitated and/or constrained by *the agency of others*. This theorization of the subject as facilitated/constrained through social interaction allows us to go right down to the micro-physics of hegemony, and to do so in way which is commensurate with the social ontology of poststructuralism.

While embodying a capacity for reflective thought and conscious action, and thus resembling the centered subject targeted by postmodern critique, the subject of Haugaard's theory is constituted within a particular regime of truth, and is thus circumscribed by a horizon of contingency. In other words this is not the subject of an unchanging and universal essence but a subject with specific performative capacities: on the one hand in possession of social knowledge which is circumscribed by the instituted episteme or imaginary, and on the other hand embodying the particular possibilities and constraints of complex (modern) social being, which splits the subject into "multiple interpretative horizons." The capacity for critical self-reflection—or limited autonomy—is one of gaining distance from local systems of meaning so that the subject becomes a "stranger to themselves." This may sound a little schizophrenic at first blush, but when we examine the relation between social knowledge and multiple interpretative horizons then we find a compelling account of *how* social orders characterized by domination—i.e., hegemony—are reproduced, resisted, and transformed (Haugaard 1997: 126). But note this is less about domination through consent in the naive sense of that term than it is a perpetual struggle within the instituted systems of meaning (see Roseberry 1994: 361). It should also be noted that this theorization of the power to act shares a core concern with Žižek's authentic act, the refusal of that which is meaning-given by bringing contingency into play: the mechanics of re-reification in other words.

Beginning with social knowledge, Haugaard proposes that the actor is in possession of two related levels of social knowledge pertaining to the shared systems of meaning that make social life possible, or more generally, two levels of discourse. Some regions of discourse are deeply sedimented or reified as truth, which is the doxic knowledge we think with rather than about (Bourdieu 1989; Bourdieu and Eagleton 1994; Bauman 2002b: 136, 164; Wacquant 1987). Other regions of discourse are questionable, which reflects those meanings that slide around in the orders of discourse as objects of debate, conflict, antagonism, etc.[4] What makes critical thought and radical action possible is the capacity on the part of the social agent to use the levels of discourse against each other, in effect problematizing those meanings which have become reified. While clearly reflecting a subject-centered perspective, the problem of subjectivism is avoided by positioning the reflective and intentional agent within discursive constraints. In more general terms the duality of social knowledge maps onto the poststructuralist categories of social imaginary/myth and social antagonism. In both theoretical frameworks we are obliged to think about how reified meanings (truth/doxa/imaginary/myth) provide the "ontological" ground upon which struggles over meaning are waged. If we align the theoretical frameworks in this way then it is possible to think about how the different levels of discourse are articulated at the level of the individual subject and the (collective) social subject.

While social knowledge centers the subject as a reflective self capable of critical thought and conscious decision, the related category of multiple interpretative horizons moves in the opposite direction, in effect dispersing the individual across a variety of positions in the social field. In this sense it works in much the same way as subject position/subjectivation, but again it entails a shift in perspective from structural relations to the subject as interpretative agent. When subject position is reconceptualized as interpretative horizon it becomes one segment of a given subjectivity, encompassing a specific realm of social knowledge which corresponds to a particular sphere of social life. An interpretative horizon is a local field of perception and a local way of thinking about the world, and it has its own specific structure of meaning and logic (Haugaard 1997: 179). An individual is competent in multiple social *milieus*, and as she moves from context to context she also switches between interpretative horizons, some of which may exhibit contradictory relations, such as the bureaucrat who engages in affective relations with her family at home while reducing people to units and inputs at work. Laclau and Mouffe (2001: 124) also make reference to this phenomenon when they note that "we all participate in a number of mutually contradictory belief systems," but they insist that no antagonism emerges from this. Haugaard disagrees and maintains that under certain conditions interpretative horizons can be used against each other to problematize a local system of meanings, and this in turn may instantiate antagonism (1997: 179-80).

The move from subject position to interpretative horizon entails a significant shift in perspective, which leaves us with the question of whether this reintroduces the problem of subjectivism. In addressing this I will replace the notion of "self-reflection" with "self-transgression." This is intended to cover the self as a locus of conscious thought and action and the discursively situated individual who articulates a multiplicity of subject positions.[5] The moment of self-transgression dislodges certain meanings from the instituted orders of discourse and makes them available for rearticulation. However, unlike the poststructuralist categories of antagonism/dislocation, this can be *initiated* at the level of the self-transgressing individual. Self-transgression constitutes a gap *within* a subject position, which is not the void of poststructuralism but the act of problematizing something by inserting a wedge between interpretative horizon and social context. The enactment of this gap is a local incidence of dislocation which brings contingency into play and opens out a space for political subjectivity to emerge. I will provide an example of this shortly following a few words on the role of context.

I have noted above that purposeful agency is subject to certain constraints, so that the role of the individual in the production/contestation of hegemony is not a matter of unconstrained autonomy. An innovation at the level of the individual, and this is the centered counterpart to Žižek's authentic act, must, in Haugaard's exact words, work *through the agency of others*. In the same way that Wittgenstein and Saussure tell us that *langue* is not the property of the individual, so individual innovation does not necessarily lead to change at the level of discourse. Individual innovation, like the invention of a new word, is in itself meaningless unless it is taken up and affirmed by others, which brings us to the role of context in the production and transformation of hegemony. The moment of self-transgression is not (yet) the radical act. In itself it is but a tiny rupture in the social fabric of hegemony, sufficient to bring contingency into play but not (yet) implicated in structural transformation. To become a radical act the moment of self-transgression must resonate in its context, and a resonant context is a specific modality of power with the potential to disrupt hegemony. In other words the structural fault lines and antagonistic relations pertaining to hegemony and counterhegemony must be enacted—this is its performative dimension, which is always more than the individual but can nonetheless be initiated at the level of the individual.

John Woo's 1997 movie *Face Off* provides a useful textual illustration of this. The Manichean plot pitches an altruistic good guy, FBI agent Sean Archer, against the egomaniacal terrorist Castor Troy. Troy has planted a bomb in Los Angeles and is the only one who knows its location, and when Archer manages to track him down they engage in combat, with Troy lapsing into a coma after he is seriously injured. With the bomb's whereabouts locked inside Troy's mind and time fast running out, Archer decides to *become* Troy so as to infiltrate his world and secure the vital information. But this is to be no ordinary undercover operation relying on physical disguise and an alias. Instead Archer agrees to undergo a revolutionary new medical procedure to have his own face literally removed and the face of Troy grafted to his head, a covert mission to be known only to a select few. His objective is to slide seamlessly into Troy's life by simulating his exact physical form. Unfortunately for Archer, back in the clinic Troy comes out of his coma and, finding himself faceless, takes his revenge by forcing the surgeon to give him Archer's face, proceeding in turn to take up the FBI agent's life: making love to his wife, teaching violent combat techniques to his daughter, and becoming a public hero by diffusing the very same bomb that the "real" Archer is attempting to track down. This is the twist in the plot. Troy-as-Archer has killed all those who know about the mission, and by diffusing the bomb he essentially locks the real Archer out of his real life. Archer-as-Troy and Troy-as-Archer are constructs which bring together incongruous interpretative horizons and social contexts.

In an act akin to the trope of catachresis, Haugaard's subject uses an interpretative horizon inappropriately to gain critical distance from the reified meanings that constitute her subjectivity and structure her context. Archer-as-Troy and Troy-as-Archer provide us with a purely fictional analogy, one involving a process of mechanical addition, but this does allow us to see how Haugaard's theory of catachrestic action works: as the antagonist and protagonist are folded into each other, so each is compelled to transgress his self. In formal terms Archer and Troy—the agent of US hegemony and the anti-hegemonic terrorist—are subject positions that can be taken up by anyone. But they are also

situated individuals within a specific social context, and the context is a relatively well-defined yet essentially indeterminate matrix of possibilities and constraints which is reproduced/transformed at the level of social interaction. Because our impostors are working within strange contexts they inevitably exhibit
behavioral traits which are entirely inconsistent with the "real" Archer and the
"real" Troy. Yet those who populate their respective circles—lovers, family,
friends, colleagues, etc.—believe them to be who they claim to be, even to the
point of modifying their perceptions in order to accommodate the new Troy and
the new Archer. There are limits to this willingness to repair the damaged context however, and in both cases the impostors are obliged to bring other forces
into play in order to keep the pretence going: Archer-as-Troy enlists support
from Troy's girlfriend by tacitly including her in his dangerous secret; Troy-as-
Archer resorts to bravado and bullying, abusing the authority that comes with his
office. In their respective attempts to create power resources (Haugaard 1997:
172, 190) both are using interpretative horizons that go against the grain of his
context, and both lack the social knowledge required to fully inhabit the subjectivity they are attempting to simulate. While Archer-as-Troy attempts to account
for the slips and accidents that might give him away, Troy-as-Archer revels in
deliberate acts of deviancy, but common to both is the way they disrupt and
modify local systems of meaning. But this is possible only insofar as these modi-
fications are *affirmed* by others within the field: the extent to which a novel action resonates in its context. Because they have created a gap *within* a subject
position—between interpretative horizon and social context—so they are implicated in acts of meaning-creation and truth production, but the outcome is never
wholly within their sphere of control (see Haugaard 1997: 172, 190). As local
universes of meaning are disrupted, so they must be *intersubjectively* repaired: a
strictly discursive process. But note this is not (necessarily) a rational-delibera-
tive consensus of the Habermasian type; instead the resonant context is constructed antagonistically. This allows us to recenter the purposeful agent within
the social ontology of poststructuralism without rehabilitating the subject as an
autonomous author of meaning and, with respect to Habermasian discourse ethics, without fetishizing consensus.

Locating the Radical Act

It was noted above that Laclau and Mouffe theorize hegemony as a decision
which successfully articulates and directs political identification toward specific
structural relations. David Howarth (2000: 122) notes a tendency in this to conflate what are in fact two modes of conflict: conflict within a structure and conflict which is implicated in structural change.[6] These are not necessarily distinct
concerns, as demonstrated by the example of feminism.

In their account of feminism, Laclau and Mouffe do not subscribe to the
idea of a unified and essential subject of feminism or a single mechanism of
women's oppression, but they do insist that it is possible to work with the idea of

a sex/gender system: a feminine pole subordinated to a masculine pole (2001: 117-8). This positing of a societal *division* makes it possible to theorize feminism as the formation of a political frontier. They also draw an important distinction between relations of subordination and relations of oppression. A relation of subordination is defined as one in which an agent is subjected to the decisions of another by virtue of "the way things are," as in the case of patriarchal forms of organization whereby men are by default cast in a privileged position above women. Relations of oppression by contrast are sites of antagonism wherein sedimented meanings have been destabilized and social structures partly dislocated. Relations of subordination correspond roughly to the category of subject position in the Althusserian sense, while relations of oppression correspond to dislocation and antagonism. The transformation from subordination to oppression is accounted for by the series: dislocation—antagonism—rearticulation—frontier formation. Applying this to the case of feminism, Laclau and Mouffe tell us that feminism could not emerge as a movement until democratic discourse provided the means to produce a strategic displacement of meaning. It is only in the context of the democratic revolution that the sedimented meanings invested in the subject positioning of "woman" could be questioned, and thus it became possible to transform subordination into a political struggle against oppression. Mary Wollstonecraft's 1792 *Vindication of the Rights of Woman* provides the example of how democratic discourse was put to practical use by displacing it from the field of political equality between citizens to the field of equality between the sexes (Laclau and Mouffe 2001: 153-4). Crucially, the condition of possibility for this displacement is not critical reflection on the part of Mary Wollstonecraft as a self, but the availability of the democratic principles of liberty and equality in the emerging social imaginary (2001: 155). The genesis of feminism is cast along the horizon of the democratic imaginary; it is but one—albeit very significant—dimension of structural dislocation and hegemonic re-formation. "Wollstonecraft" symbolizes the lack embodied in the collective subject of "woman," and the condition of possibility for its manifestation is the new horizon of possibilities constituted by the democratic revolution of the 17th and 18th centuries. At the generalized level of explanation the account is compelling, but it tends to preclude an investigation into precisely how dislocation might be enacted.

For Haugaard, a woman born into a patriarchal society tends to absorb the patriarchal world view so that it forms part of her interpretative horizon—she accepts the meanings invested in the social role of women (1997: 126). However, although born into patriarchal social circumstances she is not trapped by her cultural experience and under certain circumstances she may adopt a critical attitude to her socially-ascribed role. We are not told what the catalyst for this critical shift in perspective might be, which is presumably context-specific (and may be explained by the account above), but we are told why and how she rejects her complicity in patriarchal hegemony. The why relates to the fact that power is not conferred equally within the social system, and as the standing conditions privilege some individuals and groups at the expense of others so it makes "strategic sense" for those who are disempowered to engage in conflict over the prevailing structures (1997: 138-9). The how relates to the way that interpretative horizons can be used against each other to deconstruct and objectify a specific region of social knowledge (an alternative explanation for Wollstonecraft's act of displacement). The shift in interpretative horizons sees the woman in question "taking the stance of third person with respect to herself—the position of an outsider who does not take for granted the same things as the members of the patriarchal society" (Haugaard 1997: 126). In creating a gap within a subject position, that is, a gap between interpretative horizon and social context, this particular subject has come to perceive her subject position *as such*: an arbitrary construction within which her subjectivity is cast. In re-perceiving her socially ascribed position as contingent rather than meaning-given, that is, by coming into conscious possession of the fact that the particular meanings invested in "woman" have been socially produced and could therefore be otherwise, she becomes a political agent capable of transgressing her self. She is in possession of the means to politicize the meaning of "woman." However as discussed above, and this is crucial, she must now communicate this insight to others, who may agree wholeheartedly, may be willing to listen skeptically, or may dismiss her as an eccentric or someone who has lost her mind.

Both accounts provide plausible explanations for the emergence of a new political subject. However while Laclau and Mouffe work within the context of antagonism/dislocation and frontier formation, Haugaard opens out the possibility for innovation on the part of the individual. If we combine the poststructuralist terminology of "subordination" and "oppression" with Haugaard's framework then we can say that the subordinated individual has not found a way to disclose the arbitrariness of her subjection, and so she works within a realm of social knowledge or discourse whereby she reproduces the reified meanings invested in her subject position: she accepts the truth of "woman" and is thus implicated in the reproduction of hegemony. Alternatively, the oppressed individual has discovered the arbitrariness of her subjection, and using her repertoire of interpretative horizons against each other she gains the critical distance required to contest the meanings invested in "woman." By switching between interpretative horizons the individual transgresses her self insofar as she has been cast by the conventional meanings invested in the subject position of "woman." This in turn problematizes a specific region of hegemony as meanings are dislodged or dislocated from their place of reified inscription. A double displacement thus takes place at the levels of the subject and the structure, with the necessity of truth/hegemony transformed into contingency.

To sum up: the radical act cannot be reduced to the moment of self-transgression but must incorporate the context, and once constituted as a resonant context then the act may be local and transient or may extend in scope and become implicated in significant structural change. The act may or may not be the genesis of articulatory practices pertaining to a counterhegemonic social movement. Yet even if local and transient it may still have effects. And this raises an important line of research in view of the question derived from Hardt and Negri.

If it is credible to speak of a new global apparatus of rule in the way that *Empire* proposes, then it may be the multiplicity and proliferation of locally creative acts that prevents hegemonic closure and opens out the possibility for alternatives. In this sense it would be an error to foreclose on the possibility of studying the articulation of power at the level of individual innovations.

Conclusion

Poststructuralist thought tells us that a totally ordered society comprising fully constituted social identities would mean the eradication of politics and power. While this would be an end state of conciliation and harmony, it would also be a world emptied of alternatives and closed to new ways of being: a logical and empirical impossibility within the social ontology of poststructuralism. If hegemony is the necessary form of politics today and is immanent to the world we inhabit; if it is the *how* of politics as we structure the world through the ordering and disordering of meaning, then the possibility of resistance is always already within the prevailing conditions of possibility: that which is excluded by the decision. The constitutive surplus is the basis of the radical act, an act that makes a strategic cut in the discursive field through which contingency pours forth as the possibility for posing alternatives. I have argued that we can retain these theoretical insights while moving beyond the negative conception of the subject as lack or void. This is not about rehabilitating the subject as "unified and unifying essence" (Laclau and Mouffe 2001: 116). Instead it reconsiders the role of individually enacted and discursively situated innovations in social formation and transformation. What is proposed is to shift the locus of the radical act from the negativity of a void to a positive center of innovation within the orders of discourse.

The answer to the problem of hegemony is not necessarily its mirror image. Unless there is one big answer to the problems of today, a scenario that surely presents its own dangers, then resistance and alterity are necessarily mobile, fleeting and partial in the sense of guerrilla tactics rather than a Gramscian war of position. Thinking about power and the political in terms of structural instability and frontier-formation should not preclude examining political conflict in terms of a multiplicity of transient alliances, oppositions, innovations and transgressions. A very Foucaultian scenario to be sure, and one criticized by Newman in the proceeding chapter, yet these need not be seen in either/or terms. While guerrilla tactics may not lead to a (counter) hegemonic frontier, they are nonetheless capable of preventing closure over the social field, and this is an important—possibly even vital—dimension of contemporary political life.

Notes

1. The nodal point is derived from the Lacanian "point de capiton" or "master signifier" (see Žižek 1989; Stavrakakis 1999; Fink 1995).

2. This is similar to the episteme in Foucault's early work (see Foucault 1972).

3. Mouffe derives this usage of "grammar" from Wittgenstein's *Philosophical Investigations*.

4. Haugaard builds on Anthony Giddens' (1984) theory of structuration, where Freud's scheme of Id, Ego, and Superego is reformulated as Discursive Consciousness (DC), Practical Consciousness (PC), and Unconscious (UC).

5. I am using this term in a different way to Bauman in his *Liquid Modernity* (2002: 209-10). For Bauman it denotes a state of perpetual becoming: an individualized subject and a fragile self who is moving so fast that she overlooks the fact that what appears to be *destiny* is in fact *fate*. Jason Glynos (2004) has also surveyed the notion of self-transgression, himself developing a Lacanian account. The latter concerns the violation of ideals which are central to one's conception of self, such as publicly upholding the ideal of sexual equality while at the same time availing of opportunities to use sexist language, tell sexist jokes, or participate in sexual practices more generally (the example is Glynos' own). Again, my use of the concept differs from this.

6. This is similar to the way in which power can be analyzed both episodically and relationally *within* a given hegemony and as a struggle to *overturn* or *transform* a hegemonic formation (see Haugaard 1997: 68-9).

Conclusion

Chapter Eleven

Dynamics and Complexity in Politics

Howard H. Lentner

As argued by Haugaard in chapter one, the debate about political power is a long-standing and complex one. Yet that debate has been greatly enriched by its confrontation with the debate about hegemony. Fontana's presentation of both historical views and those of Gramsci, plus his analysis of the complex interactions of civil society and state, demonstrate how rich the thinking about hegemony has been. In both of these chapters as well as others the authors have shown that hegemony represents different dimensions of power. First, it includes activities associated with organization of political power through education, intellectual activity, rhetoric, and the mobilization of consent to achieve power. Second, it includes rule through domination and putting into place an enduring order. Third, it includes both resistance and the activities associated with forming alliances that aspire to replace the dominant order, that is, counterhegemonic activities.

Haugaard's discussion in Chapter Three interprets hegemony as a specific manifestation of power, and, by relying on Foucault and Laclau and Mouffe, he reinterprets hegemony as discourse. In the end for Haugaard ideology in Gramsci's analysis gets replaced by "an essentially arbitrary set of conventions" and a psychological analysis of "ontological security." By ending his essay with commentary on American policy toward Iraq, Haugaard reveals some overlap between social theory and realist thinking about power. He cites Tuke's understanding that "true power over an individual is created . . . through the soft tissues of the mind." Similarly, Morgenthau (1973: 28, 29) writes: "Political power is a psychological relation between those exercise it and those over whom it is exercised" and "[p]olitical power must be distinguished from force in the sense of the actual exercise of physical violence." Haugaard points to the limits of power and to the distinction between coercion and governance. Morgenthau (1973), Waltz (1979), and Schelling (1960) all agree that the actual use of force shows a breakdown of power, that power does not always produce control, and that, as Waltz (1979: 191) puts it, "Conquering and governing are different processes." At the same time, they point to the utility of threats of forceful action and of latent violence in politics and governing. Further work on the relationship of latent violence within systems of governance might be prompted by incorporating these concerns from international politics scholarship into general social analyses of power.

Cerny continues the discussion of American foreign policy, specifically and analytically by elaborating four "fault lines" in the practice of hegemony. Applying a neoliberal approach Cerny invokes issue-area analysis and treats the difficulties of institutionalization. He also notes a parallel in Lukes' work on power with hegemonic analysis. Finally, treating hegemony as a systemic phenomenon, he points to the inherent tensions between pursuit of the interests of the hegemon and its stabilizing functions for the system as a whole. Central to his analysis is the emphasis he places on the role of subalterns who stabilize the system by accepting, sometimes internalizing, and at other times tolerating domination. This rich consideration of the complexity of operationalizing theory reflects an ongoing tension in analysis between historical action and broader theory that seeks to explain phenomena at a general level.

In his chapter Lentner continues attention to international affairs and makes explicit the differing conceptions of hegemony and power that exist particularly in international politics theory but also in thinking about domestic politics. This treatment emphasizes the different tradition in this field in which Dahl's conception, dominant in political analysis over the past half-century, has been explicitly rejected by leading writers. Also emphasized are the different ways in which distribution of power has been handled in political analysis, which is mostly concerned with democracy, and in international politics, which is primarily concerned with stability. Lentner also attempts at the end of the chapter to show the utility of both the international and domestic literatures to inform and enrich the other.

Goverde's nuanced, layered analysis of the tensions in the hegemonic North Atlantic alliance led by the United States continues attention to international relations, but he also includes a treatment of the agency within political units. In the author's view realist theory has been restored, with states and security taking center stage, and the divergences between leader and followers provoking fissures that may not heal unless policies take cognizance of longer-term interests as well as immediate ones.

Hattori too pursues attention to international relations, but his chapter offers the significantly different perspective of "critical naturalism." This approach combines material and symbolic relations to examine hegemony in the capitalist system, and it treats foreign aid as a manifestation of structural power rather than as an individualistic set of relations among autonomous states. In addition to deepening our understanding of relations of power, the chapter also brings in the ethical dimension that accompanies all transactions and positional relationships.

Penttinen's examination of Finnish feminists' campaign to protect foreign women working as prostitutes employs a conception of security drawn from international relations theory. But the analyst also brings in postmodern thinking to expose the fundamentally power-infused relationship between protectors and victims which denies agency to the protected. More explicitly than in some of the other chapters, Penttinen draws attention to normative concerns in political analysis.

In his chapter treating a radical agenda within a more fragmented political environment, Newman demonstrates the no longer so germane conceptions of Foucault and goes on to think from the position of Lacan and his "void." The author notes the overlap in the individual of both particular and universal, pointing to the immense complexity of power in the modern world. In both this and the following chapter, the analysis is driven by a normative concern for finding guidance for radical action.

Ryan confronts the Lacanian notion of void but joins forces with Žižek to find "quilting points" for forging hegemony. Meanings can be contested within many different relationships, but through radical action the void is reduced to a starting rather than resting point. From this creative consideration of postmodernism, Ryan circles back to Haugaard's multiple interpretive horizons as a source for resolution of political problems in contemporary society.

Like the old story of several blind men describing an elephant, postmodern ideas resist the conception of overarching hegemonic ideologies and coercive political systems and claim that truth can only be described in part and from particular vantage points. The many viewpoints of the authors of this book offer testimony to remarkably varied approaches to and conceptualizations of power and hegemony. Both of the central concepts have been treated in quite diverse ways, and definitions and meanings are contested. Apart from the discrete treatments, the authors bring very different intellectual traditions to bear. Modern and postmodern modes of thinking appear here. Especially in the later chapters, references are made to lost Marxist categories. Yet, the book contains the thread of continuity with even the ancient past of political thought. While the classic distinction between international and domestic political systems remains, a couple of authors treat them as overlapping and mutually informative, subject to comparative analysis. Despite the great differences among the authors brought together here to consider power and hegemony in conjunction with each other, the result has advanced the power debate and the hegemony debate.

In the long debate about political power some attention has been paid to ideology as a means to justify domination (Haugaard 2000), but there has never before been such an explicit confrontation of the concepts power and hegemony. The latter contains the most systematic conception of the role of ideology not just in justification or legitimation of but also in organizing systems of domination. In Gramsci's conception hegemony and material power resources are combined to produce rule of some groups over others. Even so, hegemony remains limited in Gramsci's conception, for those not accepting of a leading group's direction of society have to be suppressed or exterminated by material power. Such a limitation is implied in contemporary American foreign policy which excludes from cooperation certain states characterized as "rogue states" and "states supporting terrorism," although in practice the United States does engage in diplomatic negotiations with some of the states so designated, such as North Korea. Another meaning of hegemony has long been used in the international politics literature; here, hegemony equates with domination of a single power over others, thus being devoid of any ideational content. An older meaning of hegemony—that articulated by ancient Greek historians including Thucydides—lies closer to Gramsci's conception in that it includes a leader possessing power but also other resources and an alliance of led, each ally remaining autonomous, and without common citizenship. These differences of definition and conceptualization offer numerous puzzles to be sorted out.

Immediately, the confrontation of hegemony and power promises important results by returning the discourse of power to political analysis, for it is clear that politics is involved in the operations of power and hegemony, and new debates are immediately generated in the confrontation. For example, the most famous formulation of power, Weber's (1957) and Dahl's (1957, 1968), indicates that consent is not part of a power relationship in which one is able to gain the cooperation of another despite resistance or to induce another to act against his own wishes. In contrast, the Gramscian conception of hegemony places consent at its center. Furthermore, the Weberian-Dahlian notion relies upon individualistic analysis in which two autonomous persons or groups have a relationship in which one is dominant and the other submissive. The Greek-Gramscian conception, in stark contrast, employs a set of cooperating agents: essential to Gramsci's argument, for example, are leaders, organic intellectuals, and followers arrayed in a pattern of domination with each unit collaborating rather than resisting. This basic conception, together with an essential counterhegemony that forms part of the analysis, also includes a political process of interaction and change over time that is both more political than and inconsistent with the repetitious and static character of the structural power formulations of Foucault (1980, 1982) and Clegg (1989).

The confrontation also gives new emphasis to the old question of the relationship between stability and change. Gramsci treats hegemony as the key to stability through permanent consent to power and domination, with counterhegemony representing change. On the other hand, Lukes (2001: 687) has written, "At its most general, *power* simply denotes the capacity of agents to bring changes." Any attention to change immediately raises the question of the meaning and degree of change. Gramsci draws a distinction between "small politics" and revolutionary or "grand politics." Gilpin's (1981) classification of system (nature of actors) change, systemic (governance) change, and interaction (processes) change offers another useful way of distinguishing and weighing change. In the discourse following our book's advance it will be necessary to deal with change and stability within power relations. In doing so, it will be well to remember that Gramsci's conception of counterhegemony grows in the context and out of a hegemonic arrangement. Thus, it seems unlikely, as Cerny in his chapter has argued so forcefully, that a counterhegemonic tendency can be created and established by a foreign power ruled under an alien hegemonic system.

In this dynamic conception, the process necessarily involves consideration of the origins of hegemony and then of counterhegemony and the formation and com-position of ideology. Lentner (2005) has noted that ideology occurs in the context of a politics that assumes conflict among groups and that hegemony stems from fear of domination, drive for autonomy, and aspiration to dominate others. Similarly, ideology results from a quest to understand one's own situation and a need to con-vince others to join a political project as well as to provide policy guidance. Wolf (1999: 44) has exposed Gramsci's thinking on hegemony "not as a fixed state of affairs but as a continuous process of contestation." Wolf (1999: 283-84) has also offered the insight that the imaginary worlds of ideology postulate cosmologies; "cosmologies, in turn, articulate with ideologies that assign to the wielders of power the role of mediators or executors on behalf of larger cosmic forces and grant them the 'natural' rights to dominate society as delegates of the cosmic order."

The very notion of hegemony in the Greek historians-Gramsci mode implies that allies or followers possess autonomy, for these subordinates, in giving their consent to leadership or domination, have by implication the ability to refuse inclu-sion in a hegemonic arrangement. In view of the fact that all systems of domination —consensual or coercive, allied or imperial, democratic or authoritarian/totali-tarian—employ ideology as a justification and guide to action, it is autonomy rather than ideology that provides the distinguishing trait of hegemonic arrangements (Lentner 2005).

In considering autonomy, Castoriadis (1991: 113-64) has shown that autonomy is a social property in which a specific kind of hegemony, a polity that embraces freedom of speech and self-governance, foments individual autonomy. Similarly, Clarke (1999: 276) emphasizes that autonomy means that actual choices remain available and that these are supplied by the society. These views clarify one type of autonomy, that which exists within hegemony, the autonomy of followers who make significant choices that nevertheless fall within the boundaries of an existing hege-monic ideology. In addition, Lentner (2005) has elaborated two other types of autonomy. Counterhegemony, contained in Gramsci's thought, is the second type that embodies the tensions within a hegemonic arrangement but which represents an aspiration to formulate an alternative ideology and to promote change to a differ-ent hegemonic arrangement. The third type of autonomy gets expressed in an op-posed hegemony, like the Communist Soviet hegemonic arrangement during the Cold War, that exists outside the boundaries of an existing hegemonic system such as the United States-led set of alliances during the same period.

Perhaps the clearest generalization that emerges from the confrontation of hegemony and power is the simple reiteration of old wisdom that politics operates through both violence and speech, both coercion and consent. In the Greek view, virtuous leadership and sensible policy decisions are crucial to the perpetuation of a hegemonic alliance. At the same time, power remains an important ingredient but also a dangerous one, for leaders are tempted to develop toward an empire through domination. Similarly, there are temptations within coherent domestic political systems for leaders to acquire tyrannical power. In both cases, the Greek historians (Wickersham 1994) have taught us that power is never separable from circumstances, strategic thinking, education, and virtue.

Although there are connections between the Greek view and the modern one from Gramsci, both of which emphasize politics and rhetoric as important components in forging and maintaining alliances, it is important to keep in mind the differences. For one, Gramsci did not give any systematic consideration to autonomy even though he assumed it; for example, he (Gramsci 1971: 9) held that in some sense every individual is an intellectual with the ability to think about politics. Neither did he concern himself with virtue, policy and strategy, and other qualities that characterize agents.

Thus, the confrontation of hegemony and power that this book offers results in a renewed emphasis on the complexity of politics. Power remains a central concept in analyzing politics but it is lent through our analysis a dynamic quality absent from some recent treatments. Furthermore, we have argued that ideas and power go together in a process in which leaders and followers interact in both cooperation and counteraction. Power can no longer be thought to supplant politics. Following this analysis, students of power will need to keep in mind the complexity of politics, the place of power within it, and the nature of struggle over domination and common action.

References

Abubakar, Jibrin 2005. "African Union Fails to Produce Candidates for UN." *Daily Trust (Abuja)*, July 6, accessed at http://allafrica.com/stories/200507060688.html.

Adamson, Walter L. 1980. *Hegemony and Revolution: A Study of Antonio Gramsci's Cultural and Political Theory*. Berkeley: University of California Press.

Adamson, Walter L. 1987. "Gramsci and the Politics of Civil Society." *Praxis Intenational* 3-4: 320-39.

Al-Madhagi, Ahmed Nomen 1994. *Yemen and USA: A Superpower and a Small State Relationship, 1962-1992*. London: I. B. Tauris.

Almond, Gabriel A., and Sidney Verba 1963. *The Civic Culture: Political Attitudes and Democracy in Five Nations*. Princeton: Princeton University Press.

Almond, Gabriel A., and Sidney Verba 1980. *The Civic Culture Revisited*. Boston: Little Brown.

Althusser, Louis 1994. "Ideology and Ideological State Apparatuses." In *Essays in Ideology*, Louis Althusser. London: Verso.

Ambrose, Stephen E. 1971. *Rise to Globalism: American Foreign Policy 1938-1970*. Baltimore: Penguin.

Anderson, James 2003. "American Hegemony after 11 September: Allies, Rivals and Contradictions." *Geopolitics* 8, 3: 35-60.

Anderson, Perry 1976-77. "The Antinomies of Antonio Gramsci." *New Left Review* 100: 4-78.

Appadurai, Arjun 1996. *Modernity at Large: Cultural Dimensions of Globalization*. Minneapolis: University of Minnesota Press.

Arendt, Hannah 1958. *The Human Condition*. Chicago: University of Chicago Press.

Arendt, Hannah 1970. *On Violence*. London: Penguin.

Aristotle 1941. *The Basic Works of Aristotle*, edited by Richard McKeon. New York: Random House.

Aristotle 2002. *Politics*. Loeb Classical Library. Cambridge, Mass: Harvard University Press.

Arts, Bas 2004. "Counterhegemonic Power: Transnational Social Movements," paper prepared for presentation at Interim Meeting of IPSA Research Committee on Power, New York (June).

Arvin, B. M. 1997. "Untied Aid and Export: Do Untied Aid Disbursements Create Goodwill for Donor Exports?" *Canadian Journal of Development Studies* 18: 9-22.

Augelli, Enrico, and Craig Murphy 1988. *American Quest for Supremacy and the Third World: A Gramscian Analysis*. London: Pinter.

Avineri, Shlomo. 1971. *The Social and Political Thought of Karl Marx*. Cambridge: Cambridge University Press.

Ayoob, Mohammed 1995. *The Third World Security Predicament: State Making, Regional Conflict, and the International System*. Boulder: Lynne Rienner.

Bachrach, Peter, and Morton S. Baratz 1962. "The Two Faces of Power." *American Political Science Review* 56, 4 (December): 947-52.

Bachrach, Peter, and Morton S. Baratz 1963. "Decisions and Nondecisions: An Analytical Framework." *American Political Science Review* 57, 3 (September): 641-51.

Bachrach, Peter, and Morton S. Baratz 1970. *Power and Poverty: Theory and Practice*. New York: Oxford University Press.

Bakunin, Mikhail 1984. *Political Philosophy: Scientific Anarchism.*. Edited by G.P Maximoff. London: Free Press of Glencoe.

Balibar, Etienne 1995. "Ambiguous Universality." *Differences: A Journal of Feminist Cultural Studies*, 7,1: 48-72.

Balibar, Etienne 2002. *Politics and the Other Scene*. Trans. by Christine Jones et al. London: Verso.

Baldwin, David A. 1966a. *Economic Development and American Foreign Policy: 1943-1962*. Chicago: University of Chicago Press.

Baldwin, David A. 1966b. *Foreign Aid and American Foreign Policy: A Documentary Analysis*. New York: Praeger.

Baldwin, David A. 1978. "Power and Social Exchange." *American Political Science Review* 72 (December): 1229-42.

Baldwin, David A. 1985. *Economic Statecraft*. Princeton, NJ: Princeton University Press.

Baldwin, David A. 1989. *Paradoxes of Power*. New York: Blackwell.

Baldwin, David A. 1998. "Exchange Theory and International Relations." *International Negotiation* 3: 139-49.

Baldwin, David A. 2002. "Power and International Relations." In *Handbook of International Relations*, edited by Walter Carlsnaes, Thomas Risse, and Beth A. Simmons. London: Sage.

Barnes, Barry 1988. *The Nature of Power*. Cambridge: Polity.

Barnes, John R. 1987. *An Introduction to Religious Foundations in the Ottoman Empire*. Leiden, the Netherlands: E. J. Brill.

Barnett, Michael, and Raymond Duvall, "Power in International Politics." *International Organization* 59 (Winter 2005): 39-75.

Bauman, Zygmunt 1989. *Modernity and the Holocaust*. Cambridge: Polity.

Bauman, Zygmunt 1991. *Modernity and Ambivalence*. Cambridge: Polity.

Bauman, Zygmunt 2002a. *Liquid Modernity*. Cambridge: Polity.

Bauman, Zygmunt 2002b. *Society Under Siege*. Cambridge: Polity.

Beasley-Murray, Jon 2003. "On Posthegemony." *Bulletin of Latin American Research* 22, 1: 117-125

Beck, Ulrich 1992. *Risk Society: Towards a New Modernity*. London: Sage.

Beetham, David 1991. *The Legitimation of Power*. London: Macmillan.

Berndtson, Erkki. "Globalization as Americanization." In *Power in Contemporary Politics: Theories, Practices, Globalizations*, edited by Henri Goverde et al. London: Sage, 2000: 155-169.

Berzins, Chris, and Patrick Cullen 2003. "Terrorism and Neomedievalism." *Civil Wars* 6, 2 (Summer): 8-32.

Bhaskar, Roy 1989. *The Possibility of Naturalism*, 2nd ed. Hemel Hempstead, Hertfordshire, UK: Harvester Wheatsheaf.

Bhaskar, Roy 1997. *A Realist Theory of Science*. New York: Verso.

Blau, Peter 1964. *Exchange and Power in Social Life*. New York: John Wiley, 1964).

Bobbio, Norberto 1975. "Gramsci e la concezione della società civile." In *Gramsci e la cultura contemporanea*, edited by Pietro Rossi. Rome: Riuniti-Istituto Gramsci.

Boot, Max 2002. *The Savage Wars of Peace: Small Wars and the Rise of American Power*. New York: Basic Books.

Bourdieu, Pierre 1977. *Outline of a Theory of Practice*. New York: Cambridge University Press.

Bourdieu, Pierre 1979. "Symbolic Power." *Critique of Anthropology* 4: 77-85.

Bourdieu, Pierre 1979. *Algeria 1960: The Disenchantment of the World*. Cambridge: Cambridge University Press.

Bourdieu, Pierre 1989. "Social Space and Symbolic Power." *Sociological Theory* 7, 1 Spring: 14-25.

Bourdieu, Pierre 1990. *The Logic of Practice*. Cambridge: Polity Press.

Bourdieu, Pierre, Jean-Claude Chamboredon, and Jean-Claude Passeron 1991. *The Craft of Sociology: Epistemological Preliminaries*. Berlin: Walter de Gruyter.

Bourdieu, Pierre, and Loic J. D. Wacquant 1992. *An Invitation to Reflexive Sociology*. Chicago: University of Chicago Press.

Bourdieu, Pierre and Terry Eagleton 1994. "Doxa and Common Life: An Interview." In *Mapping Ideology*, edited by Slavoj Žižek. London and New York: Verso.

Boyce, J. K., and Manuel Pastor 1998. "Aid for Peace: Can International Financial Institutions Help Prevent Conflict?" *World Policy Journal* 15: 42-9.

Brenner, Neil 2004. *New State Spaces: Urban Governance and the Rescaling of Statehood*. New York: Oxford University Press.

Brodie, Bernard ed. 1946. *The Absolute Weapon: Atomic Power and World Order*. New York: Harcourt, Brace.

Brodie, Bernard 1965. *Strategy in the Missile Age*. Princeton: Princeton University Press.

Brodie, Bernard 1973. *War and Politics*. New York: Macmillan.

Brown, Thomas Ford 1977. "Ideological Hegemony and Global Governance." *Journal of World Systems Research* 3: 250-258.

Brzezinski, Zbigniew 2004. *The Choice: Domination or Leadership*. New York: Basic Books.

Buci-Glucksman, Christine. 1975. *Gramsci et l'Etat: pour une théorie matérialiste de la philosophie*. Paris: Fayard.

Bull, Hedley 1977. *The Anarchical Society: A Study of Order in World Politics*. New York: Columbia University Press.

Burke, Anthony 2002. "Aporias of Security." *Alternatives* 27, 1: 1-27.

Butler, Judith 1993. *Bodies that Matter: On the Discursive Limits of Sex*. London: Routledge.

Butler, Judith 1997. *The Psychic Life of Power: Theories in Subjection*. Stanford: Stanford University Press.

Butler, Judith, Ernesto Laclau and Slavoj Žižek 2000. *Contingency, Hegemony, Universality: Contemporary Dialogues on the Left*. London: Verso.

Buttigieg, Joseph A. 1990. "Gramsci's Method." *boundary 2*, 17: 60-81.

Buttigieg, Joseph A. 1993. "Introduction." In Antonio Gramsci, *Prison Notebooks*, edited and translated by Joseph A. Buttigieg. New York: Columbia University Press.

Buttigieg, Joseph A. 1994. "Philology and Politics: Returning to the Text of Antonio Gramsci." *boundary 2*, 21: 98-138.

Buttigieg, Joseph A. 1995. "Gramsci on Civil society." *boundary 2*, 22: 1-32.

Cammett, John. 1967. *Antonio Gramsci and the Origins of Italian Communism*. Stanford: Stanford University Press.

Cassen, Robert, and Associates 1994. *Does Aid Work? Report to an Intergovernmental Task Force*, 2nd ed. New York: Oxford University Press.

Castells, Manuel 1996-1999. *The Information Age*.Three volumes: *The Rise of the Network Society* (1996), *The Power of Identity* (1997), and *The End of Millenium* (1999), Oxford: Blackwell.

Castoriadis, Cornelius 1991. *Philosophy, Politics, Autonomy*. Edited and translated by David Ames Curtis. New York: Oxford University Press.

Catrina, Christian 1988. *Arms Transfer and Dependence*. New York: Taylor and Francis.

Central Women's Union in Finland 2005. *Statement After Spring Meeting April 22-23*.

Helsinki. www.naisjarjestojenkeskuslitto.fi.

Cerny, Philip G. 2000. "Globalization and the Disarticulation of Power: Towards a New Middle Ages?" In *Power in Contemporary Politics: Theories, Practices, Globalizations*, edited by Henri Goverde, Philip G. Cerny, Mark Haugaard, and Howard H. Lentner. London: Sage.

Cerny, Philip G. 2000. "The New Security Dilemma: Divisibility, Defection and Disorder in the Global Era," *Review of International Studies* 26, 3 (October): 623-46.

Cerny, Philip G. 2005. "Terrorism and the New Security Dilemma." *Naval War College Review* 58, 1 (Winter): 11-33.

Chomsky, Noam 2003. *Hegemony or Survival: America's Quest for Global Dominance.* London: Hamish Hamilton.

Clark, Martin. 1977. *Antonio Gramsci and the Revolution That Failed.* New Haven: Yale University Press.

Clark, Richard 2004. *Against All Enemies. Inside America's War on Terror.* New York: Free Press.

Clarke, Paul Berry 1999. *Autonomy Unbound.* Aldershot: Ashgate.

Claude, Inis L. 1962. *Power and International Relations.* New York: Random House.

Clegg, Stewart 1989. *Frameworks of Power.* London: Sage.

Coalition Against Trafficking in Women 2005. www.catwinternational.org/.

Cohen, Jean, and Andrew Arato. 1992. *Civil Society and Political Theory.* Cambridge, Mass: MIT Press.

Cohen, Youssef 1987. "Democracy From Above: The Political Origins of Military Dictatorship in Brazil." *World Politics* XL, 1 (October): 30-55.

Cohn, Carol, and Cynthia Enloe 2003. "A Conversation with Cynthia Enloe: Feminists Look at Masculinity and the Men Who Wage War." *Signs* 28, 41: 1187-1207.

Cohn, Theodore 2000. *Global Political Economy: Theory and Practice.* New York: Addison Wesley Longman.

Collier, Andrew 1994. *Critical Realism: An Introduction to Roy Bhaskar's Philosophy.* New York: Verso.

Collier, Andrew 1999. *Being and Worth.* New York: Routledge.

Cox, Robert W. 1981. "Social Forces, States and World Orders: Beyond International Relations Theory" *Journal of International Studies, Millenium* 10, 2: 385-424.

Cox, Robert W., with Timothy J. Sinclair 1996. *Approaches to World Order.* Cambridge: Cambridge University Press.

Crenson, Matthew A. 1971. *The Un-Politics of Air Pollution: A Study of Non-Decision-Making in the Cities.* Baltimore: Johns Hopkins University Press.

Critchley, Simon 1998. "Metaphysics in the Dark: A Response to Richard Rorty and Ernesto Laclau." *Political Theory* 26, 6: 803-17.

Cronin, Bruce 2001. "The Paradox of Hegemony: America's Ambiguous Relationship with the United Nations." *European Journal of International Relations* 7, 1: 103-30.

Daalder, Ivo H., and James M. Lindsay 2003. *America Unbound: The Bush Revolution in Foreign Policy.* Washington, DC: Brookings Institution Press.

DAC (Development Assistance Committee of the Organization for Economic Cooperation and Development). *Development Assistance* (1962-71), *Development Cooperation* (1972-2001), and *DAC Journal* (2002-present). Paris: OECD.

Dahl, Robert 1957. "The Concept of Power." *Behavioral Science* II (July): 201-215.

Dahl, Robert A. 1958. "A Critique of the Ruling Elite Model." *American Political Science Review* 58: 463-64.

Dahl, Robert 1961. *Who Governs? Democracy and Power in an American City.* New

Haven: Yale University Press.

Dahl, Robert A. 1968. "Power." In *International Encyclopedia of the Social Sciences, Vol. 12*, edited by David L. Shills. New York: Macmillan.

Davidson, Alastair. 1977. *Antonio Gramsci: Towards an Intellectual Biography.* London: Merlin Press.

Dean, Mitchell 1999. *Governmentality: Power and Rule in Modern Society.* London: Sage.

Derrida, Jacques 1997. *The Politics of Friendship.* New York: Verso.

de Soto, Hernando 2000. *The Mystery of Capital: Why Capitalism Triumphs in the West and Fails Everywhere Else.* New York: Basic Books.

Domhoff, G. William 1968. *Who Rules America.* Englewood Cliffs, NJ: Prentice Hall.

Domhoff, G. William 1978. *Who Really Rules.* Englewood Cliffs, NJ: Prentice Hall.

Donnelly, Jack 1998. *International Human Rights*, 2nd ed. Boulder: Westview Press.

Donzelot, Jacques 1979. "The Poverty of Political Culture." *Ideology & Consciousness*: 73-86.

Durkheim, Emile 1986. *Durkheim on Politics and the State*, edited by Anthony Giddens, translated by W.D. Halls. Cambridge: Polity Press.

Ehrenburg, Victor. 1960. *The Greek State.* New York: Norton.

Ehrenburg, Victor. 1973. *From Solon to Socrates: Greek History and Civilization During the 6th and 5th Centuries BC.* London: Meuthen Books.

Elias, Norbert 2000. *The Civilizing Process.* Oxford: Basil Blackwell.

Elman, Colin, and Miriam Fendius Elman, eds. 2001. *Bridges and Boundaries: Historians, Political Scientists, and the Study of International Relations.* Cambridge, Mass.: MIT Press.

Engels, Friedrich 1968. "The Origin of the Family, Private Property, and the State." In Karl Marx and Friedrich Engels, *Selected Works.* Moscow: International Publishers.

Enloe, Cynthia 1988. *Bananas, Beaches, Bases: Making Feminist Sense of International Relations.* Berkeley: University of California Press.

Enloe, Cynthia 1993. *The Morning After: Sexual Politics at the End of the Cold War.* Berkeley: University of California Press.

Enloe, Cynthia 2004. "'Gender' Is Not Enough; The Need for a Feminist Consciousness." *International Affairs* 80, 1: 195-98.

Evans, Peter 1995. *Embedded Autonomy: States and Industrial Transformation.* Princeton: Princeton University Press.

Evans, Peter 1997. "The Eclipse of the State? Reflections on Stateness in an Era of Globalization." *World Politics* 50 (October): 62-87.

Faulks, Keith 1999. *Political Sociology. A Critical Introduction.* Edinburgh: Edinburgh University Press.

Femia, Joseph V. 1987. *Gramsci's Political Thought: Hegemony, Consciousness, and the Revolutionary Process.* Oxford: Clarendon Press

Ferguson, James 1990. *The Anti-Politics Machine: "Development," Depoliticization and Bureaucratic Power in Lesotho.* New York: Cambridge University Press.

Ferguson, Niall 2003. "Think Again: Power." *Foreign Policy* 134 (January/February): 18-24.

Ferguson, Niall 2004. *Colossus: The Price of America's Empire.* New York: Penguin.

Fink, Bruce 1995. *The Lacanian Subject: Between Language and Jouissance.* Princeton: Princeton Univerity Press.

Finland, Legislation 2004. www.finlex.fi/fi/laki/alkup/2004/2004/20040650.

Finland, Ministry of Justice 2004. www.om.fi/25076.htm.

Flint, Colin 2001. "The Geopolitics of Laughter and Forgetting: A World-Systems Interpretation of the Post-Modern Geopolitical Condition." *Geopolitics* 6, 3: 1-16.

Flynn, Maureen 1989. *Sacred Charity: Confraternities and Social Welfare in Spain, 1400-1700*. Ithaca: Cornell University Press.

Fontana, Benedetto. 1993. *Hegemony and Power: On the Relation Between Gramsci and Machiavelli*. Minneapolis: University of Minnesota Press.

Fontana, Benedetto 2000. "*Logos* and *Kratos*: Gramsci and the Ancients on Hegemony." *Journal of the History of Ideas* 61: 305-326.

Fontana, Benedetto 2005. "Hegemony." In *New Dictionary of the History of Ideas*, edited by Maryanne Cline Horowitz. New York: Scribner's.

Fontana, Benedetto forthcoming. "Liberty and Domination: Civil Society in Gramsci." *boundary 2*.

Fontana, Benedetto 2006 forthcoming. "The Democratic Philosopher: Rhetoric as Hegemony in Gramsci." *Italian Culture*.

Foot, Rosemary, S. Neil McFarlane, and Michael Mastanduno 2003. *U.S. Hegemony and International Organizations*. Oxford: Oxford University Press.

Foucault, Michel 1970. *The Order of Things: An Archaeology of Human Sciences*. New York: Random House.

Foucault, Michel 1971. *Madness and Civilization: A History of Insanity in the Age of Reason*. London: Tavistock.

Foucault, Michel 1972. *The Archaeology of Knowledge and the Discourse on Language*. London: Tavistock.

Foucault, Michel 1973. *The Order of Things: An Archaeology of the Human Sciences*. New York: Vintage.

Foucault, Michel 1975. *The Birth of the Clinic: An Archaeology of Medical Perception*. New York: Vintage.

Foucault, Michel, ed. 1975. *I, Pierre Riviere, Having Slaughtered My Mother, My Sister and My Brother...A Case of Parricide in the 19th Century*. Harmondsworth: Penguin.

Foucault, Michel 1977. *Discipline and Punish: the Birth of the Prison*. Harmondsworth: Penguin.

Foucault, Michel 1978. *The History of Sexuality VI: Introduction*, translated by R. Hunter. New York: Vintage Books.

Foucault, Michel 1979. *Discipline and Punish: The Birth of the Prison*. New York: Vintage.

Foucault, Michel 1980. *Power/Knowledge: Selected Interviews and Other Writings 1972-1977*. Edited by Colin Gordon. New York: Pantheon.

Foucault, Michel 1980. "Truth and Power." In *Power/Knowledge: Selected Interviews and Other Writings 1972-77*, edited by Colin Gordon. New York: Harvester Press.

Foucault, Michel 1981. *History of Sexuality*, Vol 1. Harmondsworth: Penguin.

Foucault, Michel 1982. "The Subject and Power." In *Michel Foucault: Beyond Structuralism and Hermeneutics*, Second Edition, edited by Hubert L. Dreyfus and Paul Rabinow. Chicago: University of Chicago Press.

Foucault, Michel 1983. "Afterword, The Subject and Power." In *Michel Foucault Beyond Structuralism and Hermeneutics*, edited by Hubert L. Dreyfus and Paul Rabinow. Chicago: The University of Chicago Press.

Foucault, Michel 1984. *The Foucault Reader*, edited by P. Rabinow. New York: Pantheon.

Foucault, Michel 1984. "Nietzsche, Genealogy, History." In *The Foucault Reader*, edited by Paul Rabinow. New York: Pantheon Books.

Foucault, Michel 1988. *Madness and Civilization: A History of Insanity in the Age of Reason*. New York: Vintage.

Foucault, Michel 1991. "Questions of Method." In *The Foucault Effect: Studies in Governmentality*, edited by Graham Burchell, Colin Gordon, and Peter Miller. Hertfordshire: Harvester Wheatsheaf.

Foucault, Michel 1991. "Governmentality." In *The Foucault Effect: Studies in Governmentality*, edited by Colin Gordon et al. Chicago: University of Chicago Press.

Foucault, Michel 1997. In *Ethics, Subjectivity and Truth: Essential Works of Foucault 1954-1984 Vol. 1*, edited by Paul Rabinow. New York: The New Press.

Foucault, Michel 2003. *Society Must Be Defended: Lectures at the College de France 1975-76.* Translated by David Macey. London: Allen Lane.

Frank, Justin A. 2004. *Bush on the Couch: Inside the Mind of the President.* New York: Regan Books.

Fraser, Nancy 1985. "Michel Foucault: A 'Young Conservative.'" *Ethics* 96:165-184.

Freud, Sigmund 1995. "Group Psychology and the Analysis of the Ego." In *The Freud Reader*, edited by Peter Gay. London: Vintage.

Freud, Sigmund 1940. "Splitting of the Ego in the Process of Defence." In *Standard Edition of the Complete Psychological Works of Sigmund Freud, Vol. 23*, edited and translated by James Strachey. London: Hogarth Press.

Frisch, H., and M. Hofnung 1997. "State Formation and International Aid: The Emergence of the Palestinian Authority." *World Development* 25: 1243-55.

Fukuyama, Francis 1989. "The End of History?" *The National Interest* 16 (Summer): 3-18.

Fukuyama, Francis 2004. *State Building: Governance and World Order in the Twenty-First Century.* London: Profile Books.

Gallie, W.B. 1955/56. "Essentially Contested Concepts." *Proceedings of the Aristotelian Society* 56: 167-98.

Gardner, Lloyd C. 1971. *Economic Aspects of New Deal Diplomacy.* Boston: Beacon Press.

Gardner, Richard N. 1980. *Sterling-Dollar Diplomacy in Current Perspective*, revised edition. New York: Columbia University Press.

Garfinkel, Harold 1984. *Studies in Ethnomethodology.* Cambridge: Polity.

Garin, Eugenio 1975. "Politica e cultura in Gramsci (ilproblema degli intellettuali)." In *Gramsci e la cultura contemporanea*, edited by Pietro Rossi. Rome: Riuniti-Istituto Gramsci.

Garton Ash, Timothy 2003a. "Het rode hart van Vaclav Havel" *NRC Handelsblad* 31.1.

Garton Ash, Timothy 2003b. "Anti-Europeanism in America" *New York Review of Books* L (February 13): 32-34.

Garton Ash, Timothy 2003c. "Europa moet Polen bijstaan in Irak" *NRC Handelsblad* 16.5.

Garton Ash, Timothy 2003d. "Tijd om te dansen voor Europa en de VS" *NRC Handelsblad* 30.5.

Gaventa, John 1980. *Power and Powerlessness: Quiescence and Rebellion in an Appalachian Valley.* Urbana: University of Illinois Press.

Gellner Ernest 1983. *Nations and Nationalism.* Oxford: Blackwell.

Germino, Dante. 1990. *Antonio Gramsci: Architect of A New Politics.* Baton Rouge: Louisiana State University Press.

Giddens, Anthony 1984. *The Constitution of Society.* Cambridge: Polity.

Giddens, Anthony 1987. *The Nation-State and Violence: Volume 2 of A Contemporary Critique of Historical Materialism.* Berkeley: University of California Press.

Gill, Stephen 1990. *American Hegemony and the Trilateral Commission.* Cambridge: Cambridge University Press.

Gill, Stephen 1993. "Epistemology, Ontology, and the 'Italian School.'" In *Gramsci, Historical Materialism, and International Relations*, edited by Stephen Gill. New York: Cambridge University Press.

Gill, Stephen 2003. *Power and Resistance in the New World Order*. New York: Palgrave Macmillan.

Gilpin, Robert 1981. *War and Change in World Politics*. Cambridge: Cambridge University Press.

Gilpin, Robert, with the assistance of Jean M. Gilpin 1987. *The Political Economy of International Relations*. Princeton: Princeton University Press.

Gilpin, Robert with the assistance of Jean M. Gilpin 2001. *Global Political Economy: Understanding the International Economic Order*. Princeton: Princeton University Press.

Glynos, Jason 2000. "Sex and the Limits of Discourse." In *Discourse Theory and Political Analysis*, edited by David Howarth, Aletta J. Norval, and Yannis Stavrakakis. Manchester: Manchester University Press.

Glynos, Jason 2004. "Self-Transgression and Freedom." *Critical Review of International Social and Political Philosophy* 6, 2: 1-20.

Gould, Arthur 2003. "Ruotsin prostituutiolaki: feminismi, huumeet ja ulkomailta tuleva uhka." In *Prostituutio*, edited by Susanne Thorbek and Bandana Pattanaik. Helsinki: Like.

Gouldner, Alvin W. 1960. "The Norm of Reciprocity: A Preliminary Statement." *American Sociological Review* 25: 161-78.

Goverde, Henri, Philip G. Cerny, Mark Haugaard, and Howard H. Lentner, eds. 2000. *Power in Contemporary Politics: Theories, Practices, Globalizations*. London: Sage.

Goverde, Henri, Henk de Haan, Mireia Baylina, eds. 2004. *Power and Gender in European Rural Development*. Aldershot: Ashgate.

Gowa, Joanne 1983. *Closing the Gold Window: Domestic Politics and the End of Bretton Woods*. Ithaca: Cornell University Press.

Gramsci, Antonio. 1958. *Scritti giovanili*. Turin: Einaudi.

Gramsci, Antonio. 1965. *Lettere dal carcere*. Edited by Sergio Caprioglio and Elsa Fubini. Turin: Einaudi.

Gramsci, Antonio. 1971. *Selections from the Prison Notebooks*. Edited and translated by Quintin Hoare and Geoffrey Nowell Smith. New York: International Publishers.

Gramsci, Antonio. 1975. *Quaderni del carcere*. Turin: Einaudi.

Gramsci, Antonio. 1975. *Scritti giovanili 1914-1918*. Turin: Einaudi.

Gramsci, Antonio. 1977. *Selections from Political Writings 1910-1920*. Edited and translated by John Mathews. New York: International Publishers.

Green, Donald, and Ian Shapiro 1994. *Pathologies of Rational Choice Theory: A Critique of Applications in Political Science*. New Haven: Yale University Press.

Greider, William 1998. *Fortress America: The American Military and the Consequences of Peace*. New York: Public Affairs.

Gusterson, Hugh 1998. *Nuclear Rites*. Berkeley: University of California Press.

Guthrie, W.K.C. 1971. *The Sophists*. Cambridge: Cambridge University Press.

Haimson, Leopold. 1966. *The Russian Marxists and the Origins of Bolshevism*. Boston: Beacon Press.

Hands, Arthur R. 1968. *Charities and Social Aid in Greece and Rome*. Ithaca: Cornell University Press.

Harding, Sandra 1991. *Whose Science? Whose Knowledge: Thinking from Women's Lives*. Buckingham: Open University Press.

Hardt, Michael, and Antonio Negri 2001. *Empire*. Cambridge, Mass.: Harvard University Press.

Hattori, Tomohisa 2001. "Reconceptualizing Foreign Aid." *Review of International Political Economy* 8: 633-60.

Hattori, Tomohisa 2003. "Giving as a Mechanism of Consent: International Aid Organizations and the Ethical Hegemony of Capitalism." *International Relations* 17: 153-73.

Haugaard, Mark 1997. *The Constitution of Power*. Manchester: Manchester University Press.

Haugaard, Mark 2000. "Power, Ideology and Legitimacy." In *Power in Contemporary Politics: Theories, Practices, Globalizations*, edited by Henri Goverde et al. London: Sage.

Haugaard, Mark 2002. *Power: A Reader*. Manchester: Manchester University Press.

Haugaard, Mark 2003. "Reflections on Seven Ways of Creating Power." *European Journal of Social Theory* 6: 78-114.

Harvey, David 2003. *The New Imperialism*. Oxford: Oxford University Press.

Havel, Vaclav 1985. "The Power of the Powerlessness." In *The Power of the Powerlessness*, edited by Vaclav Havel. Armonk, NY: M. E. Sharpe.

Havel, Vaclav 2002. "Bestrijd het kwaad niet met leugens." *NRC Handelsblad* 11.21: 9.

Hayek, Friedrich. 1944. *The Road to Serfdom*. London: Routledge.

Hay, Colin 1996. *Re-Stating Social and Political Change*. Buckingham: Open University Press.

Heidegger, Martin 1962. *Being and Time*. Oxford: Blackwell.

Heikka, Taneli 2005. Interview with Minister of Justice Johannes Koskinen. *Aamulehti*, September 18, B16.

Held, David 2000/1996. *Models of Democracy*, second edition. Oxford: Blackwell.

Held, David and Anthony McGrew, eds. 2002. *Governing Globalization: Power, Authority and Global Governance*. Cambridge: Polity.

Heller, Agnes and Ferenc Fehér 1988. *The Postmodern Political Condition*. Cambridge: Polity.

Heywood, Andrew 2002. *Politics*, second edition. Houndmills: Palgrave.

Hindess, Barry 1996. *Discourses on Power: From Hobbes to Foucault*. Oxford: Blackwell.

Hirsch, Fred, and Michael Doyle 1977. "Politicization in the World Economy: Necessary Conditions for an International Economic Order." In *Alternatives to Monetary Disorder*, edited by Hirsch and Doyle. New York: McGraw Hill.

Hobbes, Thomas. 1968. *Leviathan*. Harmondsworth: Penguin Books.

Höglund, Anna T. 2002. "Gender Aspects of the Legitimisation of Military Force—a Post-September 11 Perspective." *Utsikt mot utveckling* 19. Collegium for Development Studies at Uppsala University, Sweden.

Höglund, Anna T. 2003. "Justice for Women in War? Feminist Ethics and Human Rights for Women." *Feminist Theology*, 11, 3: 346-361.

Holsti, K.J. 1985. *The Dividing Discipline: Hegemony and Diversity in International Theory*. Boston: Allen & Unwin.

Homans, George 1958. "Social Behavior as Exchange." *American Journal of Sociology* 63 (May): 597-606.

Homans, George 1961. *Social Behavior: Its Elementary Forms*, first edition. New York: Harcourt, Brace & World.

Howarth, David 2000. *Discourse*. Buckingham: Open University Press.

Hunter, Floyd 1953. *Community Power Structure: A Study of Decision-makers*. Chapel Hill: University of North Carolina Press.

Huntington, Samuel P. 1991. *The Third Wave: Democratization in the Late Twentieth Century*. Norman: University of Oklahoma Press.

Ikenberry, G. John 2001. *After Victory: Institutions, Strategic Restraint, and the Rebuilding of Order After Major Wars*. Princeton: Princeton University Press.

Ilchman, Warren F., Stanley N. Katz, and Edward L. Queen, eds. 1998. *Philanthropy in the World's Traditions*. Bloomington: Indiana University Press.

International Monetary Fund 1962-2005. *Annual Report*. Washington, D.C.: IMF.

Irigaray, Luce 1985. *This Sex Which Is Not One*. Translated by Catherine Porter. Ithaca: Cornell University Press.

Isaac, Jeffrey C. 1987. *Power and Marxist Theory: A Realist View*. Ithaca: Cornell University Press.

Isocrates. 2000. *Panegyricus*. Loeb Classical Library. Cambridge, Mass.: Harvard University Press.

Ives, Peter 2004. *Language and Hegemony in Gramsci*. London: Pluto.

Ives, Peter 2004. *Gramsci's Politics of Language: Engaging the Bakhtin Circle and the Frankfurt School*. Toronto: University of Toronto Press.

Janis, Irving L. 1982. *Groupthink: Psychological Studies of Policy Decisions and Fiascoes*. Boston: Houghton Mifflin Company.

Jessop, Bob 2002. *The Future of the Capitalist State*. Cambridge: Polity.

Jones, R. J. Barry, ed. 2001a. *Routledge Encyclopedia of International Political Economy*. London: Routledge.

Jones, R.J. Barry 2001b. "Hegemony." In *Routledge Encyclopedia of International Political Economy*, edited by R.J. Barry Jones. London: Routledge.

Joseph, J. 2002. *Hegemony: A Realist Analysis*. London: Routledge.

Kagan, Robert 2002. "Power and Weakness." *Policy Review* 113 (June and July): 3-28.

Kagan, Robert 2003. *Of Paradise and Power: American and Europe in the New World Order*. New York: Knopf.

Kagan, Robert 2004. "America's Crisis of Legitimacy." *Foreign Affairs* 83, 2 (March/April) : 65-87.

Kaldor, Mary 1982. *The Baroque Arsenal*. London: Andre Deutsch.

Kaldor, Mary 1999. *New and Old Wars: Organized Violence in a Global Era*. Cambridge: Polity

Katzenstein, Peter J., Robert O. Keohane, and Stephen D. Krasner 1998. "International Organization and the Study of World Politics," *International Organization* 52 (Autumn): 645-685.

Kearney, Christine 1993. "Creditor Clubs: Paris and London." In *Dealing with Debt*, edited by Thomas Biersteker. Boulder: Westview.

Kennedy, David 2004. *The Dark Sides of Virtue*. New York: Routledge.

Kennedy, Paul 1988. *The Rise and Fall of the Great Powers 1500-2000*. London: Allen & Unwin.

Keohane, Robert O. 1984. *After Hegemony: Cooperation and Discord in the World Political Economy*. Princeton: Princeton University Press.

Keohane, Robert O. 2002. "Ironies of Sovereignty: The European Union and the United States." *Journal of Common Market Studies* 40, 4: 743-65.

Keohane, Robert O., and Joseph S. Nye 1989. *Power and Interdependence*, Second Edition. Glenview, Ill.: Scott, Foresman.

Khalilzad, Zalmay 1995. "Losing the Moment? The United States and the World after the Cold War." *Washington Quarterly* 18, 2: 87-107.

Kindleberger, Charles P. 1973. *The World in Depression, 1929-1939*. Berkeley: University of California Press.

Kingdon, John W. 1984. *Agendas, Alternatives, and Public Policies*. New York: Harper Collins.

Kleinschmidt, Harald 2000. *The Nemesis of Power: A History of International Relations Theories*. London: Reaktion Books.

Knack, Stephen 2004. "Does Foreign Aid Promote Democracy?" *International Studies Quarterly* 48): 251-66.

Kropotkin, Peter 1947. *Ethics: Origin & Development*. Translated by L.S Friedland. New York: Tudor.

Krasner, Stephen D. 1976. "State Power and the Structure of International Trade." *World Politics* 28, 3 (April): 317-47.

Krasner, Stephen D. 1999. *Sovereignty: Organized Hypocrisy*. Princeton: Princeton University Press.

Kuhn, Thomas S. 1970. *The Structure of Scientific Revolutions*. Chicago: The University of Chicago Press.

Kupchan, Charles A., Emanuel Adler, Jean-Marc Coicaud, and Yuen Foon Khong 2001. *Power in Transition: The Peaceful Change of International Order*. Tokyo: United Nations University Press.

Kvinnoforum 2005. Swedish Women's Rights Organization website: http://www.kvinnoforum. se/english/.

Lacan, Jacques 1977. *Ecrits: A Selection*. Translated by Alan Sheridan. London: Tavistok.

Lacan, Jacques 1997. *The Seminar of Jacques Lacan. Book III: The Psychoses 1955-1956*. Translated by, Russell Grigg. New York and London: W.W Norton & Co.

Lacan, Jacques 1998. *The Seminar. Book XI. The Four Fundamental Concepts of Psychoanalysis*. Edited by J-A Miller and translated by A. Sheridan. London: W.W Norton & Co.

Laclau, Ernesto 1990. *New Reflections on the Revolution of Our Time*. London and New York: Verso.

Laclau, Ernesto 1996. *Emancipation(s)*. London: Verso.

Laclau, Ernesto 2000. "Structure, History and the Political." In *Contingency, Hegemony, and Universality Contemporary Dialogues of the Left*, edited by Judith Butler, Ernesto Laclau and Slavoj Žižek. London: Verso.

Laclau, Ernesto 2001. "Democracy and the Question of Power." *Constellations* 8,1: 3-14.

Laclau, Ernesto and Chantal Mouffe 1987. "Post-Marxism Without Apologies." *New Left Review* 166: 79-106.

Laclau, Ernesto and Chantal Mouffe 2001. *Hegemony and Socialist Strategy: Towards a Radical Democratic Politics*, second edition. London: Verso.

Lash, Scott 2002. *Critique of Information*. London: Sage.

Lasswell, Harold, and Abraham Kaplan 1950. *Power and Society*. New Haven: Yale University Press.

Lawson, Tony 1997. *Economics and Reality: Economics As Social Theory*. New York: Routledge.

Leffler, Melvyn P. 1992. *A Preponderance of Power: National Security, the Truman Administration, and the Cold War*. Stanford: Stanford University Press.

Lefort, Claude 1986. *The Political Forms of Modern Society: Bureaucracy, Democracy, Totalitarianism*. Cambridge: Polity Press.

Lefort, Claude 1988. *Democracy and Political Theory*. Cambridge, UK: Polity Press.

Leng, Russell J. 1998. "Reciprocity in Recurring Crisis." *International Negotiation* 3: 197-226.

Lentner, Howard H. 2000. "Globalization and Power," in *Rethinking Globalization(s): From Corporate Transnationalism to Local Interventions*, edited by Michael G. Schechter and Preet Aulakh. London: Macmillan.

Lentner, Howard H. 2004. *Power and Politics in Globalization: The Indispensable State*. New York: Routledge.

Lentner, Howard H. 2005. "Hegemony and Autonomy." *Political Studies* 53: 735-52.

Leopold. Joseph, and George Shambaugh 1998. "Rethinking the Notion of Reciprocal Exchange in International Negotiation: Sino-American Relations, 1969-1997." *International Negotiation* 3: 226-52.

Lichtheim, George. 1970. *Marxism: An Historical and Critical Study*. New York: Praeger Publishers.

Lobell, Steven E. 2003. *The Challenge of Hegemony: Grand Strategy, Trade, and Domestic Politics*. Ann Arbor: University of Michigan Press.

LoPiparo, Franco 1979. *Lingua, Intellettuali, Egemonia in Gramsci*. Bari: Laterza.

Luard, Evan 1992. *Basic Texts in International Relations: The Evolution of Ideas about International Society*. New York: St. Martin's Press.

Lukács, Geörgy 1971. *History and Class Consciousness*. Translated by Rodney Livingstone. London: Merlin.

Lukes, Steven 1973. *Individualism: Key Concepts in the Social Sciences*. Oxford, UK: Blackwell.

Lukes, Steven 1974. *Power: A Radical View*. London: Macmillan.

Lukes, Steven 2001. "Power." In *The Oxford Companion to the Politics of the World*, Second Edition. Oxford: Oxford University Press.

Lukes, Steven 2005. *Power: A Radical View*, Second Edition. Basingstoke: Palgrave Macmillan.

Machiavelli, Niccolò. 1985. *The Prince*. Introduction and translation by Harvey C. Mansfield, Jr. Chicago: University of Chicago Press.

Machiavelli, Niccolò 1531/1997. *Discorsi. Gedachten over Staat en Politiek* (Discorsi sopra la prima deca di Tito Livio). Amsterdam, Leuven: Ambo/Kritak.

Maddison, Angus 1982. *Phases of Capitalist Development*. Oxford: Oxford University Press.

Malesevic Sinisa and Mark Haugaard, eds. 2002. *Making Sense of Collectivity*. London: Pluto.

Mann, Michael 1986. *The Sources of Social Power, Volume 1: A History of Power From the Beginning to A.D. 1760*. Cambridge: Cambridge University Press.

Mann, Michael 2003. *Incoherent Empire*. London: Verso.

Martin, James 1998. *Gramsci's Political Analysis: A Critical Introduction*. Hampshire: Macmillan.

Marx, Karl 1973. "The Eighteenth Brumaire of Louis Bonaparte." In *Surveys from Exile*, edited by D. Fernbach. Harmondsworth: Penguin.

Marx, Karl 1974. "The Civil War in France." In *The First International and After*, edited by D. Fernbach. Harmondsworth: Penguin.

Marx, Karl 1978. "Contribution to the Critique of Hegel's *Philosophy of Right*: Introduction." In *The Marx-Engels Reader*, edited by Robert Tucker. New York: Norton.

Mauss, Marcel 1967. *The Gift: Forms and Functions of Exchange in Archaic Societies*. New York: Norton.

McChesney, R. D. 1991. *Waqf in Central Asia: Four Hundred Years in the History of a Muslim Shrine, 1480-1800*. Princeton: Princeton University Press.

Mead, Walter Russell 2004. *Power, Terror, Peace and War: America's Grand Strategy in a World at Risk*. New York: Knopf.

Mearsheimer, John J. 2001. *The Tragedy of Great Power Politics*. New York: W.W. Norton.

Mills, C. Wright 1956. *The Power Elite*. Oxford: Oxford University Press.

Mintz, Beth, and Michael Schwartz 1985. *The Power Structure of American Business*. Chicago: University of Chicago Press.

MIT 2005. *Electronic Journal of Middle East Studies* 5 (Spring). http://web.mit.edu/cis/www/mitejmes/

Modelski, George 1987. *Long Cycles in World Politics*. Seattle: University of Washington Press.

Mohanty, Chandra Talpade 1994. "Under Western Eyes: Feminist Scholarship and Colonial Discourses." In *Colonial Discourse and Postcolonial Theory*, edited by Patrick Williams and Laura Chrisham. London: Harwester Wheatsheaf.

Moïsi, Dominique 2001. "The Real Crisis over the Atlantic." *Foreign Affairs* 80 (July/August): 149-53.

Morgenthau, Hans J. 1973. *Politics Among Nations: The Struggle for Power and Peace*, Fifth Edition. New York: Knopf.

Mouffe, Chantal 2000. *The Democratic Paradox*. London: Verso.

Mueller, John 1989. *Retreat from Doomsday: The Obsolescence of Major War*. New York: Basic Books.

Mueller, John 1995. *Quiet Cataclysm: Reflections on the Recent Transformation of World Politics*. New York: HarperCollins.

Münkler, Herfried 2005. *Imperien: Die Logik der Weltherrschaft vom Alten Rom bis zu den Vereinigten Staaten.* Berlin: Rowohlt.

Nardone, Giorgio. 1971. *Il pensiero di Gramsci.* Bari: De Donato.

Nietzsche, Friedrich. 1966. *Beyond Good and Evil: Prelude to a Philosophy of the Future.* Translated by Walter Kaufmann. New York: Vintage Books.

The 9/11 Commission Report 2004. *Final Report of the National Commission on Terrorist Attacks upon the United States.* Baton Rouge: Claiter's Publishing Division.

Norval, Aletta J. 2000 "Trajectories of Future Research in Discourse Theory." In *Discourse Theory and Political Analysis*, edited by David Howarth, Aletta J. Norval, and Yannis Stavrakakis. Manchester: Manchester University Press.

Nye, Joseph S. Jr. 1990. *Bound to Lead: The Changing Nature of American Power.* New York: Basic Books.

Nye, Joseph S., Jr. 2001. "Military Deglobalization? Long-Distance Military Interdependence is Taking New Forms." *Foreign Policy* 122 (January/February): 82-83.

Nye, Joseph S. Jr. 2002. *The Paradox of American Power: Why America Must Join the World in Order to Lead It.* Oxford: Oxford University Press.

Nye, Joseph S. Jr. 2004. *Soft Power: The Means to Success in World Politics.* New York: Public Affairs.

Nye, Joseph S., Jr. 2005. *Understanding International Conflicts: An Introduction to Theory and History*, fifth edition. New York: Pearson, Longman.

Nyoni, T. S. 1998. "Foreign Aid and Economic Performance in Tanzania." *World Development* 26: 1235-40.

Ollman, Bertell 1976. *Alienation: Marx's Conception of Man in Capitalist Society*, second edition. New York: Cambridge University Press.

Ollman, Bertell 1993. *Dialectical Investigation.* New York: Routledge.

Olson, Mancur 1971. *The Logic of Collective Action: Public Goods and the Theory of Groups*, revised edition. Cambridge: Harvard University Press.

Owen, David 1964. *English Philanthropy, 1660-1960.* Cambridge, Mass.: Harvard University Press.

Oye, Kenneth A., ed. 1986. *Cooperation Under Anarchy.* Princeton: Princeton University Press.

Parry, Jonathan 1986. "The Gift, the Indian Gift, and the 'Indian' Gift." *Man* 21: 454-73.

Parsons, Talcott 1963. "On the Concept of Political Power." *Proceedings of the American Philosophical Society* 107: 232-62.

Patchen, Martin 1998. "When Does Reciprocity in the Action of Nations Occur?" *International Negotiation* 3: 171-96.

Penrose, E.F. 1953. *Economic Planning for the Peace.* Princeton: Princeton University Press.

Penttinen, Elina 2004. *Corporeal Globalization: Narratives of Subjectivity and Otherness in the Sexscapes of Globalization.* Tapri publication. Tampere University Press, Oy Juvenes Print.

Peterson, V. Spike 1992. "Security and Sovereign States: What is at Stake in Taking Feminism Seriously?" In *Gendered States: Feminist (Re)visions of International Relations Theory*, edited by V. Spike Peterson. Boulder: Lynne Rienner.

Peterson, V. Spike and Anne Sisson Runyan 1993. *Global Gender Issues.* Boulder: Westview.

Piven, Francis Fox, and Richard A. Cloward 1971. *Regulating the Poor: The Function of Public Welfare.* New York: Pantheon Books.

Plato. 2000. *Republic.* Loeb Classical Library. Cambridge, Mass.: Harvard University Press.

Pogge, Thomas 2002. *World Poverty and Human Rights: Cosmopolitan Responsibilities and Reforms.* Cambridge: Polity.

Poggi, Gianfranco 2000. *Forms of Power.* Cambridge: Polity.

Pøkiæ, François 1997. "End of the Cold War and Democratisation in Sub-Saharan Africa: The Emergence of Transnational Rebel Territories in Today's Conflicts." Paper presented to the Workshop on Democratisation and the Changing Global Order, Annual Joint Sessions of Workshops, European Consortium for Political Research, Bern, Switzerland, 27 February-4 March.

Polsby, Nelson 1980. *Community Power and Political Theory*. New Haven: Yale University Press.

Rasler, Karen, and William R. Thompson 1994. *The Great Powers and Global Struggle, 1490-1990*. Lexington: University of Kentucky Press.

Rawls, John 1971. *A Theory of Justice*. Oxford: Oxford University Press.

The Responsibility to Protect 2001. Report of the International Commission on Intervention and State Sovereignty. Ottawa: International Development Research Centre.

Reus-Smit, Christian 2004. *American Power and World Order*. Cambridge: Polity.

Rice, Condoleezza 2000. "Promoting the National Interest" *Foreign Affairs*, 79, 1: 45-62.

Rietbergen, Peter 1998. *Europe: A Cultural History*. London: Routledge.

Rietbergen, Peter 1994. *Dromen van Europa: Een cultuurgeschiedenis*. Amersfoort: Bekking.

Robinson, William I. 1996. *Promoting Polyarchy: Globalization, US Intervention, and Hegemony*. Cambridge: Cambridge University Press.

Roelofs, Joan 2003. *Foundations and Public Policy: The Masks of Pluralism*. Albany: State University of New York Press.

Rorty, Richard 1989. *Contingency, Irony and Solidarity*. Cambridge: Polity.

Rosecrance, Richard, ed. 2001. *The New Great Power Coalition: Toward a World Concert of Nations*. Lanham: Rowman & Littlefield.

Roseberry, William 1994. "Hegemony and the Language of Contention." In *Everyday Forms of State Formation: Revolution and the Negotiation of Rule in Modern Mexico*, edited by G. M. Joseph and D. Nugent. Durham: Duke University Press.

Rosenthal, Joel T. 1972. *The Purchase of Paradise: Gift Giving and the Aristocracy, 1307-1485*. London: Routledge and Kegan Paul.

Rubin, Miri 1987. *Charity and Community in Medieval Cambridge*. New York: Cambridge University Press.

Ruggie, John G. 1982. "International Regimes, Transactions, and Change: Embedded Liberalism in the Postwar Economic Order." *International Organization* 36, 2 (Spring): 379-415.

Ruggie, John Gerard 1983. "Continuity and Transformation in the World Polity: Toward a Neorealist Synthesis." *World Politics* 35 (January): 261-85.

Ruggie, John Gerard 1998. *Constructing the World Polity: Essays on International Institutionalization*. London: Routledge.

Sabra, Adam 2000. *Poverty and Charity in Medieval Islam: Mamluk Egypt, 1250-1517*. New York: Cambridge University Press.

Sahlins, Marshall 1972. *Stone Age Economics*. Chicago: Aldine.

Salli 2005. Website. http://www.salli.org/.

de Saussure, Ferdinand (1960) *Course in General Linguistics*. London: Peter Owen Limited.

Sayer, Andrew 1995. *Radical Political Economy: A Critique*. New York: Routledge.

Sagan, Scott D., and Kenneth N. Waltz 2003. *The Spread of Nuclear Weapons: A Debate Renewed*. New York: W.W. Norton.

Schelling, Thomas C. 1960. *The Strategy of Conflict*. Cambridge, Mass.: Harvard University Press.

Schelling, Thomas C. 1966. *Arms and Influence*. New Haven: Yale University Press.

Schendelen, Rinus van 2003. *Machiavelli in Brussels. The Art of Lobbying the EU*. Amsterdam: Amsterdam University Press.

Schutz, Alfred 1971. *Collected Papers, Vol 1*. The Hague: Dryden Press.

Scott, James C. 1990. *Domination and the Arts of Resistance: Hidden Transcripts*. New Haven: Yale University Press.

Scott, John 2001. *Power*. Cambridge: Polity.

Scruton, Roger. 1982. *A Dictionary of Political Thought*. New York: Hill and Wang.

Singer, Amy 2002. *Constructing Ottoman Beneficence: An Imperial Soup Kitchen in Jerusalem*. Albany, NY: State University of New York Press.

Singer, Peter 2002. *One World: The Ethics of Globalization*. New Haven: Yale University Press.

Smith, Anne-Marie 1994. *New Right Discourse on Race and Sexuality: Britain 1968-90*. Cambridge: Cambridge University Press.

Smith, Neil 2002. "Scales of Terror: The Manufacturing of Nationalism and the War for US Globalisation." In *After the World Trade Center: Rethinking New York City*, edited by Michael Sorkin and Sharon Zukin. New York: Routledge: 97-108.

Snyder, Glenn H., and Paul Diesing 1977. *Conflict Among Nations: Bargaining, Decision Making, and System Structure in International Crises*. Princeton: Princeton University Press.

Sprout, Harold and Margaret 1951. *Foundations of National Power: Readings on World Politics and American Security*, Second Edition. Toronto: D. Van Nostrand.

Staden, Alfred van 2005. *Power and Legitimacy. The Quest for Order in a Unipolar World*. The Hague: Netherlands Institute for International relations, Clingendael Diplomacy Papers no 1.

Starr, Paul. 2004. *The Creation of the Media: Political Origins of Modern Communications*. New York: Basic Books.

Stavrakakis, Yannis 1999. *Lacan and the Political*. New York: Routledge.

Steans, Jill 1998. *Gender and International Relations: An Introduction*. Cambridge: Polity.

Strange, Susan 1987. "The Persistent Myth of Lost Hegemony." *International Organization* 41, 4 (Autumn): 551-574.

Strange, Susan 1988. *States and Markets*. London: Pinter.

Strange, Susan 1996. *The Retreat of the State: The Diffusion of Power in the World Economy*. Cambridge: Cambridge University Press.

Sylvester, Christine 1994. *Feminist Theory and International Relations in a Postmodern Era*. Cambridge: Cambridge University Press.

Sylvester, Christine 2002. *Feminist International Relations: An Unfinished Journey*. Cambridge: Cambridge University Press.

Taylor, Charles 1984. "Foucault on Freedom and Truth." *Political Theory* 12, 1: 52-83.

Taylor, Peter J. and Colin Flint 2000. *Political Geography: World-economy, Nation-state & Locality*, fourth edition. Harlow: Prentice Hall.

Texier, J. 1989. "Sur les sens de 'société civile' chez Gramsci." *Actuel Marx* 5: 50-68.

Thompson, John B. 1991. "Editor's Introduction." In Pierre Bourdieu, *Language and Symbolic Power*, edited by John B. Thompson. Cambridge, Mass: Harvard University Press.

Thucydides. 2002. *The Pelopnnesian War*. Loeb Classical Library. Cambridge, Mass.: Harvard University Press.

Tickner Ann 1992. *Gender in International Relations: Feminist Perspectives on Achieving Global Security*. New York: Columbia University Press.

Torfing, Jacob 1999. *New Theories of Discourse:Laclau, Mouffe and Žižek*. Oxford: Blackwell.

Tucker, Robert C. 1969. *The Marxian Revolutionary Idea*. New York: Norton.

Unioni Naisasialiitto Suomessa RY:N (Women's Union of Finland) 2003. *Lausunto koskien naiskauppaa ... (Statement of the Board concerning trafficking in women ...)*. Helsinki, April 29. www.naisunioni.fi/naiskauppa.htm.

Urquhart, Brian 2004. "A Matter of Truth." *New York Review of Books* LI, 8: 8-12.

Useem, Michael 1983. *The Inner Circle: Large Corporations and Business Politics in the U.S. and U.K.* New York: Oxford University Press.

van der Pijl, Kees 1998. *Transnational Classes and International Relations.* New York: Routledge.

Veyne, Paul 1990. *Bread and Circuses: Historical Sociology and Political Pluralism.* New York: Penguin.

Vico, Giambattista. 1988. *On the Most Ancient Wisdom of the Italians Unearthed from the Origins of the Latin Language: Including the Disputation with the Giornale de' letterati d'Italia.* Translated by Lucia M. Palmer. Ithaca: Cornell University Press.

Vidal, Gore 2002. "De oliejunta van Bush." *De Groene Amsterdammer* 9,11: 21-30.

Villepin, Dominique de 2004. "Sleutel voor de nieuwe wereld ligt in het recht." (Key for the New World Order is situated in International Law; speech). The Hague: Academy for International Law. www.nrc.nl/doc.

Wacquant, L. J. D. 1987. "Towards a Reflexive Sociology: A Workshop with Pierre Bourdieu." *Sociological Theory* 7, 1 (Spring): 26-63.

Wallerstein, Immanuel 1974. *The Modern World System: Capitalist Agriculture and the Origins of the European World Economy in the Sixteenth Century.* New York: Academic Press.

Wallerstein, Immanuel 1979. *The Capitalist World-Economy.* New York: Cambridge University Press.

Waltz, Kenneth N. 1979. *Theory of International Politics.* Reading, Mass.: Addison-Wesley.

Waltz, Kenneth N. 1990. "Nuclear Myths and Political Realities." *American Political Science Review* 84 (September): 731-45.

Wang, T. Y. 1999. "US Foreign Aid and UN Voting: An Analysis of Important Issues." *International Studies Quarterly* 43: 199-210.

Warner, Daniel 1991. *The Ethic of Responsibility.* Boulder: Westview.

Weber, Max 1948. *From Max Weber: Essays in Sociology.* London: Routledge and Kegan Paul.

Weber, Max 1957 [1922]. *The Theory of Social and Economic Organization*, edited by Talcott Parsons. Glencoe, Ill.: Free Press.

Weber Max 1964. *The Theory of Social and Economic Organization.* New York: Free Press.

Weber, Max 1978. *Economy and Society.* Two volumes. Berkeley: University of California Press.

Weiss, Linda 1998. *The Myth of the Powerless State.* Ithaca: Cornell University Press.

Wendt, Alexander 1987. "The Agent-Structure Problem in International Relations Theory." *International Organization* 41: 335-70.

Wendt, Alexander 1999. *Social Theory of International Politics.* New York: Cambridge University Press.

Wickersham, John 1994. *Hegemony and Greek Historians.* Lanham: Rowman & Littlefield.

Wight, Martin 1946. *Power Politics.* London: Royal Institute of International Affairs.

Wilde, Jaap de 2002. "Robert Kagans moeras van de machtspolitiek." *Internationale Spectator* LVI, 11: 531-35.

Williams, Gwyn A. 1960. "The Concept of 'Egemonia' in the Thought of Antonio Gramsci: Some Notes on Interpretation." *Journal of the History of Ideas* 21: 586-597.

Williams, R. 1977. "Hegemony." In *Marxism and Literature.* Oxford: Oxford University Press: 108-14.

Williamson, John 1990. "What Washington Means by Policy Reform." In *Latin American Adjustment: How Much Has Happened*, edited by John Williamson. Washington, DC: Institute of International Economics: 5-20.

Wittgenstein, Ludwig 1968. *Philosophical Investigations.* Translated by G.E.M. Anscombe. Oxford: Blackwell.

Wolf, Eric R. 1999. *Envisioning Power: Ideologies of Dominance and Crisis.* Berkeley: University of California Press.

Wolferen, K.G. van 2003. "Europa moet nu Amerika redden." *NRC Handelsblad* (May 18).

Wolfowitz, Paul 1997. "Re-building the Anti-Saddam Coalition." *Wall Street Journal,* (November 18): A22.

Wolin, Sheldon. 2004. *Politics and Vision: Continuity and Innovation in Western Political Thought.* Princeton: Princeton University Press.

World Bank 1962-2005. *Annual Report.* Washington, D.C.: World Bank.

World Bank 1998. *Assessing Aid.* New York: Oxford University Press.

Wrong, Denis 1995. *Power: Its Forms Bases and Uses.* New Brunswick, NJ: Transaction Publishers.

Yergin, Daniel 1977. *Shattered Peace: The Origins of the Cold War and the National Security State.* Boston: Houghton Mifflin.

Young, Iris Marion 2003. "The Logic of Masculinist Protection: Reflections on the Current Security State." *Signs.* 29,1: 1-25.

Youngs, Gillian 2004. "Feminist International Relations: A Contradiction in Terms? Or Why Women and Gender Are Essential to Understanding the World 'We' Live In." *International Affairs* 80, 1: 75-88.

Žižek, Slavoj 1989. *The Sublime Object of Ideology.* London: Verso.

Žižek, Slavoj 1990. "Beyond Discourse-Analysis." In *New Reflections on the Revolution of Our Time, edited by Ernesto Laclau. London: Verso.*

Žižek, Slavoj 1996. *The Indivisible Remainder: An Essay on Schelling and Related Matters.* London: Verso.

Žižek, Slavoj 1999. "The Specter of Ideology." In *The Žižek Reader,* edited by Elizabeth Wright and Edmond Wright. Oxford: Blackwell.

Žižek, Slavoj 2000. "Class Struggle or Postmodernism? Yes, Please!" In *Contingency, Hegemony, and Universality Contemporary Dialogues of the Left,* edited by Judith Butler, Ernesto Laclau and Slavoj Žižek. London: Verso.

Zunes, Stephen 1996. "Strategic Functions of US Aid to Israel." *Middle East Policy* 4: 90-101.

Index

class-consciousness, 46
classical dualism, remaining in
    hegemony, 4
class interests, 61
class structure, in Gramsci, 111
class struggle, 179, 196
Claude, Inis L., Jr., 92
Clegg, Stewart, 96
Clinton, William J., 75
Clinton administration, 80
clock-time, 52
closing the gold window, 77
Coalition Against Trafficking in
    Women, 147
coalition-building, 70
coercion, 5, 54, 62-64
coercive power, 90
cognitive dissonance, 7
Cold War, deterrence in, 80; emphasis
    on military, 75, 92; international
    system, 74, 102, 217; U.S.
    position and policy in, 71, 78, 82
collective interests, in alliance, 8
collective will, of subaltern classes, 7,
    9, 173, 187, 188
common norms, in globalization, 15
common will, 47
community and consensus, in Gramsci,
    30
complex interdependence, 93, 100-101
Communism, 102, 180, 187
community power theorists, 104
comprador elites, 85
conditionality, 85
conflict, Foucault's concept of, 57
conflicts, deep ontological, 56
confirming-structuration, 51, 52, 53,
    58, 59
Congo, 130n4
Congress, 80
consciousness raising, 7
consensual leadership, 12
consensus, 50, 52
consent, 5, 6, 8, 31, 37
consequences of action, 95
consequences, unwilled, 89
Constituent Assembly, dispersal of in
    1918, 27
constructivism, 102, 103, 107

contradiction between national interests
    and systemic hegemony, 85-87
cosmopolitanism, 101
counterhegemonic debate on
    criminalization of prostitution in
    Finland, 136, 142
counterhegemonic strategy, 7, 58
counterhegemony, 8-9, 12, 40-42, 45,
    49, 198; absence of, 85
crime syndicates, 145
criminalization, of buying of sexual
    services, 133, 134, 135, 136, 142
critical realism, 15-16
critical understanding of self, 40
Cronin, Bruce, 117
crony capitalism, 85
cyclical time, 52
Czechoslovakia, 115

Dahl, Robert A., 14, 81, 89, 92, 93, 96,
    104, 152, 154, 155, 216
Daalder, Ivo H., and James M. Lindsay,
    70, 124, 126
deaths of Americans and Iraqis, 80
death of the subject, 185
Debt Crisis, 160
decolonization, 53
defense spending, 75
Delian League, 24, 25
democracy, concentration of power in,
    104; different meanings of, 52; as
    liberal mechanism, 70
democratic discourse, as resource, 199;
    concerning feminism, 207
democratic theory, in Mouffe, 49;
    normative concerns, 14
democratic revolution, Lenin's view of,
    26
democratization, from above, 75; and
    socioeconomic issues, 75-77
Denmark, 121
desire, imperative in Lacan, 179
destructuration, 53, 58, 59, 63, 135;
    rejection of, 51
destructuring reactions, in deep
    ontological conflicts, 56
deterrence, nuclear, 74, 99
Derrida, Jacques, 58, 59, 189
developing countries, 81

development theory, 84
dichotomies in American and European
    projects, 117
difference-creating practice, 162
discourse, 49; analysis, 182; as
    interpretive horizon, 48; language
    of replaces ideology, 47;
    masculinist, 16-17; theory, 17
discourse formation, 49
discourses, 126, 128
discursive exterior, 126
discursive formulation, 9
discursive validation, 7
disempowerment, in structured
    relations, 52
dispute settlement mechanism of World
    Trade Organization, 81
Divine Right, 171
Dodge line, 76
domain of power, 156
dominating discourse, in Finland, 133,
    134
domination, consent to, 5; exercise of
    political power, 28; global system
    of, 102; reproduction of, 55;
    reliance on in Italian unification,
    30; and resistance in international
    politics, 89; structured relations
    of, 52
domination/leadership polarity, 30
donor-recipient relation, 15, 163
Donzelot, Jacques, 173
doxa, 161
doxic experience, 153, 158, 160, 161
drones, 80
drug traffickers, 100
dualism, between domination and
    leadership, 12
dual nature of politics, force/
    persuasion, 30
dual perspective, in political action, 28
Durkheim, Emile, 107

Eastern Europe, women trafficked
    from, 16
Eastern girl, 143
economic public goods, 69
economy of violence, 44
election, as basis of authority, 53

Elias, Norbert, 64
embourgeoization, 6
empire, 4, 91, 200
empowerment, 52
empty place, 184, 195
end of history, 84
ends and means, 93
energetai, 159, 162
Enloe, Cynthia, 136
episteme, 201
epistemological individualism, 156
equaliberty, 18, 189
equality, principle of, 189
essentialist claims, 47
essential logic, of quilting points, 49-50
ethical discourse, of philanthropic
    organizations, 162, 163
ethics, moment of madness in, 188, 189
ethics of place, 188-90
ethnic cleansing, 140
ethnicity, 136
Europe, 76, 114, 127, 128. *See also*
    European Union
European civilization, 116
European constitution, 121, 122
European divide, 110
European internationalist belief system,
    128
European project, 120-22
European Union, 81, 113, 120-21, 122,
    130n4; as ally, 127, 129n3
European Union/France/Germany, 115
European-US divide, 122
everyday social practices, 7
exchange approach to foreign aid, 155-
    58
exchange theory, 15-16
exchanges, 155
exchange value, in Marx, 52
exclusion, of alternative meanings, 52;
    workings of, 48

Face Off, 205
false consciousness, 46, 47, 111
fault lines, in American hegemony, 71,
    72
Faulks, Keith, 118
fear, 100
Femia, Joseph V., 7

Index

About the Contributors

Philip G. Cerny is Professor of Global Affairs at Rutgers University—Newark, New Jersey. He is coeditor of *Internalizing Globalization: The Rise of Neoliberalism and the Erosion of National Varieties of Capitalism* (Palgrave, 2005) and author of "The New Security Dilemma: Divisibility, Defection and Disorder in the Global Era," *Review of International Studies* (2000), "Terrorism and the New Security Dilemma," *Naval War College Review* (2005), and "Pluralism, Plurality and Power: Elements of Pluralist Analysis in an Age of Globalization," in Rainer Eisfeld, ed., *Pluralism: Developments in the Theory and Practice of Democracy* (Leske and Budrich for the International Political Science Association, 2006). He is currently completing a book on *Multi-Nodal Politics: Political Dynamics of a Globalizing World*.

Benedetto Fontana teaches political philosophy at Baruch College of the City University of New York. He is the author of *Hegemony and Power: On the Relation Between Gramsci and Machiavelli* (University of Minnesota Press, 1993). In addition to Gramsci, he has published on Machiavelli and the ancients, as well as on democratic politics and rhetoric. Recently he has edited (with Cary J. Nederman and Gary Remer) *Talking Democracy: Historical Perspectives on Rhetoric and Democracy* (Pennsylvania State University Press, 2004).

Henri Goverde is Associate Professor of Public Administration in the Nijmegen School of Management, Department of Public Affairs and Public Administration, and Endowed Professor of Political Science, Wageningen University and Research Center. Since 1994 he has been chair of the Research Committee "Political Power" of the International Political Science Association. His research focuses on power, policy networks, and European multi-level governance. His most recent (edited) book is *Power and Gender in European Rural Development* (2004).

Tomohisa Hattori is an Assistant Professor of Political Science at Lehman College, the City University of New York. His recent articles include: "Giving as a Mechanism of Consent," *International Relations* 17 (2003); "The Moral Politics of Foreign Aid," *Review of International Studies* 29 (2003); and "Reconceptualizing Foreign Aid," *Review of International Political Economy* 8 (2001).

Mark Haugaard lectures in the Department of Sociology and Politics at the National University of Ireland, Galway. His recent publications on power include

"Reflections on Seven Forms of Power," *European Journal of Social Theory* 6 (2003) and *Power: A Reader*, Manchester University Press (2002).

Howard H. Lentner is Professor Emeritus at the City University of New York. His most recent book is *Power and Politics in Globalization: The Indispensable State* (Routledge, 2004) and his most recent articles are "Hegemony and Auton- omy," *Political Studies* 53 (2005) and "Public Policy and Foreign Policy: Diver- gences, Intersections, Exchange," *Review of Policy Research* 23 (2006).

Saul Newman is a Lecturer in Politics at Goldsmiths College, University of Lon- don. His most recent book is *Power and Politics in Poststructuralist Thought: New Theories of the Political* (Routledge 2005), and he is working on a new book on radical politics for Manchester University Press. He has published widely in the area of contemporary political and social thought.

Elina Penttinen, Ph.D., is a postdoctoral researcher at Tampere Peace Research Institute, University of Tampere, Finland. Her current research project involves the study of gendered construction of security and insecurity through analyzing the experiences of women peacekeepers and women refugees as subjects and objects of security. Her research interests are the application of feminist methodology and new ethnography in the field of International Relations. However, currently she enjoys her role as a full-time stay- at-home mom of her three small children. Her doctoral thesis (2004) was titled, *Corporeal Globalization: Narratives of Subjectiv- ity and Otherness in the Sexscapes of Gobalization.* She has published several articles, including "The Marriage Deal Between a Young Finnish-Saame Man and Former Russian Prostitute in Northern Finland," *Canadian Women Studies* 3,4 (2003), and "Whose Voices Matter: Feminists Stretch the Boundaries of Interna- tional Relations Discipline," in *Power In Focus: Perspectives From Multiple Disciplines,* edited by Subhash Durlabhji (Lima, Ohio: Wyndham Hall Press, 2004).

Kevin Ryan lectures in Sociology and Political Theory at the Department of Politi- cal Science and Sociology, National University of Ireland Galway. He is author of *Social Exclusion and the Politics of Order*, forthcoming with Manchester University Press, and is currently researching power and exclusion in modernity and postmodernity.